Personal Landscapes

Personal Landscapes

by
JEROME MALITZ

TIMBER PRESS
Portland, Oregon

ISBN 0-88192-131-9
Printed in Hong Kong

TIMBER PRESS, INC.
9999 SW Wilshire
Portland, Oregon 97225

Library of Congress Cataloging-in-Publication Data

Malitz, Jerome.
    Personal landscapes / by Jerome Malitz.
        p.   cm.
    Bibliography: p.
    Includes index.
    ISBN 0-88192-131-9
    1. Gardens--Design. 2. Landscape gardening.   I. Title.
SB473.M268 1989
    712'.6--dc19   89-30114
                                                       CIP

Contents

Acknowledgments

Another volume would be required to justly acknowledge all the horti-culturists, plantsmen, and garden hobbyists who so patiently endured my questions and so unselfishly shared their knowledge with me. However, several individuals were so instrumental in bringing this book into being that they must be mentioned.

I am indebted to Richard Abel of Timber Press for his encouragement and many helpful suggestions. Special thanks to my son, Seth, who read the manuscript with critical care and the expertise gained from a dozen years of avid plant collecting and gardening. Thanks also to Carolyn Morganstern who elicited many of my more off-the-wall remarks. The project owes a great debt to Frieda and Dick Holley, long-term friends, colleagues, and gardening associates. Many of their recommendations have been incorporated into the text, and many of the ideas in the text were honed in heated conversations with them. Frieda's critcal reading of the manuscript is largely responsible for the writing having some resemblance to English. Most of all, my gratitude and thanks go to my ever-patient, ever-supportive, long-suffering wife, Susan, whose help was crucial at every stage of the book's evolution.

My thanks to the following institutions and corporations for granting me permission to use my photographs of their gardens: Denver Botanic Garden, Denver, Colorado; Golden Gate Park, San Francisco, California; Longwood Gardens, Kennett Square, Pennsylvania; and Washington Park Arboretum, University of Washington, XD-10, Seattle, WA 98195. Thanks to the Hewlett-Packard Corp. and EDAW Landscaping both of Ft. Collins, CO for the use of photographs of gardens designed by Herbert Schall.

Several people graciously consented to have their photographs appear in this book. Thanks to Peter Bloomer (p. 164), Jodi Malitz (p. 51), Seth Malitz (p. 52, 53, 83, 87, 98, 157), Susan Malitz (p. 85, 176), and Charles Holley (p. 85). The extraordinary photograph of the Hien Shrine garden was taken by William Corey. The photo on p. 177 is used by permission from Shufunotomo Co., Ltd., Tokyo. They are the co-publishers, with Timber Press, Inc., of *Essentials of Bonsai* (1982). All the other photographs are the author's.

The cartoons on p. 26 and p. 147 are the work of young Dutch cartoonist, Daniel "Dadara" Rozenberg, drawn three years ago when he was sixteen.

Introduction

The personal garden is one of the last, great, remaining luxuries. Exploding populations, dwindling resources and economic necessities will make it even more so. A life spent in an asphalt and concrete landscape may so deaden the senses that the desire for this amenity might be blunted, but the need never will be.

The purpose of this book is to facilitate the planning of a garden that will be of interest during all seasons. Perennial beds, vegetable gardens, bulb displays, etc. are not our main concerns. What does concern us is the over-all structure of the garden, the stage and backdrop against which these and other interests will be played.

We are primarily interested in the garden as an environment. Its interior decoration can continually provide enjoyment and exercise the owner's creativity and interests. But it will be the large scale structure of the garden, the placement of trees, shrubs and stones that will concern us here. These features largely determine its character and appeal, and so to a large extent, influence our mood as we view it, and stroll its paths.

The focus is on gardens of the temperate region, although most of the principles discussed are relevant to garden design in any climate. I have had relatively little experience with gardens of the tropics or subtropics and have developed less of a rapport with them than with temperate gardens. I have had a bit to do with gardens in the maritime influenced climates of California and Chile. About arctic gardens I know nothing.

The book is divided into two parts. The first considers design sources, various goals that a landscape can achieve, and some of the materials and methods available for attaining these goals. The second part describes an expedient method of creating a landscape plan.

The chapters in each part consist of a collection of short essays, diatribes, and harangues.

Chapter 1 discusses various garden styles that can inspire a personal garden. Both ready-made gardens found in nature and gardens designed by man are considered and illustrated as potential sources of landscape ideas.

The major physical components of garden design are discussed in Chapter 2. Various kinds of trees and shrubs are compared with respect to their design potential and impact. In a general way, perennials, ground covers, rocks, and garden structures are also discussed.

Chapter 3 has two sections. The first is devoted to a discussion of existing plants that are my personal favorites for landscaping. The second entails wishful thinking about plants that don't exist but would be among my favorites if they did exist.

In Chapter 4 the problem of incorporating personal hobbies and interests within the garden without compromising its design is considered. The pros and cons of back-yard rockeries, bogs, rose gardens, perennial beds, and animal sanctuaries are weighted.

Chapter 5 deals with the technique of plant management, in particular the care and grooming of trees and shrubs for design purposes.

Chapter 6 focuses on the choices that must be made initially in the design process, and the discussion includes the choice of style, plant materials, rocks and so on.

The last chapter of Part I, Chapter 7, contains some mental meanderings through several real and imagined gardens along with a few off-the-wall reflections on gardening in general.

Part II of the book describes a method for creating overhead and ground-level views of a landscape in various stages of growth, in leaf as well as deciduated.

The first section of Part II describes the method which requires transparent overlays for its implementation.

The drawings from which the overlays are made and the descriptions of their intended function conclude Part II.

The reader should be warned that my own aesthetic preferences and opinions of what constitutes a satisfactory personal garden are presented throughout, and that I hold them with bulldog tenacity. However, I do not want the reader to see this as arrogant dogma which must be followed if one is to succeed in realizing his own Eden, but rather as strongly held personal tenets begging for strong concurrence or strong disagreement. The main objective is to encourage the reader to formulate his own ideas of the perfect garden, perfect for him at least, and to formulate them clearly and with conviction.

Throughout I offer some general principles, guidelines, and cautionary advice. The latter is given in the hopes that the reader will avoid the mistakes and pitfalls that ensnared this gardener and some of his friends and acquaintances. The former is offered as a ploy designed to goad the reader into taking stock of his own goals and resources, and to harden his resolve to put together that personal dream garden.

PART I:
SOURCES AND STYLES, MATERIALS AND METHODS

CHAPTER 1 *Sources*

[1.1] INTENT

Pass through the gates of any great garden and you enter a perfect universe, an example of the most congenial collaboration between man and nature. Stroll the paths and every step opens up new pleasures, every turn is met with delightful surprises.

The garden can evoke the tranquility of a misty, lichen-draped rain forest or a sun-drenched, alpine tundra. It can call to mind a rocky, wave-lashed shore, or a river-worn canyon. The garden is an ombudsman between us and all the expressions of nature from its gentlest manifestations to its harshest, always presenting them in a non-threatening way but nevertheless forcefully, convincingly, and poetically.

Within this idealized fragment of nature one can withdraw for awhile, isolate oneself from our citified, high-speed, high-tech, high-rise existence, and touch a world that seems more remote but more essential everyday. Perhaps this is what we seek most in a garden, its ability to evoke the presence of nature, to transport us in a few steps to a microcosm that is not all bright and shiny, molded, cut, and cast out of concrete, steel, and glass.

The goal is to design such a garden for private use, a personal sanctuary where one can retreat from the hassles of our over-urbanized existence and rekindle our sensibilities to the splendors of nature.

It is as unlikely in the garden arts as it is in the plastic arts that a unique and personal style will spring full-blown out of the blue with the first attempt. There has to be time to pursue dead-end paths and make errors before a style can be honed to clarity and conviction.

Since the gardener is a one-painting artist, there is little opportunity to develop a truly novel and individual style. A concerted attempt to be uniquely original is quite likely to produce something amateurish, unconvincing, or simply an outright abomination.

So it is far safer to fashion the design after some existing garden, man-made or God-given. Models and examples are in endless supply and there is considerable opportunity to express individuality both in the initial choices and in the translation and realization of the design.

What sources can we tap that will provide us with ideas on which to plan such a landscape? Certainly the designs of nature, the infinite variety of wild gardens, provide the most inexhaustible source. Most of the styles of the past and present were inspired by the designs of nature, and the great gardens that were created in these styles also offer an abundant source of ideas. A step further removed from nature but still in a direct line of descent, landscape painting and various painting styles can provide ideas. Even tray landscapes and the art of dwarfing trees, saikei and bonsai, can be used.

Our aim here is to discuss and compare some of these sources with a view to their applicability in designing a personal garden.

[1.2] NATURE

The principle source of inspiration for most of our gardens has always been found in the wild scenery with which this planet is so abundantly blessed. Even the most abstract gardens of Noguchi and Nagare are indebted to nature for much of their inspiration. Those few styles that lean more on geometry, toeing the line set by straightedge and compass, seem more appropriate for the planting of a city thoroughfare or the perimeter of a parking lot, than for the design of a personal garden.

There are so many natural landscapes to furnish suitable models for a personal garden that the problem lies not in finding one, but rather in selecting one. Although the tourist's inclination is to search out the most spectacular landscapes and those that have the most unusual features, it is the subtler features of the more common places, the ordinary forests, ponds, meadows, and streams, that most readily and convincingly transcribe to the personal garden. Moreover, the designs which follow such models seem particularly well suited to provide the amenities which seem so desirable in a garden today—lasting interest and beauty, privacy, and a sense of retreat.

Forests of Birch, Aspen, and Pine

Perhaps no landscape is as hospitable and comforting as a forest, and perhaps none can supply as rich a cache of design ideas. Although there are many different kinds of forests, each with its own mood and spirit, not all can be emulated in the garden. But fortunately, a great many can.

On the East Coast there are forests of Paper Birch, bright and airy even in full leaf, glorious in the gold of fall, and spectacularly austere in winter, when slender columns of white are patterned against the white snow. No forest communicates the rush of spring as vibrantly as when the birch speckle themselves in the brilliant yellow-green of their newly emerging leaves.

West of the Paper Birch forests the Aspen come into their own and offer a more than fair substitute. Their bark may not be as pristine white as that of the Paper Birch, but it is striking enough in its ivory hue, and the responsiveness of the foliage to the gentlest breezes brings an animation and sparkle to the forest unmatched by any other. When the alchemy of autumn gilds this forest and the breezes set the translucent leaves in motion, entire hillsides possess the shimmer and sparkle of a zircon lake. The course of this yearly spectacle is closely monitored by the newspapers and newscasts, and during the peak of the season the highways are so clogged by Aspen watchers that minimum speed limits are ignored and practical travel is impossible.

This golden outburst is not the Aspens' final statement for the year. Laid bare by the winds of October, they reach their season of greatest refinement and delicacy. Large stands cover the mountain sides like the clinging morning mists in shades of gray and mauve. But only close at hand can one fully appreciate the creamy white bark and the elegance of their individual

forms. The Aspen is a tree for all seasons, and what it offers in each is unique for that season, making a garden of continuing interest throughout the year.

On a north facing hill the Aspen may be mixed with an occasional young Blue Spruce, and on a south facing hill Aspen and pine mingle to form stands of remarkable contrast but with perfect harmony in every season. The dark pines and blue-green spruce are the ideal foil for the Aspens' golden fall color and its lime-green spring hues. Summer sees the Aspens' leaves flutter dull green and silver in breezes too slight to move the rugged conifers; now the color composition is all harmony and the contrast is in the choreography. But this pairing is at its best in winter when the white, open elegance of the Aspen is bared against the dark, massive conifers.

Here is an example for the best of gardens, those that are a joy in each season and pique our anticipation of the next with the promise of dramatic change. The landscaper can do no better than create such a design, one that will be as responsive to the seasons and reflect each with as much beauty.

The effect of a birch or Aspen grove is rather easy to duplicate on a small scale in the garden since both trees are relatively fast growing and of modest size. But one must be more patient and possess more space to conjure up the look and feel of the great hardwood forests of the East. The trees that inhabit these forests, the Red Maples and Sugar Maples and oaks, are noble, tall, spreading trees at maturity, too large for the average garden. In youth they are too sparse and awkward to make a significant showing. But the scarlet, orange and yellow fall color display is so spectacular, and the dense shade in the heat of summer is so welcome that one can reach for an approximation using smaller trees like the maples *Acer truncatum, A. grandindentatum, A. circinatum, A. palmatum, A. japonicum,* and the like.

The coniferous forests are still slower in reaching maturity. Perhaps more somber than forests where deciduous trees predominate, no other gives the feeling of protected seclusion to the same degree. The Ponderosa forests of the Rockies give me particular pleasure. The pines here are not of the same variety as the giants of the Sierras and they lack the boldly checkered, bright golden bark that is such a spectacular feature of their western relatives. But this smaller stature makes the individuality of their forms and the organization of their groupings more apparent, and so more suggestive of designs for a personal garden.

Overleaf. Aspen role out a golden carpet to celebrate the arrival of autumn. Cub Lake Trail, Rocky Mountain National Park, Colorado.

The Big Trees

However, not every scene that moves one is a candidate for modeling in the garden. The scale may be inappropriate, or the time required to obtain the desired outcome might make the project unrealistic. For example, there is no match for the grandeur and majesty of the redwood forests of the Pacific Coast. Here the giant trees tower 365 ft. above the forest floor, with boles that reach a diameter of 25 ft. Their massiveness and the directness of their ascent is in strong contrast to their thin, horizontal limbs and delicate fans of needle foliage. The spongy forest floor is rich and dark, built up from the decay of centuries of fallen giants. Sorrels, ginger, and ferns cover the ground, and since sunlight seldom finds its way there, few trees and shrubs dare challenge the redwoods. But occasionally some Bigleaf or Vine Maple will find a place, and here and there a young redwood will stretch itself up beside some ancient ancestor. When sunlight does find its way to the forest floor, it streams down in distinct beams, delineating the leaves and branches in gleaming silver. No man-made cathedral can evoke such wonder and awe.

However, the creation of such a forest is not measured in human lifetimes, and nothing remotely approaching the effect can be achieved in a garden started from scratch. In spite of their fast initial growth the effect of a young stand of coastal redwoods is delicate and airy. The individual trees have a spindly grace with perhaps a bit of gawkiness that gives some hint of their future stature. The young grove will have its own beauty and its appearance will change with fair rapidity, but not until centuries later will it take on the commanding majesty of a mature redwood forest.

The forests of the Giant Sequoia (*Sequoiadendron giganteum*) in the high Sierras are an equally inappropriate model. Though not as tall as their coastal relatives, the Giant Sequoias reach heights of 325 ft. and a trunk girth of 40 ft., making them the world's most massive trees. Their whipcord foliage is held in billowing clumps which accentuates the sheer brawn of the trees. They stand in small groves, co-mingling with other giant species like Sugar Pines and several enormous firs, and this competition steals a bit of their thunder. In the garden the young trees look like some hyperthyroidic juniper or thuja for a couple of hundred years, and in no way display the venerable majesty of mature specimens.

Rain Forests

The great, coniferous rain forests of the Pacific Northwest offer a completely different mood. Darker and more somber, they are immersed in a soft air, moist enough to coddle ferns and mosses growing epiphytically 20 ft. above the forest floor. Light, color, and sound are all muted, and in the timeless hush, growth proceeds upon growth, layer upon layer, seemingly with such speed that you might hear the rush. But it's only witnessed by a deep, absorbent silence. Petasites, sorrel, ferns, and mosses cover the ground. Fallen trees in rapid decomposition host rows of young trees implanted on their trunks. Vine Maples, with their delicate, bright lime-green leaves and graceful stems, provide a counterpoint to the somber foliage and massive trunks of the cedars and Douglas Fir. It's a garden of gentle contrasts, a soothing garden of privacy and intimacy in spite of the overwhelming majesty of the trees. Again not an effect easily obtained on a quarter acre in one lifetime. But the look and feel of the forest floor and the mid-forest canopy of maples, along with some larger trees that offer shade can be approximated within a reasonable span of years and resources.

Scale and the time needed to achieve the desired result are not the only criteria for the rejection of a landscape model. The Coloradan might long for the lush exuberance of the tropical forest but will find that the reality of the climate permits only the weakest approximation.

There are many landscapes that are renowned thanks to features which are unique and unusual, or even strange and bizarre. The Devil's Post Pile, Bryce Canyon, Monument Valley, the Painted Desert are great places to visit, but I would not want to live there. And I would not want to model a garden after any of them either. The transcription and necessary miniaturization would be unconvincing, out-of-joint kitsch, without any of the amenities we associate with a garden. No shade, little privacy, nearly devoid of the companionship of plants—such a garden would have little to offer. The grotesque aspect of this kind of scenery is quite likely to wear quickly on the person who sees it day after day, and that person might soon long for the tranquility, privacy, and ever changing interest that other gardens offer. But there are other exotic landscapes in inhospitable places that do transcribe readily into personal gardens of great beauty and interest.

Mountain, Desert and Jungle Gardens

In the high alpine regions, where ice and snow yield reluctantly to a brief summer, the landscape reflects the harshness of the environment with a bold simplicity and heroic quality.

Ancient trees, thickened and twisted by the gales and bent by the snows stand alone or in small groves. Sometimes they crouch in the lee of great boulders or lean against them for protection and support. Sometimes they dare the elements in the most exposed sites so as to capture as much of the sunlight as possible. What shrubs there are, alpine birch and some willows, creep along the ground, or huddle inconspicuously in the protection of the rocks. Except for the lay of the land, this is an open landscape, alternately baked by the intense, crisp sunlight, and battered by an endless succession of storms. Inhospitable? For sure, but majestic and awesomely beautiful.

This is a setting that has been a model for gardens for hundreds of years. To affect the look of timberline in the garden the land is strongly contoured, the contours are stabilized and clarified by the placement of large boulders and rock formations, and then planted with wind-sculpted trees dug from the mountains.

Such a garden can evoke the drama and grandeur of the remote peaks in a convenient and hospitable setting. But for this kind of garden you trade the gentle grace and comfort of other designs for heroic forms and hard-won character. There is little shade for the stroller and little protection from the wind. The changes in the garden in response to the seasons will be slight and subtle. There is little opportunity to incorporate other garden interests into the design without destroying its integrity. But nevertheless, here is a style to stir the imagination and delight the eye for many, many years.

The mountains also provide gentler models. In the moraines and alpine meadows grow some of the most exquisite miniature plants, tiny specialists in mountain survival. They use the rocks for shelter from the wind and sun, protection from extreme temperature fluctuations, and tap the cracks and

ustralian tree fern in
e garden of tree
rns in Golden Gate
ark, San Francisco,
alifornia.

fissures for the water that seeps in and the sparse nutrients that accumulate. Many of these plants flower prodigiously, all out of proportion to their size, mantling themselves in the most delicate bloom in a brave show of defiance against the brevity of summer and the harshness of winter—the only other season. These are the places that inspire our rockeries and alpine gardens. Light and airy gardens, washed over by wave after wave of color from the end of one winter to the beginning of the next. They are water-wise, space-frugal, and relatively quickly established.

Even the deserts provide a design source for some, and it has to be admitted that many of the most extraordinary plant forms and most exquisite blossoms belong to plants that dwell in the dry lands. The cactus and other succulents in particular embody this Beauty-and-the-Beast contrast, the fat and spiny plants giving rise to flowers that are often gigantic in size, stunningly colored, and delicately scented. The individual plants are curiosities and showpieces, and some gardeners will go to any extreme in order to grow and display them. Few people are aware of the diversity of succulents that can be grown as far north as Zone 4. Cactus of many genera, yuccas, agaves, an infinity of sedums, and all sorts of shrubby desert dwellers succeed quite easily in cold climates providing that excessive winter damp can be avoided. Again this is a garden of light and warmth requiring very little maintenance, and like the rockery is likely to be the choice of the hobbyist who is at least as much concerned with housing a collection of interesting plants as in establishing a garden for its intrinsic beauty and atmosphere.

At the other extreme from the spare and ascetic landscapes of the deserts and alpine tundra is the model of the tropical forest. Here a bold and easy lushness prevails; a flamboyance of color, an extravagance of leaf shapes, and an exuberance of growth that is unbridled by a true winter. The garden is primarily evergreen, and except for an endless cycle of exotic flowers, ignores the calendar's seasons. I enjoy these gardens enormously, and visit them or glasshouse replicas whenever possible. But if I lived in the tropics I would soon come to miss the sculptural integrity of the more northerly trees, which show all the character of growth hard-won in the yearly battle against the elements and the seasons. I would resent the crowding that masks the individuality of the trees. I would miss the compositional clarity afforded by the play of open spaces against planted ones. But most of all, I would sorely miss the great seasonal changes which compose the gardening year into four distinct movements.

Water Music

Almost any hiking trail will lead to some lake or waterfall and offer up a full portfolio of ideas for the use of water in the garden. How many times has a picnic lunch been postponed until it could be enjoyed beside some pond or stream? Such places have a universal fascination and appeal. You expect the plants to have a special lushness and beauty where their leaves enjoy a softer air, and their roots tap moisture whenever needed. Those along the south or west shore will be particularly vigorous, getting a full issue of sunlight directly and by reflection. Many plants demonstrate a strong preference for a waterside existence and are rarely found elsewhere. Swamp Cypress, Tupelo, Red Maple, Clethra, many ferns and irises never show their full beauty away from water. Even the smallest seep trickling down the face of a rock is likely to host some unusual plant forms, maybe a primrose, or a carnivorous butterwort, and offer up a measure of beauty all out of proportion to its size. This is surely a place where the hiker will pause to refresh himself at least as much by the scenery as by a splash of water on the neck.

A lake or pond has a way of intensifying and concentrating the beauty around it while softening and blurring the images. The scene is twice enjoyed, directly and by reflection. Reality is splintered into sparkling fragments. Boulders, grasses, and trees stand on their own reflections, the sky above and below, in a mirage of free floating sculpture on the grandest scale. Moving water adds its own life and music to the landscape. Even the smallest stream or thread waterfall animates and enlivens the scene to capture and sustain our interest.

In the garden most of the moods of water can be emulated. But the gentler manifestations—the tranquility of a pond or a meandering stream—are the most easily captured, and perhaps the most suitable, satisfying, and have the greatest enduring interest. Even a small stream or waterfall can so focus our attention that distractions from outside the garden vanish, and we are convinced that the place is a forest. In a larger garden one might accommodate a series of ponds or a lake, edged with boulders and set with bog plants of all kinds. Stepping stones, bridges, or a waterside bench would not be inappropriate. Many of the great classic gardens of Japan feature a lake as their most conspicuous design element, and invariably there is a pavilion or viewing station strategically placed so that the water can be enjoyed night and day, and in every season.

Every kind of terrain and climate, every mood of nature has inspired the design of some garden. You can take your lead from the gentle and hospitable, or those that are awesome and inhospitable. Of course you have to take care that the model is horticulturally feasible, that it is appropriate in scale and character to the setting and architecture. And the design has to be one that you will not tire of, one that will nurture your interests over the long run.

[1.3] GARDENS OF MAN

The great gardens of man offer another rich store of design ideas. A certain amount of abstraction accompanies any transcription of nature into a garden setting, and the more disparate the two in scale or location, the more abstract will be the realization. If we take our lead from existing gardens, the abstraction is no longer a concern, and this removes some of the difficulty of the design processes and some of the challenge. It is easier to make a copy of a portait than it is to draw a portrait from life. Even those styles that are out of vogue or impractical can be useful in delineating goals more clearly and focusing attention on what is wanted and can be accomplished.

My aim here is not to present a comprehensive survey of garden styles but rather to focus on a few that seem particularly germane to today's personal garden.

When considering gardens of the past it is important to keep our awe, respect, and reverence of ancient things in check in order to evaluate their relevance to contemporary design. The ancient gardens have a historical interest that can cloud the critical eye. Some of these gardens, if duplicated today, would be ridiculed as contrived, overripe, out of place, or even pure kitsch. On the other hand, some of their aesthetic principles are just as relevant today as they were when they were built. Since there has been so much uncritical praise written about these ancient gardens, I shall try to keep enthusiasm and admiration for them in control and be as irreverent as possible.

Every great garden presents its own unique view of nature: in part, it is this strong personalization, this unity, that justifies these gardens as works of art. On the other hand, their strong identity can easily cramp the viewer's imagination. They seem so right, so perfect, that for the moment no alternative approach can be seen or imagined even when something entirely different would be much more suited to the purpose.

But for one's personal landscape, uniqueness or creative originality in the context of garden design is not likely to be the primary concern.

It is far safer and more convenient to plan the work along some established design which is known to work horticulturally and has strong appeal, than to hazard the considerable time and expense on some "new" design conceived primarily for the sake of displaying creativity. Besides, the garden will have its stamp of uniqueness under any circumstance since sites vary in their surroundings and in their horticultural restraints, and the design will depend on the commercial availability of plants, stones, gravel, and the like. Moreover, trees and other plants have a way of ignoring the desires of the gardener and expressing their own individuality. And no one follows a plan so slavishly that all alterations that personalize it are avoided. So each garden develops a personality of its own no matter what the original intention might have been.

[1.3.1] GARDENS OF THE ORIENT

Certainly the styles that evolved in China and Japan have to be considered as being among the most influential and germane, not simply because of horticultural compatibility and scale considerations but because of a poetic sense which many of us find deeply moving.

The ancient gardens that have survived over the centuries pose a curious dilemma. Valued as masterpieces of garden art, set aside, protected and preserved, they change. There is even some question about the immutability of the dry landscapes, like the renowned Royan-ji in Kyoto. Evidence in the form of ancient woodblock prints indicates that a flowering cherry graced this garden in the past, planted off center but well within its interior. It must have been a far different garden then, belying recent interpretations that it represents clusters of islands in an expanse of ocean.

The problem is especially pronounced in gardens featuring large, long-lived trees, like the pines. In some instances preserving the trees requires extraordinary measures. Supports the size of telephone poles are installed beside them. In the winter the branches are trussed up against the weight of the snow by tying them to the top of the pole, and often additional struts and crutches support the limbs from below. To my eye, these Daliesque devices strongly detract from the design of the garden. They introduce new, unplanned, and inharmonious elements into the composition. The sense of strength and nobility that these trees could offer is countered by these heroic measures to preserve them, and renders them weak-looking, even grotesque and pitiable.

Today such a garden is a stage-full of King Lears, each vying for the viewer's attention, wonder, and sympathy, whereas in the original conception the importance of individual trees was quite likely subservient to the design of the whole. In these cases a superabundance of respect and reverence has led to the preservation of individual trees at the expense of the over-all plan, so a once-great garden is transformed over the centuries into a museum of haggard, time-worn specimens.

This gives rise to a three-horned dilemma. Continue the exaggeration and characterization as long as possible; let the trees age and die naturally, pruned and shaped by the elements; or yank some out and start young trees in their place. No decision can be made without thinking of the time required to again have an acceptable garden, and generations might pass before the garden hints of its former glory.

Perhaps the ancient trees can be replaced piecemeal, one by one, on a continuing basis. The transition would not be as wrenching, but the result is likely to compromise the original conception, and the discordance brought on by the clash between old trees and new is not likely to be pleasing.

In those gardens employing smaller clones and species, or in those in which trees are kept small by skillful management, the problem is ameliorated to a considerable extent. With today's tree moving machinery and horticultural techniques, even a 20 ft. tree can be balled and burlapped, and set into place with relatively little shock, and this permits continual renewal without a major disruption in the design. If the design calls for a stand of vibrant young trees rather than a bunch of hoary ancients, such replacement will be welcomed.

However, in many gardens replacement is unthinkable since it would blunt the aura of antiquity which contributes so much to their mystique and esteem, and so the great old trees are nursed over the centuries until they are caricatures of ancientness, and the original design has been fragmented into individual stations of interest.

Of course, there are many gardens in China and Japan of recent origin and smaller scale which do not display these shortcomings, and perhaps it is these gardens that have the most to teach us.

Chinese Gardens

The classic gardens of China and Japan share many of the same stylistic features and principles of design. This is to be expected since so many cultural traditions infiltrated Japan from China. But the way these principles are expressed is often markedly different. Although both base their aesthetics securely on the designs of nature, the ancient gardens of China seem much more exotic and contrived, often to the point of caricature. The plan is often less cohesive and more jumbled. It is common for a single garden to have a series of stations each featuring a different kind of scene, something like the different stalls of a home and garden show, or in some cases, more like the sideshow stalls at a carnival.

Many of these gardens experienced a spasmodic evolution, alternately undergoing periods of destruction and neglect, with periods of refurbishment. Now they reflect the inhomogeneous inspiration of the many minds that directed the expansion of buildings, walkways, and stonework until the gardens were dominated by their inanimate architecture.

The rocks, plants, and man-made features seem chosen primarily for their strangeness, or extravagant decorativeness bordering on the crass, as for example, in the Liu Garden, Suzhou Provence, which boasts as its dominant feature a huge rock sculpted by nature into a misshapen chunk of Swiss cheese, giving an effect that would embarrass even Gaudi.

This garden also features a rubble of rock of one texture sprawling between two upended, pumpernickel-shaped boulders of a completely different texture to affect a reclining, bullet-breasted Venus poised to launch her mammaries into deep space. The renowned Lion Forest Garden in Suzhou features an enormous Crackerjack arrangement of carmel-corn rock glued together in a haphazard amalgam with surprise prizes—stiletto obelisks—jutting up here and there, seemingly placed at random.

On the other hand, the rockwork in the Tiger Hill Garden also in Suzhow, is massive, blocky, powerfully impressive, and natural even to a westerner's eyes.

But strange and exotic as these landscapes seem to us, they often accurately represent the natural, local scenery. Many are surrounded by weird and wonderful landscapes, such as the stone forest of Yunnan, looking like something disgorged from the innards of Carlesbad Caverns and left to bake and weather in the sun.

Although the source material might be wondrous, translation and compromise can bastardize the effect. What is unusual and fascinating when encountered in nature can be contrived and freakish in a garden setting. Certainly the United States boasts of some of the world's most awesome, beautiful, and geologically interesting features on this planet, but you have to pick and choose your models.

Most of these gardens do not work for me much beyond the nostalgia, curiosity and fascination for ancient times and peoples that they evoke.

That is not to say that I fail to appreciate the important role their design principles played in the evolution of the Japanese garden and the gardens of Europe and the United States. But I am not sympathetic to the way these principles are realized in the classic Chinese garden. The buildings and other structures that bind together the various scenes comprising the garden play such an important role in the over-all design that it is unlikely to be effectively imitated by a split-level pavilion in suburban Peoria. Out of scale and context, this kind of design evokes none of its original lavish grandeur, and is nothing more than a humbled, cloying homage to a style that evolved as a grand reflection of royal taste and royal means in a place and at a time when such ostentatious display was more acceptable than it is now.

Japanese Gardens

No group of styles has influenced our ideas about garden design more than those which evolved over the past eight hundred years in Japan.

There is no such thing as "the Japanese garden". Japanese gardens, even before the 20th Century, embraced a great number of wonderfully diverse styles serving different goals, although there is a common and distinct sensibility governing them all. They share many of the same principles, devices, and materials, but this only partly explains their strongly unique character as a group. Perhaps it is the reflection of the profound Japanese sensitivity to the most subtle expressions of nature that gives some over-all unity to these various garden styles.

The emphasis is on understatement and suggestion rather than on the brash and explicit. Gentle modulation of form, texture, and color are prized; not the wrenching color discords of beds of tulips and petunias. These are gardens to nurture long-term interest and contemplation, rather than grandstage for a "wow" from the casual passerby.

In many of the gardens, even the stroll gardens, the design was arranged to evoke a sense of some larger natural scene, usually by excerpting a significant and characteristic feature and representing it in reduced scale. Sometimes, as is the case in Ryoan-ji or Daitoku-ji, the reduction in scale is enormous. But this reduction in scale makes for a landscape to be looked at rather than be surrounded by. The viewer is an outsider not a participant. Such gardens work in a Japanese setting but given a backdrop of western non-style, suburban architecture, such miniaturizations are usually unconvincing and integrate poorly into the architectural setting.

Perhaps it is Japan's more modern private gardens gracing courtyards and entranceways of homes and places of business that are the most germane for our purposes. In spite of their small size they offer up a full measure of that uniquely Japanese sensibility that weds a reverence for nature with a spare and almost ascetic design sense. Being relatively new creations, they do not display the amalgam of disparate ideas that successive designers have piled on some of the renown older gardens over the centuries. Nor do we see a design in which the plant components have overgrown their intended role, and now grossly over-act it. The design seen in these modern gardens is the design the viewer was intended to see.

There are several reasons for the contemporary appeal and relevance of these gardens. Their small size is commensurate with today's smaller lots. Their clear, uncluttered, direct conception is in sympathy with our notions of modern design. And moreover, most require relatively little maintenance.

It is true that in order to be at their best they have to be clean, weed free, and finely tonsured. But their small scale and extensive use of paving stones and unraked gravel, and their spare use of plants keeps these chores to a bare minimum.

Many westerners find the Japanese gardens mannered, contrived, and a bit cutesy in spite of their obvious homage to nature. Some object to them as being overly manicured, with their clipped azaleas and boxwoods and shaped trees, making larger examples dependent on a considerable amount of drudgery in order to maintain their form. The dry landscapes, and others employing raked sand and carefully trained miniature trees and shrubs are sometimes criticized as being too precious and impractical. Many see the modern entranceway and courtyard gardens as set pieces, like large-scale ikabana, designed to be looked at from without, and not as an environment to be enjoyed from within. Others complain that their delicateness is out of place with our bolder and more massive architecture. And some gardeners will see these designs as so perfect that there is no room left to garden in. The enjoyment is static because the tight coherence of the design does not permit embellishments and experimentation, and those who enjoy gardening at least as much as they enjoy gardens may not be happy over the long run with this kind of plan.

All of these are valid criticisms, but they should not prevent us from appreciating the contributions these gardens can make to our own designs. Principles such as "framing", "borrowed landscape", "the great in the small", are relevant and useful, and we will discuss them in Chapter 6. More complex notions involving placement or composition, ideas which are not easily verbalized, are tellingly illustrated in the Japanese gardens. Even their integration of landscape and architecture is extremely instructive. But most of all, it is that profoundly sensitive and poetic interpretation of nature that is so appealing and so desirable to many garden designers.

The Japanese Style in the West

Where the climate is sympathetic to the flora traditionally used in Japan, it is not surprising to find gardens that are stylistically close to classic Japanese gardens. San Francisco's Golden Gate Park, and Seattle's Washington Park Arboretum are outstanding examples. But in places where traditional pines, maples, cherries and bamboos can not be grown, it is surprising to find convincing examples of gardens that honor the Japanese principles without using the plants that most consider essential to the character of these gardens.

The Japanese gardens in Lethbridge, Alberta, Canada and in Denver, Colorado reflect both a profound understanding of the aesthetic principles underlying the traditional Japanese garden and a deep knowledge of regional horticulture. After all, the climate of Lethbridge is not the climate of Kyoto, and the sun-drenched high plain around Denver is not the cool, mist-enshrouded environ of San Francisco. But compromises were struck between the necessities of horticulture and the demands of art without compromising either.

In the Lethbridge garden Ginnela Maples stand in for Japanese Maples, Austrian Pines for Japanese Black Pines, and crabapples for flowering cherries. Russian Olives replace who knows what, but they are not at all out of place, with their silver foliage conjuring up a light frost or a mist even in the clear brightness of an August afternoon, in wonderful contrast to the rough, black bark and strong angularity of their framework.

The Denver garden features a surprising number of species that are typically grown in Japanese gardens. However, a price is paid for including these exotics. It's amusing to see Japanese cherries wintering over under a thick, thatch skirt covered with a thick, cloth blanket, all cord-wrapped. But these devices do not enhance the winter aspect of the garden in any way.

There is a clarity of design about the Denver Garden, an openness to it, a spacious quality that befits its location on the plains skirting the Rockies. However, this clarity was obtained by arranging dwarfed trees in isolation or in groups widely separated from one another, and this resulted in some tradeoffs. The design is highly suggestive of mountain scenery. But the small scale cannot help but impose a Gulliver-in-Lilliput aura to the garden, and the unmoderated July–August sun does not invite the stroller to pause and contemplate its many superb features.

Nevertheless, as a servant of two masters with conflicting demands,

18

adherence to the principles of the Japanese stroll garden and planting a garden capable of surviving Denver's climate, it's a wonder.

Bonsai and Saikei

In excerpting a fragment of a wild garden and transcribing it to one's lot there is inevitably some process of abstraction. For example, a few boulders may be obliged to play the role of a mountain range, a 3 ft. wide ribbon of pebbles might be assigned the task of suggesting a river, or a 10 ft. × 10 ft. bed of raked gravel may be required to conjure up the image of the ocean vastness. When this is done successfully, a miniature world is created which you can enter mentally but not physically. It can evoke reminiscences of places like those represented, and, to some extent, elicit the same emotions experienced there, much in the same way that a landscape painting does.

But much of the enjoyment comes from the art itself, from the realization that this is a miniaturized representation of some great fragment of nature. The very artfulness of the piece and the skill evident in its realization play a major role in the appreciation of it.

The art of bonsai is a good example. Here a tree, or even a grove of trees is dwarfed to a height of perhaps 1–3 ft. by judiciously pruning the roots and tops, restricting the root run and amount of nutrients, and carefully bending the trunks and limbs. In the great examples of the art, the bonsai develops the character of a full-grown tree or stand. Its character can be that of a noble elm, unchallenged in its domain, wide-spreading and symmetric, or a wind tortured pine clinging to some rocky crag, or a gentle grove of maples in a field of moss. Some of the most renown examples were plucked from timberline, "krummholtz" that were locked in battle with the winds and snows and baking summer sun. Every tortured and twisted limb shows the fight and the indomitable tenacity of the plant. Those that are nursery grown are often modeled after these noble specimens and can convincingly suggest the high mountain environment.

But a bonsai is no more of a garden than a landscape painting. The windswept heights may be suggested but you won't feel the wind, the shaded forest is implied, but doesn't cool you on an August afternoon. The birds don't flock to it, and if they did, would appear to be ostriches on the wing. The pleasures derived from these arts is, in some sense, more cerebral and abstract, less physical and direct, and so perhaps less convincing and moving. The thing itself, and the cleverness, skill, and patience of the artist who created it, take center stage. It's bonsai, it's not a garden.

The horticultural craft involved in dwarfing the trees and the sculptural art of shaping them to evoke the character of the mature tree and the environment that shaped it over the centuries combine to make great bonsai. It's the interaction of these two facets of the art that is so enthralling. That is why I find more pleasure and wonder in those examples that use trees which if left to their own would reach majestic proportions, rather than in those which use genetically dwarfed trees and shrubs to simulate forest giants.

On the other hand, in a full scale garden I prefer not to be distracted by ingenious horticultural practices, or awed by the cleverness of the designer; not that ingenuity or cleverness are ever absent in a great garden, but when present in adequate measure, they never need to be flaunted.

The gardens that move me most, perfect and creative though they may

the Japanese rden, Golden Gate rk, San Francisco, alifornia.

19

be, have an artlessness about them which makes their representation of nature more convincing. Caught up in the mood of one of these gardens there is no great need to marvel at the skill of its originator or the state of his psyche at the moment of its conception. All this excess baggage impedes the appreciation and enjoyment of the garden for its own sake.

This does not imply that the garden should show no signs of having been designed, just a chunk of the wilderness at the doorstep. Nor does a roped-off boundary delineating a piece of forest define a garden. There should be some evidence of human intelligence and creativity, without this being its primary purpose. An awareness that the garden is an expression of the human sensibility certainly doesn't lessen enjoyment, and in fact it is likely to add an additional component to an appreciation of it, as long as the creative aspect is not its sole point.

Moreover, it is unlikely that a small plot can reach any semblance of a design goal if it is not managed. Without some control the plot would soon evolve into a Darwinean arena in which the plants fight it out in a test for the fittest, making the garden into a disorganized jumble of the most prodigious seeders and rampant growers. But the line between controlled and contrived is a fine one, and each gardener must set the line for himself.

One should not confuse controlled with formal. The formal garden is certainly highly controlled, but gardens based on natural precepts can also be highly controlled, as is the case with most of the gardens of China and Japan. Indeed, these gardens strike many as being so controlled as to be contrived, while others argue that any idealization is automatically contrived.

To the extent that "contrived" and "idealized" overlap, bonsai and saikei are as contrived a representation of the landscape as any other. But what wondrously poetic contrivances these are, and one can learn a great deal from them regarding the shapes of trees, the shaping of trees, and the arrangement of groups of trees in a landscape. In fact, if there was an easy way to do it, if miniature trees of various kinds and sizes were readily obtainable, saikei could be used as a model to work out the design problems of a proposed landscape in much the same way that the traditional sculptor uses a maquette to work out the design problems of a larger piece.

[1.3.2] GARDENS OF THE OCCIDENT

In spite of our fascination with the gardens of the Orient and the relevance of their design principles, most of our garden aesthetic is dominated by European traditions. This is a rich heritage embracing a diversity of styles, and bringing with it a plethora of plants bred and selected for use in designs adhering to these styles. European breeders have been so successful in developing "improved" varieties that these are the dominant plants in most nurseries today. The potent visual impact on the landscape that many of these varieties have practically assures any design using them will adhere to traditional European canons. Moreover, the spectacular nature of many of these plants, the wealth of horticultural experience in growing them, and their resultant availability has impeded the discovery and use of other species and varieties which are much more suited to contemporary tastes and much more adapted to climates unlike those of England and continental Europe.

Nevertheless, these traditional styles can not be ignored for they are exemplified by masterpieces, designs of extraordinary integrity and beauty, and these gardens are supported by a broad base of horticultural knowledge which has wide relevance. We can enjoy these styles for what they are, ignore the coercion of tradition, and choose those aspects to emulate that best suit our needs and tastes.

Formal (Geometric) Gardens

Perhaps the great formal gardens with their adherence to strict geometric principles were beaten into Pythagorean submission in an effort to display the owner's mastery over his universe. To no small extent these are gardens for the ostentatious display of power and wealth. The proper maintenance of their weed-free lawns, their geometric hedges, their pristine pools, their straight-edged walks, and rows of regimented roses requires the employment of a mindless workforce engaged in the worst kind of drudgery that a garden can call forth. Diametrically opposed to this canon is the Japanese view that the garden should bring one humbly and contemplatingly to the threshold of nature and pique his awareness and sensibilities so that he may more keenly appreciate it. In this view the architect sees himself as being in harmony with nature and not as a potential master bent on complete submission.

I don't believe that a satisfactory garden can be designed on the precepts of geometry, or that of any other mathematical discipline for that matter. It's not that I have anything against these most cerebral of all arts; indeed, I have a special fondness for them and appreciate their rich applicability to everything from physics to biology. But a garden given over to simple geometric shapes, to straight-line paths, and boxwood hedges pampered into parallelepipeds, is a pitifully uninteresting representation of mathematical order. The problem is that mathematics is too austere and cerebral to be applicable to an art with which we expect to have some emotional rapport. Mathematics will never make you weep, unless you discover a hole in a proof and the proof is yours. No theorem that I know of will give you the hots. It may be the correct model for chemistry and physics, but it seems largely irrelevant to the art of today's personal garden.

We also have objections to the formal garden that are less philosophical. We find most of these formal gardens dreadfully boring. We miss the irregularities with which nature offers us delightful surprises. Cubes, circles and rectangles are too commonplace to be surprising or interesting in a garden. It seems too easy to plan a landscape around these elements. This type of design already abounds in our concrete and asphalt environment, dictated by necessity and expedience. What most of us need in a garden is some respite from this harsh geometry, and some contact with the freeform exhuberance of nature.

Of course, spacious lawns and broad straight paths do offer some amenities. One can snift a brandy or walk with the hands clasped behind the back while discussing politics, without fear that concern over the national debt or G.N.P. will distract and cause one to stumble into a well-manured strawberry bed or get hung up in the blackberry patch. Broad lawns can host a genteel game of croquet or a bit of lawn bowling. Even soccer, football, lawn tennis, or badminton can be enjoyed if there is enough room to provide a new site for the court every week or so.

But in the restricted confines of our quarter-acre lots a weekly game of badminton will so screw up the lawn that it could pass as the grazing ground of a herd of buffalo.

The Outdoor Room

A style of recent vintage and burgeoning popularity, especially in the milder, more laid-back zones, was introduced by the architect Thomas Church at about 1955 in his book *Gardens Are For People*. The title suggests that plants are barred from his gardens, but this is not entirely true.

This style is based on the premise that a private garden should be an extension of the dwelling, sort of an outdoor room whose design and function extend the amenities of our houses by incorporating such features as a pool, a barbecue, and plenty of furniture.

The idea of melding the interior with the landscape is certainly not new. The Chinese framed some of their choicest garden views through doors and windows in the shape of vases, leaves, and flowers. To further the link between interior and exterior, halls within the building continued as garden paths outside, and roofed paths and bridges connected one wing of the building to another, providing close-up viewpoints for the enjoyment of the garden in all weather. The Japanese honored the intent of this principle while elaborating and customizing it. Their architecture evolved into a lighter and more open structure. Mortar and stone were replaced by wood and paper. Thick, opaque walls were abandoned in favor of sliding translucent panels that opened an entire side of the building to the garden, removing the boundary between exterior and interior altogether.

But where the landscape masters of the Far East sought to bring the amenities of nature into the home, Church's scheme proposes to extend the banality of indoor decoration out into the landscape. Maybe it's because Church lived and worked on the other side of the globe that caused him to get it backwards.

The style easily lends itself to many amusing perversions. The outdoor barbecue grill becomes a center of focus. Kitschy-curly, wrought-iron, lawn furniture replaces natural seats of wood or stone; the plastic umbrella in decorator colors functions as a short but efficient shade tree; the tennis court serves as a mini-meadow devoid of flowers, neatly striped, lined, and painted with one of those rare greens that is antithical to any imparted by chlorophyll. The chlorinated, acid blue pool is your lily pond, the lilies replaced by multi-colored bathing caps, and the hot tub replaces some spring. A couple of gimlets and a dip in the tub and no one notices the difference. Outdoor living at its most plastic and sterile.

[1.4] ART AND THE ART OF THE GARDEN

*It has come to this,—that the lover of art is one, and the lover of nature,
another, though true art is but the expression of our love of nature. It is
monstrous when one cares little about trees and much about Corinthian
columns, and yet this is exceedingly common.*

Henry David Thoreau

Garden design has enjoyed a long and fruitful reciprocity with other
arts, inspiring painters and poets, and in return being inspired by them.

For the gardener, painting and drawing of natural scenes are an obvious
source of ideas, and examples can be found that readily transcribe to garden
designs, although usually the original will allow enough artistic license to
make the transcription more of a creative interpretation and more of a work
of art than a copy.

However, paintings can be used as a design source in a more indirect
way. The style itself, independent of any representational content, can
suggest a garden.

Impressionism

For example, the soft atmosphere of the impressionists can be simu-
lated by a planting that features plants having a very fine texture. Honey
Locusts, Albizia, False Spirea, pea shrubs, heaths and heathers, Smoke Bush
for its flowers, cut-leaved maples and birch, and all sorts of perennials such as
Astilbe, Fillipendula, Aruncus, and fine-textured ferns, and many, many
more are candidates for creating this effect. Even pointillism, that most
orthodox form of impressionism, can be approximated by an appropriate
choice of design and plant material.

Abstract Expressionism

Those habituated to a more frenetic environment can capture some
frenzied exuberance of abstract expressionism in the garden. The vast
canvases of Jackson Pollock, with their many-layered, interwoven trickles
and spatters of paint, conjure up images of the great rain forests of the Pacific
Northwest, draped with an entanglement of lichen-covered branches and
vines. In the garden this effect might be suggested by an understory of
Corkscrew Willows, or Vine Maples (grown in the shade), or by larger
shrubs and trees supporting vines of Akebia, Climbing Hydrangea,
honeysuckle, and clematis.

On a much smaller scale, taking inspiration more from Mark Tobey than
Pollock, perennials like Boltonia, Grambe, Threadleaf Coreopsis, and Baby's
Breath can provide an approximation to the rich linear embroidery of the
style.

Indeed, almost any style that moves you deeply and sustains your interest is a candidate for a garden design. Anything, from a Frankenthaler cum
Burl Marx juxtaposition of broad swaths of high-intensity color, to the
amorphous intermingling of subtler hues in the color-field approach of Jules
Olitski, can be approximated using perennials for paint, and the good earth as
the support.

Geometric Abstraction

The great "dry landscape" tradition of Japan has modern day disciples like Masayuki Nagare and Isamu Noguchi. They updated the style, replacing the raked gravel by tiled paths, and the found boulders by sculpted stones. Often, the contour of the paths and the pattern of the tiles suggest moving water, as does the raked sand of the earlier gardens, and the abstract sculpture evokes images of mountains, islands, and rocky prominences. The austere and mysterious spirit is still there, but these new gardens are unmistakably products of this century.

The ancient counterparts were designed to be viewed from the perimeter of the garden—footprints on the raked sand would not only destroy its pattern but even suggest that someone had walked on water, an inappropriate symbol for a Buddhist garden. In contrast, the paths of the contemporary versions are designed to be walked on, and so these gardens seem less hermetic and standoffish than their precursors. Still, to most they will appear too austere and antiseptic to serve as models for a private landscape.

You might view the earthworks of Andre, Christo, Judd and the like as some further artsy abstraction of the stone gardens of Noguchi and Nagare. But whereas the latter evoke a sense of timelessness and permanence, the former are often intentionally and deservedly transitory. One must wonder if the artists responsible for these outcraps on the land have ever seen or are the least bit sensitive to the great natural earthworks, the deserts, mountains, and canyons that enrich our common garden with infinite variety and subtlety and are there without pretension or guile.

Incidentally, I am not criticizing the appropriateness of incorporating elements into the garden that are of a temporary or fleeting character. The bellflower garden or Hoshun-in, Daitoku-ji in Kyoto and bush clover garden of the Kyoto Imperial Palace emphasize this characteristic. But here the scale is different. The time, energy and money spent in the creation of these gardens or their like is commensurate with their size and effect and so are much less pretentious. Perhaps those with a more meditative bent, those who enjoy contemplating the finiteness of life more than I are more deeply moved by these gardens than I am. However, where time and space are considerations, a garden given over to a single fleeting yearly effect may not be enough compared to one boasting unflagging interest through the four seasons.

Minimalist Art

The minimalist sculpture of Tony Smith graced the cover of *Time Magazine* and the accompanying article referred to his work as a "math man's delight". What rubbish. Works like his black steel cube 6 × 6 × 6 ft. inspire no delight in any math man I know. This simple-minded geometry for the amented is not something of even the slightest interest to the mathematician—he can form a mental image of the cube with no difficulty at all, rotate it slowly in space, see its inside, float it in the middle of the Atlantic, set it on a snow-capped plateau or in the middle of the Sahara. Compared to the geometric constructs the mathematician considers on a day-to-day basis, pieces such as these are much too obvious and simplistic to be at all entertaining, and the building of one is a totally unnecessary waste of time and space.

Apologists for the minimalists argue that minimal cues best pique the imagination. But this art only leads one to wonder at the lack of imagination, the pretension, and the earnestness of the practitioners. A great deal of experimental evidence suggests that creatures with brains need a rich environment in order to keep those brains well honed and working at peak efficiency; a deprivation of stimuli only encourages the contents of the head-bone to ossify.

Of course, minimalism has its advantages. Minimalist art makes little demand on the viewer's cerebrum or soul, and the minimalist garden makes few demands on the back or buck. A void is easy to organize. Unfortunately, the number of ways of doing so is somewhat limited. However, one can give an entire lot over to a concrete deck. Paint it green to add a conceptualist twist. Perhaps a pot or two of purple petunias would please the colorist but might bastardize the effect. If the concrete can be poured from purple trucks, the entire project might be funded by the Rockefeller Foundation or photographs of the happening could be displayed at the Guggenheim.

I do not appreciate the minimalist aesthetic in the visual arts and have even less appreciation for it in the garden arts. In my own garden I much prefer a maximalist aesthetic as long as composition, harmony, and ease of maintenance are not compromised. Such an approach fosters continuing interest and pleasure in the garden, whereas the minimalist view fosters only short-term curiosity and long-term boredom.

Pop

Even pop art has its adherents among the gardening public. Just consider the number of plastic ornaments that are blow-molded specially for the garden.

Plastic carriage boys hold out a loop to which one can tie a Toyota.

Plastic palm trees are Zone 1 hardy, and unfortunately, guaranteed to be fade proof.

And few garden accouterments are as stunning as a bevy of beauteous flamingos in polyester pink, frozen in mid-stride by a Denver snowstorm.

There is a directness and honesty about it. Kitxch used intentionally as kitsch. Trash for the sake of trash. But plastic doth not a garden make.

There are many other styles that can inspire the design of a garden, but the choice has to be made carefully. Changes in an established garden are not made by rubbing out or overpainting a passage. Major changes usually necessitate major expenditures of time, effort and money, which is good reason to entertain the classic Oriental approach to art when designing a garden, rather than a more contemporary approach.

In the Far East, styles evolved slowly with each generation respectfully mindful of its artistic heritage, adding their own stamp of individuality only after assimilating the lessons of the past. Our approach, especially in this century, is to emphasize the novel, the individualistic expression, and downplay the craft. "Creativity" is the touchstone, the "raison d'etre", and all else is of secondary importance. Indeed, any hint of the influence of a prior time is likely to bring accusations of "derivative", "stodgy", and "unoriginal". With the requirements of craft relaxed, movement supersedes movement with dizzying speed. Pop is upstaged by Op and Op by Slop, and rubbish is heaped on rubbish, supported by the towering babble of a self-serving establishment. Works that were pedaled as creative and relevant a few years ago now seem dated, amateurish, and a bit silly.

The very notion of art as having some permanent worth has been questioned, as though there is an inherent tradeoff between the staying power of a piece and its ability to evoke a strong emotional response in a world ever more desensitized by the mass media and ever less mindful of craft in a time of burgeoning technology.

But the designer of the personal landscape is usually not out for a temporary, shocking effect. His goal is not to please or amuse others for a few moments. The time, money, and effort involved in establishing a landscape preclude that end, and impose a more conservative approach, one more mindful both of the past and of the future with a view toward creating something of long-term interest.

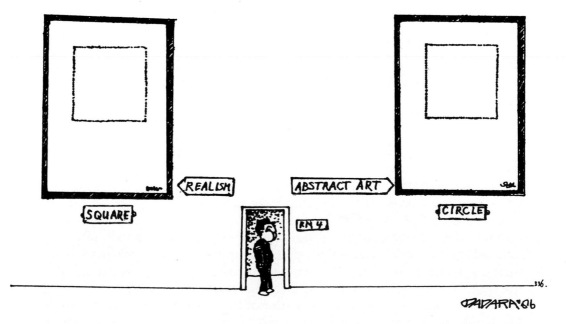

[1.5] PUBLIC PARKS, MALLS, ETC.

A few ideas can be gleaned from the landscape design of some of our public parks and the grounds of public buildings. They commonly contain all sorts of examples of what to do, and what not to do. These oases in the high-rise desert offer a good opportunity to learn something about the plants which are locally adaptable, and the form they are likely to take in your region. Frequently, however, there is a need to compromise the design for reasons that are of little concern to the architect of a personal garden. The material for a city planting has to be chosen for its ability to survive city conditions. Any tree that grows in Brooklyn is an unalloyed blessing, but the back-yard Ailanthus might look like a shabby overgrown weed. Among the restrictions that beset the designer of public parks are pollution, the shade of tall buildings and the heat reflected from them, concrete or blacktop over root runs, vandalism, and a million passing dogs. Hopefully, the home landscaper need be less concerned with these drawbacks and hazards.

Sizable parks usually offer sizable lawns and specimen trees, often with an emphasis on the most noble in height and spread. Oaks, beech, ash, and large maples are favored for their shade, their imposing character, longevity, and their toughness under city conditions. Sometimes the scale becomes so large that one can not perceive a sense of over-all design, and it becomes just a planting of individual trees grown for their own interest and for the amenities they offer strollers and picknickers. But our gardens have to be of a more personal and intimate scale, and a quarter acre has to nurture our year-long interests. Stuffing the site with a giant beech or oak will finish the landscaping and one's interest in the garden simultaneously.

The grounds of most public buildings are unfortunately designed with the aim of affecting a chic backdrop for the architecture, a splash of color that will momentarily attract the eye of the harried passerby. A planting of 1000 red tulips in a square framed by 500 yellow daffodils, to be replaced by 1000 purple petunias framed by 500 marigolds will usually suffice to draw a glance and a wow from even the most hassled motorist. Occasionally, a bench will be provided so that the stroller may pause to take in the fumes of the passing cars. Neo-knot gardens are also popular embellishments for public buildings, and almost always depict a flag, state or national, all done up in lavender, thyme, and sage. Seldom is patriotism expressed so sweetly. Rose gardens are always in vogue for city parks, and although I love taking my nose and eyes for a walk in them, I can't remember a single feature of any one which distinguishes it from any other.

Even parks which are designed to provide private garden amenities for the public—a place for strolling, picnicking, and viewing plants—often have to make compromises in order to accommodate the large number of visitors, as for example, the defacing concrete walkways at the Japanese garden in the Huntington Estate in California. But certainly there are enough great public parks to provide unlimited inspiration and design ideas.

The Hewlett Packard Garden

Occasionally one finds a truly superb and useful example of landscape architecture gracing the grounds of a corporate building. Recently and unexpectedly we found such an example in Fort Collins, Colorado. On a

Sunday afternoon in mid-April friends treated us to a tour of the grounds of the Hewlett-Packard Building . The structure is two-stories high and shaped like a squared-up letter U. The building enfolds a half-acre garden of extraordinary purity of design and incredible beauty. It's a garden of Paper Birches. They stand in groups, each group reigning over a grassy knoll studded here and there with boulders. These hillocks have no other plants, but the perimeter of the planting shelters various shade tolerant plants like Oregon Grape Holly, Burning Bush, and Redtwig Dogwood, as well as various junipers like 'Sea Green'. But center stage belongs to the birch.

Either the spacing of the trees or judicious pruning has forced each into a slender outline, emphasizing their spare elegance. Their whiteness is dramatically set off by the dark background of the building. This is a planting for all seasons, but we must have seen it at its best, with the fresh, pale green leaves of spring one quarter expanded and edge-lit by the late afternoon sun.

Walls of tinted glass permit the viewer to enjoy the planting from numerous viewpoints within the building, but strolling the paths is required in order to fully appreciate it.

The path coming into the garden from the south leads first through a grove of Austrian Black Pines, dense enough to block any view of the birch. The end of the pine grove is punctuated by two Colorado Spruce, and beyond the spruce is that exquisite birch forest.

The entire garden stands on little more than half an acre, and offers a variety of scenery and a feeling of spaciousness totally incommensurate with its modest size. It was planted only 8 years ago on naked farmland, but the trees brought in were of such a size as to give an immediate effect. Although the Paper Birch in Colorado is plagued by all sorts of problems like the Bronze Birch Borer, and the splitting of trunk and limbs due to the wrenching temperature changes, the trees here are in superb health, and have been maintained and pruned to perfection. The protection of the building is no doubt another factor contributing to their well-being.

So pure and coherent is this design that the occasional embellishments supplied by those who care for the garden, but took no part in its original conception, stand out with embarrassing clarity. A couple of Alberta Spruce occupy an out-of-the-way hilltop, seemingly too aware of their banal "klutzi-ness" to dare join the aristocratic party. A 4 ft. tall magnolia, maladjusted to the climate, exists by retaining a fifth of last year's growth, the rest having been butchered off by the weather, making a shabby but heroic picture as it bravely sets forth a few blossoms.

Here is a design to inspire a dozen variations suitable for a personal landscape, a private garden that will be a joy every day of the year, and reflect the seasonal changes with a grace and elegance that few others can match. Moreover, although it is a design which exploits all the principles of the classic Japanese garden, it shows no national idiosyncrasies, but has a unique character all its own.

It must be frustrating to work with such a design, one that is so perfect that any embellishment is immediately seen to be an afterthought by a lesser mind. With bitter grapes fermenting my enthusiasm, I wonder how many avid gardeners would be content to tend such a masterpiece, a garden too perfect to admit any improvement, a garden in which any addition, any change will diminish the effect. This is a garden in which the only remaining opportunity for active participation is relegated to the maintenance chores. On the other hand, the upkeep of such a garden should not be unduly burdensome. And for those who are not avid gardeners, are not driven to press their own stamp on the scene, and are not rabid collectors of some class of plants—those who just want to enjoy the garden as a scene or environment and take little interest in gardening per se—this garden may offer just the right model.

[1.6] CLOSING

The principal design source for our personal landscape is, as it has always been, nature. Established gardens and parks can show us how other societies and other cultures have interpreted and transcribed nature into gardens. Painting and photography can suggest styles and compositions, as can bonsai and saikei. But all of these are abstractions, one or two steps removed from the ultimate source.

I don't hike through the forest to satisfy some temporary need. But on occasion I want to indulge myself, as in some great feast, and satiate my hunger for awhile. Then I trek off to the mountains or forest to gorge my senses, my whole being, as fully as I can. There is no special season for this gluttony, for each offers up its own unmatched specialties, so I try to cram in as much as I can. However, this is an appetite that awakens every morning, and being tied to other things I can't trek off to satisfy this need as it arises. I need my own Walden, my own private bit of forest to wrap around me.

Surely there is no garden substitute for a forest walk or a hike in the mountains. Nothing we can make will match the scale and grandeur of nature's garden; nothing else will give us that tranquility and fill us with the same sense of wonder and awe. But for those of us whose sensibilities are more in sympathy with Muir and Thoreau than our professions can accommodate, the personal garden is the only alternative. And while we will be unable to enjoy the grandest symphonies of nature in this scale, at least we can have the pleasure of her chamber music day after day.

Alder at streamside along the path to
the Patriarchs, Mount Rainier National
Park, Washington.

Pteridium ferns gilded by the alchemy of autumn's first chill. On the trail to Cub Lake (above) and to Fern Lake (below). Rocky Mountain National Park, Colorado.

Time and scale are considerations.
Opposite page. The Coast Redwood, *Sequoia sempervirens*, Santa Cruz, California. This page pictures Giant Sequoia, *Sequoiadendron gigantea* in Sequoia National Park, California.
Above. Sue eyes the General Sherman Tree, wondering how to get it home, and where in the garden to place it.

The rain forest is a model of limited
climatic adaptability, but it is the finest
model of unbridled exhuberant
growth. These examples are from the
Olympic Penninsula, Washington.

A Zone 4 gardener's idea of an exotic garden—the tree fern garden in San Francisco's Golden Gate Park, California.
Above. *Gunnera chilensis* (with leaves up to 8 ft. across) is accompanied by orange flowered *Crocosmia masoniorum.*

Jungle under glass in Golden Gate Park, San Francisco, California. The photo on the left was taken shortly after the automatic misters were shut off.

Varied moods of water. On this
page Nymph Lake, Winter and
Summer, Rocky Mountain
National Park, Colorado.
To the right, a small waterfall
with a circular pool. Mount
Rainier National Park,
Washington.

40

The principles of "framing" and the "captured landscape" (left and above) exemplified on a grand scale. Mount Rainier National Park, Washington.

Above. Premonition of winter—a Daliesque trussing to fend off the coming snows. Kenroku-en Kanazawa, Japan. Photo courtesy of Charles Holley.

Left page. Shofu-en, the Japanese style garden in the Denver Botanic Garden, Denver, Colorado.

46

The Japanese garden in Golden Gate Park, San Francisco, California is pictured on this page and to the right. On the following two pages a scene in the Washington Park Arboretum, Seattle, Washington.

Longwood gardens, embodying the grandeur and scale that justifies the formal style and is justified by it. Kennett Square, Pennsylvania.

Longwood gardens. In the upper left is a gazebo—a wonderful place for a barbecue grill were it not for the open roof. T'is truly a folly. Above. A superb hyper-formal planting. Photo by Jodi Malitz
Below. The Italian water garden spouting off with obvious geometric simplicity.

51

The formal lily pools in Longwood gardens.
Above is the Queen Victoria Lily with pads up to 6 ft. across.
Left is the underside of a pad—structurally sound engineering coupled to a beautiful geometry.
On the two pages following the lilies is a nearly minimalist landscape in Santa Cruz, California.

Photo by Seth Malitz

53

Photo by Seth Malitz

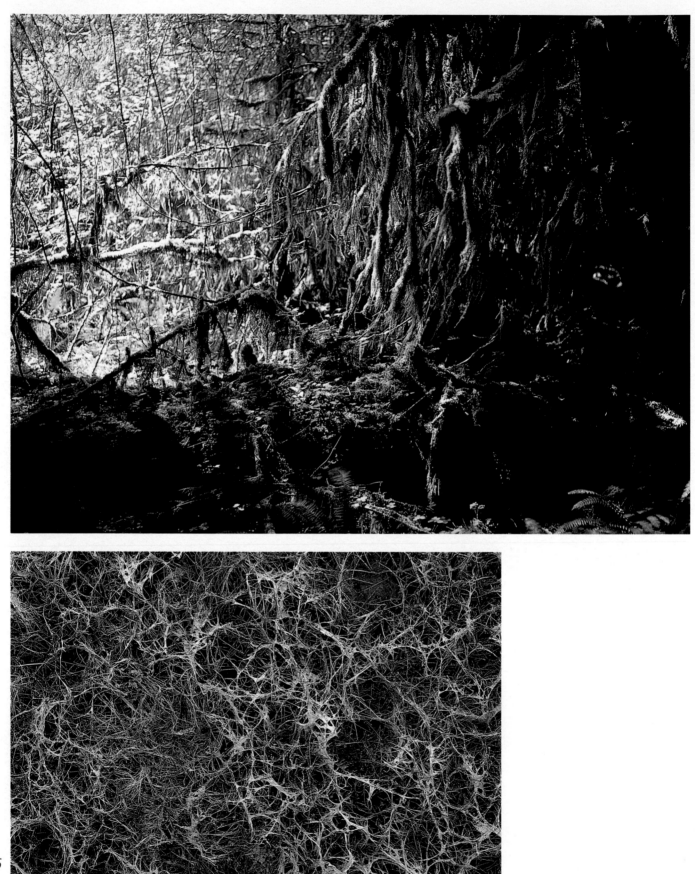

Analogies between art styles and natural scenes.
Above. An impressionist landscape near Bierstadt Lake, Rocky
Mountain National Park, Colorado.
Upper left. The Olympic Rain Forest, Washington offers a scene
reminescent of the style of Jackson Pollock.
Left. A patch of muddy grass is more in the style of Mark Tobey.

58

The Hewlett-Packard Garden in Fort Collins, Colorado, designed by Herbert Schaal of EDAW Inc. The photos on these pages are by Herbert Schaal.

59

CHAPTER 2 *Materials*

[2.1] INTENT

The landscaper is no Constable working with dabs of ocher and sienna. He works with flats of perennials, truckloads of dirt and gravel, boulders measured in tons, shrubs, and 15 ft. trees, and out of this stuff he creates a living, changing landscape. It's these materials and their use in garden design that is the focus here.

Trees and shrubs are usually a garden's dominant features. They have the greatest effect on its look and feel, and can even create a microclimate markedly different from that surrounding the garden. The substantial shadiness of a pine grove is in sharp contrast to the wispy airiness of a stand of birch or Japanese maples. The character of the design is also affected by the garden's smaller features—the perennials, rockwork, structures, and ornaments—to an extent that is more or less commensurate with their size.

Here we will consider the design potential of these various components, lumping the plant materials into groups according to their visual effect without regard to their botanical affinities. We will work our way down from the most striking and permanent large-scale features, the trees and shrubs, to what should be the least important fixtures, the ornaments and contraptions.

[2.2] GROUPIES AND LONERS

Some trees are loners, for either horticultural or design reasons, while others seem to prefer the company of their own kind and look their best when planted in groups. For example, the live oaks, phellodendrons, true cedars, and larger magnolias are best grown as isolated specimens. On the other hand a lone Aspen or Paper Birch usually looks wimpy and abandoned. Too thinly branched and too thinly foliaged to make an impression alone, but gathered together in a stand they form a significant and striking landscape feature. And where a single tree might give little usable shade, the grove provides a welcome retreat on a hot August afternoon.

A single tree planted as a specimen has to reach specimen size before it can be fully appreciated, and then the visual aspect of its majesty is best appreciated from some distance. On the other hand a grove of trees will offer a good measure of its full potential at a much younger age and from a greater variety of distances.

Whereas a grove of trees can effectively offer the look and feel of a bit of forest, a single oak specimen on a lot of the usual size is not likely to give us the sense of the oak-studded hills of coastal California.

There is more flexibility in placing a grove of relatively thin-trunked trees. For example, a window view through a small thicket of birch or Aspen might be a delight, but opening the blinds to be met by the bole of a mighty oak makes little sense.

Other trees can play either role, the majestic loner or the gregarious groupie. In this amenable lot we find certain oaks like the Red Oak (*Quercus rubra*), and the Scarlet Oak (*Q. coccinea*), certain maples like the Red Maple (*Acer rubrum*), David's Maple (*A. davidii*), and Moosewood (*A. pensylvanicum*), as well as Swamp Cypress, beeches, locusts and Honey Locust, White Poplar, walnuts and many others. With many of these the shape of the individual tree is radically altered when grown in a group. The trees grow more rapidly, at least at first, more erectly, and are more thinly branched. The eventual height of the grove, however, is usually much less than the height of a mature, isolated individual, and this can be a considerable advantage.

Even many of the noble trees that we usually think of as specimen trees like most of the oaks, beeches, and larger maples, can be grown in a small grove, closely spaced at ground level or with enough space between them to accommodate a path. The first plan often causes the planting to splay out into a gigantic fountain, giving considerably more spread than a single tree and often less height. This is the case with cottonwoods and Silver Maples. But Red Maples and Red Oaks choose to make themselves more narrow and upright, and so are well suited to a planting that allows space for walking between the trees.

On the other hand, a single mature White Oak, Sugar Maple or beech defines a landscape. Everything else is rendered insignificant. The other plants are bit players that literally act out their parts in the shadow of the principal. Such a scheme, with one strongly dominant component, is easy to devise and easy to maintain. It provides a shady picnic area and a roost for treehouses. It may cater to other garden pursuits, like the growing of shade-loving plants, And it offers superb fall color and a powerful winter outline.

But you have to acquire it full-blown. A 10 ft. oak will keep you waiting half a century before it serves up these amenities. In the meantime it will play the part of the gawky juvenile—ungainly, too thin to offer much shade, too fragile to climb in, looking lonely, but yet demanding its own space.

Moreover the lot has to be sizable to support even one mature White Oak or beech. A good quarter acre will hardly fit the bill. For the smaller lot, there are more suitable choices for a single dominant specimen. Trees like the smaller lindens and oaks, the larger flowering crabs and cherries, mountain ashes, and many others will do the job. These smaller trees are relatively fast growing and the nursery-bought 10 footer will give reasonable size and shade in 10 years or so. Place a few perennials and shrubs around the borders of the garden and you have a complete scene of charm and simplicity. Charming but boring. Too simple to be thought of as a landscape design, it's simply there. An attractive tree on a neat lawn and some pretty flowers. Pleasantly dull, and nothing much to design except the color harmony in the perennial beds and the careful placement of the tree. We want something more out of the garden, and prefer more challenging designs.

Flowering cherries on the grounds of the Heian Shrine, Kyoto, Japan. Photograph by William Corey

63

[2.3] FLOWERING TREES

Under the cherry tree
There are no strangers

Basho (1644–1694)

Surely the most exuberant heralds of Spring are the flowering trees. Giant bouquets erupt into the sky, unmuted by the greens and browns that surround the other flowering plants. And when the festivities begin, the parks where flowering cherries, crabs, and dogwoods are massed become shrines to Spring, attracting the winter-weary from near and far.

You don't stoop or kneel to view a flowering tree. You look up. You stand under it, and it surrounds you with a nebulous shawl of red, pink, or white. There is no more exhilarating spectacle in the garden. Too brash, a bit crass? Perhaps, but who can quibble at the sight of it. Look up, and the sky is studded with blossoms. Whatever clangorous dissonance might arise from the perennial bed, the trees rise above it, enveloping you in a bouquet so large that only a part of it is in clear focus at once. Often there is a delicate scent in still softer focus. Or sometimes the scent is piquant and sharp to go with the harsh pink of a flowering plum seen against a blue sky. And the display goes on for weeks. In the end, as the trees don more conservative attire, they rain petals of white, pink and red, which are blown across the ground in a high-keyed scumble over the browns and greens. The reproductive ritual is finished for a year, the landscape calms, and the trees turn to the workaday job of photosynthesis and vegetative growth.

To immerse oneself in the greatest indulgence, plant a small grove of one variety of flowering crab or cherry. Place a table and some chairs somewhere in its interior and wait for spring.

The Eastern, Western, and Chinese Dogwoods will also do the job, except that these are relatively small trees or large shrubs and their branching is horizontal and begins close to ground level. This does not allow the gardener to prune them without destroying their shape. The result is a grove that cannot be walked through or sat under. But in a mixed planting backed by evergreens or high-branching, deciduous trees, they are unexcelled.

I appreciate the large magnolias less. Most strike me as coarse and graceless. Everything about them, their habit, their leaves and twigs, and often their flowers seem clumsy and artificial, although the large ones are as spectacular in their season as any flowering tree. But in a mixed planting they fit like a fullback in a chorus line. However, there are some shrubby ones, like 'North Star', which are all class—elegant in flower, pleasant in leaf, interesting and neat in habit and structure. These are easy mixers, and can do much for the planting.

Some worry that with so much going on in the spring, the addition of a half-dozen, spring-flowering trees could overburden the senses, and so they opt for trees that flower later in the year. Choices for June include the Fringe Tree (*Chionanthus virginicus*), Japanese and Peking Tree Lilacs (*Syringa pekinensis* and *S. reticulata*), or the Japanese Snowbell (*Styrax japonicus*). The first has creamy white flowers of spidery elegance, borne in such profusion that the tree seems veiled in a clinging mist. The leaves, on the other hand, straddle the line between bold and course. The trees are dioecious, with the male flowers a bit larger and more showy, but the females offer a fall bonus of blue-black berries.

Although not as popular now as it once was, the Japanese Tree Lilac has several features to recommend it. Left to its own, it forms a large, multi-stemmed shrub to 20 ft. (30 ft. when pruned as a tree), with burnished, red stems like that of a cherry, and robust, upright form. It flowers in mid-June, long after the Common Lilac, and the white blossoms are born in huge 12 in. pannicles, more graceful and almost as showy as those of the Peegee Hydrangea. The boldness of its form and flowers borders on coarseness, making the tree difficult to assimilate in a mixed planting, but where it can be integrated into a design, it is likely to be a favorite. Some favor the Peking Tree Lilac over the Japanese Tree Lilac since it has all of the attributes of the latter but is more graceful.

No one accuses the Japanese Snowbell of being coarse. This is a small tree or shrub to 20 ft., of elegant form, gracefully open, with slender, horizontally layered branches. In early June, pendulus, bell-like, white, ¾ in. flowers hang underneath the newly opened, bright green foliage, accentuating the layered structure. All class and elegant charm, the Japanese Silverbell is widely considered to be one of the finest small trees.

The trees that flower late in the season, in July, August or September, like the Stewartias, *Franklinea altamata*, and the Golden Rain Tree (*Koelreuteria paniculata*) have particular value. All of these are four-season trees. The Golden Rain Tree covers itself with pannicles of yellow blossoms, which later give rise to curious seed pods like brown, paper Japanese Lanterns which remain decorative for over a month. The compound leaves are bold and decorative, something like those of a Staghorn Sumac, but unlike the sumac, show no fall color. On the other hand, the angular framework and the rough, black bark have considerable winter interest.

The other two are less ostentatious in flower, but the display is more sustained. Fall finds them flaunting the hottest reds and fieriest oranges in defiance of the impending cold. When finally stripped of their foliage the stewartias can give full display to their bark, a smooth patchwork richly colored in cream, tan, and sienna. There are even trees for temperate climates that flower in the winter, such as the witch hazels (*Hamameles* sp.), and Cornelian Cherry (*Cornus mas*). Their display is perhaps a bit more modest than that of the crabs and cherries, but their yellow, orange and red blossoms are sufficiently spectacular when counterpointed against the cold gray days to provide effective reassurance that this winter too will pass.

It is easy to be seduced by the flowering trees, and plant them to the exclusion of everything else. But they are the great scene stealers, and in their season one can't see the garden for the flowers. This is why the Japanese use them cautiously and sparingly. The subtle harmonies of the garden and its over-all composition are likely to be temporarily disrupted when the flowering crabs and cherries put on their audacious display. It's temptingly easy to overstep that fine line where gorgeous becomes garish, and floriferous is debased to florid. But after a long winter it is hard to resist exchanging the palette of Rembrandt for that of Monet. The trick is doing it in a way that does not violate the integrity of the design for the rest of the garden year. You don't want to squander 50 weeks of pleasure in a two-week splurge.

Fortunately, many flowering trees will hold up their end of the design throughout the year. Most hawthorns, crabs, and dogwoods are four-season performers, with attractive foliage, some with fall color, some with spectacular fruit that hangs on into winter, and many with an interesting and distinctive winter outline. So dessert before dinner need not ruin the rest of the meal.

[2.4] EVERGREEN TREES

No group of trees imposes its character on a garden more forcefully than the larger evergreens—the pines, spruce, fir, cedars and hemlocks. Large specimens assert their presence in all seasons and under all conditions, whether looming out of a mist, or cloaked in snow, or glistening in the sun of a dewy, spring morning. Their size, opacity, and noble structure often make them the dominant elements of the landscape in every season. Although there is considerable variation in shape and garden effect between the various species, we will lump together all of those that naturally form themselves into a conical spire, as do most of the spruce, fir and hemlocks, and often when we refer to spruce, we have these others in mind as well.

When considering spruce, fir, or hemlock as a major design component, one should keep in mind their disadvantages as compared to pines or deciduous trees. Their year-round opacity and conical shape offers complete shade at just the time of the year or day when it is least needed, when the sun is low. In contrast a deciduous tree lets virtually all of the warmth and sunlight pass during winter, provides shade and evaporative cooling during summer, and something in between during spring and fall. A tall pine pruned free of its lower branches will give dense shade through the summer but asks the gardener to pay the price for this amenity six months later. Because of the difference in shape between the spruce and the pine, each imparts a distinctly different character to the garden. The feeling of a spruce planting is less intimate, more standoffish than a stand of pines pruned high. One walks between and among spruces not under their protection, not close to them.

On the other hand even a small grove of pines offers a secluded retreat. Cool shade and protection from the wind can be found within its labyrinth. Extraneous sights and sounds are muted, and it offers one of the most distinctive of forest scents, a deliciously pungent, resinous aroma with a musty overlay when damp. Although the dense shade plays host to the cold and prevents snow melt in the winter, these qualities, too, can be used to good advantage. In climates where intense, winter sun coupled with brisk winds conspire to freeze-dry broad-leaved evergreens in short order, such a grove is a likely home for all sorts of shade-tolerant, evergreen material such as rhodos and azaleas, kalmias, hollies, and the larger daphnes. As an added bonus, fallen pine needles build an acidic and highly friable soil, a must for many of these species.

For the most part the landscape use of spruce is limited to the grouping of these trees. The trees do not lend themselves readily to forms other than their natural, slender, cone shape, and so the challenge and potential of shaping the individual trees is minimal.

Moreover, spruce age gracelessly. Their limbs droop weary of the weight of many winters and their cloak of needles takes on a frayed and worn appearance. More shabby than noble, more ragged than rugged, they outlive their usefulness in the landscape and become a debit for perhaps a third of their lives. Unless the designer takes himself so seriously that he envisions his quarter acre preserved for posterity, he need not be overly concerned with this aspect of the tree, but in 30 years they reach a size of major concern if their growth is not controlled, and their size is not easily controlled. Nevertheless, there is no tall screen more effective than a grove of spruce, and nothing provides a more majestic backdrop.

Pines are much longer lived than spruce, and can be trained and pruned into a diversity of shapes that emphasize their character and give them the look of noble old age, providing a garden asset to the end. The challenge lies in sculpting the trees so that their interest and individuality are increased while maintaining the integrity of the entire composition.

Winter points out other differences between them. In a light snow, both the pine and spruce retain a dusting that modulates their colors. The Blue Spruce goes to silver, and the pines to a gray-brindle. But, in a heavy snow, they wear their mantles in a distinctly different way. The spruce is more passive. It holds out giant, relaxed hands, palms downward, and catches the snow on the backs of them. The short needles provide the base for an even blanket. The heavier the fall, the more relaxed the attitude of the hands, and the smoother and narrower the outline of the tree until it is bound and wrapped into a tight spire. The pines are at first more defiant; their limbs have more spring. They hold their arms with the palms up and resist the weight of the snow as long as possible. The snow accumulates in uneven clumps in the crotches of the limbs and branches until, with enough weight, they too are forced to relax. If some snow slides clear, they may flex their limbs upward and shake themselves free. Otherwise they don greatcoats of snow and bow beneath the weight—giant snowmen hunkering against the winter.

There are other upright conifers to consider in addition to pines and spruce, fir and hemlock.

Italian Cypress and tall narrow junipers can be used to pierce a design and impart an emphatic element to the composition. But these trees have all the shortcomings of the spruce and few of their advantages. They, too, give little usable shade, can not be gardened under, and are not easily pruned into anything but their natural, stiletto shape. And the way they hold the snow makes them as boring in the winter as in other seasons.

Forget the time-honored candlestick cliche of placing a matching pair near an entryway, one on each side of the door. This device is too much used and abused to give pleasure or enjoyment, or even to be noticed.

There are all sorts of stocky upright junipers, chamaecyparis, thujas and yews but most have the grace and elegance of wallowing hippopotami.

How does one choreograph a bevy of these bloated, billowing ballerinas? They take up so much space at shoulder height and ground level and offer so little by way of visual interest that it is usually best to leave them offstage. They do not blend easily with either deciduous or evergreen trees and are too hippy to be grouped close together.

Stocky junipers are shrubs of the foothills. There they stand in isolation or in small groups, often the tallest plants around. Although I enjoy hiking among them, I see this terrain not as a goal to reach and then linger and enjoy, but rather as a temporary stretch in the hike from a more interesting place to a more interesting place. Since I do not see how to capture the effect of a natural stand on the scale of a small garden incorporated into an urban setting, I avoid them.

On the other hand, a planting of dwarf conifers has a charm and elegance that is hard to beat. Such a planting is relatively carefree, and makes an excellent collector's garden. Every imaginable shape, color, texture and size is available. There are blues, reds, yellows, and even greens; there are fuzzy balls, prickly cones, spiny hummocks in all sizes and shapes from creepers and crawlers to proper trees. Take a nibble of one and two dozen more will fail to satisfy your craving. But unhappily, the collector commonly gets the better of the designer and the garden becomes a botanical sideshow where its inhabitants are enjoyed more as individual curiosities or even freaks than as elements of an over-all design. So distinctive are these plants that even the gardener with enough self-control to stop at three or four might find it impossible to incorporate them harmoniously into the design. Realizing all of this, I confess to having succumbed to the temptation some several dozen times. Some of my favorites are the Birds Nest Spruce, *Abies balsamea* 'Nana', *Tsuga canadensis* 'Bennett' and several dwarf Mugho Pines. All of these are easy mixers.

The true cedars, *Cedrus atlantica, C. deodara,* and *C. libani,* are magnificent and majestic trees, the latter two reaching heights of 80 ft. and spreading majestically to 50 ft. At full maturity they are trees for a park or a country estate; quarter-acre lots are not sufficiently large to accommodate even one of these great trees. And, unfortunately, the young trees point to their future size and majesty with a gawkey openness of structure that many find unappealing and difficult to accommodate in any landscape plan. There are, however, several dwarf and semi-dwarf strains that tend away from this gawkiness, and mature to a much more accommodating size. I have never seen a closely spaced stand of these trees, but perhaps they can be grown this way. Such a grove would offer the design flexibility of pines with the color choice and soft texture of spruce, a combination difficult to surpass.

[2.5] SHRUBS

The design of most gardens is supported by a scaffolding of trees, which forms its skeleton, its bony core. The shrubs flesh it out and help bring it into human scale. They modulate the power and majesty of the trees and bring a greater sense of intimacy to the planting.

There is no botanical distinction between trees and shrubs. If a woody plant is tall enough and has one or a few trunks, we call it a tree; otherwise, short and multistemmed, we call it a shrub. The distinction is quite arbitrary since there is a continuum of heights, and the number of stems a plant will form is partly determined by its environment and partly by its genetic makeup. Pruning and other horticultural practices can make a tree out of a shrub and a shrub out of a tree, although this is more easily achieved with some than it is with others. In Chapter 4 I will suggest some candidates for such a metamorphosis and describe some of the techniques which can be employed to bring it about. Here we are concerned with the design potential of shrubs.

A tree pruned high enough to walk under provides a canopy of shade while occupying a relatively small area at ground level. But a shrub, on the other hand, squats on its plot to its full width so even a modest-sized specimen takes up considerably more room at ground level than a much wider tree.

Evergreen Shrubs

In climates with a distinct winter the evergreen shrubs play a special role in keeping our interest in the garden alive throughout the year. A planting with a high percentage of deciduous trees can be stark and dreary from autumn's clean sweep to the first flush of spring unless there is an understory of evergreens to soften the effect and give it some body. But ironically, the choice of evergreen shrubs, especially broad-leaved evergreens, is most limited where winters are harshest and of longest duration.

Along much of the East and West Coasts so many kinds of broad-leaved evergreens are grown and with such relative ease that just listing a few makes me envious. This is the land of azaleas and rhodos, Mountain Laurel and Cherry Laurel, boxwood and Nandina, hollies of all sorts and pieris. In the southern coastal areas the list expands to include Fatsia, *Daphne odora*, pittosporum, and on and on.

But away from the coasts, where winters are dry and sunny, and summers are dry and hot, and soils are alkaline clay, the choice is much more restricted. Kalmia are a rarity, almost no pieris will survive, and Cherry Laurel and hollies are rarely seen. When rhodos and azaleas are present they are pointed to as a sign of great horticultural skill, devotion, and luck, even though their shabby and miserable appearance is an embarrassment to the garden. And if, as is usually the case, they require the winter protection of a burlap tent or shawl, shame is heaped on embarrassment, so the garden is invariably better off without them. Even in protected sites, most will show scraggly growth, and sparse, wind-burned foliage that they roll up and hang in despair during the winter, so that one is tempted to bag them anyway in order to keep them out of sight. But when the Carolinian asks "What is that", and adds under his breath "shabby little thing", the owner can puff himself up and proudly answer, "A rhododendron".

The traditional Japanese attitude is quite different, they view the horticultural challenge as less important than the over-all appearance of the garden and the plants within it. With few exceptions, they use plants that are well suited to the climate, and grow them to perfection. There is the occasional Sago Palm that has to be protected against winter by folding its fronds down, umbrella-like, and then wrapping the entire plant in a heavy blanket secured by cord—a motionless mummy haunting the landscape; but this is not common. The Japanese are more concerned with presenting well-groomed plants in peak condition, and leave the culture of exotic varieties that are constitutionally unfit for their climate to the care of botanic gardens. This approach may seem dreadfully unadventurous, but it usually contributes to the making of a better garden.

Fortunately, there are broad-leaved evergreens that can be grown well away from the coasts, and a band of skillful breeders is steadily extending the range of other, more finicky ones. Besides the ubiquitous *Euonymous fortunei* cultivars, the Oregon Grape Holly, and some of the hardy pyracanthas like

'Gnome', and hollies like 'Blue Princess' seem to have the right stuff to thrive over much of the country. The latter two add spectacular berries to their fall-winter attributes, and the Grape Holly and true holly bronze their foliage during these seasons.

The coniferous evergreen shrubs are cause for less envy. In general, they are more widely adapted and less finicky regarding soils and exposure. Even though many chamaecyperous, thuja, yews, and hemlocks are recalcitrant growers over much of the midwest, there is so much variety among the shrubby firs, spruce, pines, and junipers that they hardly need be missed. The range of texture and shape is overwhelming, and the term "evergreen" gives no hint of the range of color that is available. The cooler hues are particularly well represented, ghostly grays and silvery blues that intensify with cold and in turn intensify our perception of it. There are purples too, but most are muddy and with little warmth. And those that are an acrimonious yellow or garish gold in summer are usually sullied to still baser hues of sickly raw sienna and raw umber by the harsher seasons. But most of the coniferous shrubs are reliable stalwarts, showing little change from season to season except when the bright, pale green burst of new spring growth is set against the past years' dark foliage, and even the commonest offer wondrous bits of winter beauty when etched in drypoint by a frost, or sporting topcoats of new snow.

How wonderful it would be if every evergreen that grows somewhere would grow here. However, in almost all parts of the country there are more than enough to design with. In this respect the Japanese approach is again worth considering. Although they have an extraordinarily wide variety of climatically suitable plants to choose from, their gardens feature only a few. This contributes to the cohesive quality of their gardens, and places greater focus on the over-all design, rather than on the individual components.

Deciduous Four-season Shrubs

Some shrubs, like *Viburnum burkwoodii*, *V. lantana*, Bayberry, and pyracantha may lose their foliage in cold climates. Sometimes referred to as semi-deciduous by the pessimist or semi-evergreen by the optimist, they hold their leaves late into the year and bud out early. Except for a month or so these can be used to fill the same design needs as the evergreens. Gambel's Oak (*Quercus gambelii*) is a favorite of mine. It may be grown as a tree, but is more suitable as a large, coarsely textured, open shrub. The leaves are as beautiful as that of any oak, a Mattisean cutout of dull green that colors up orange or red in the fall. Then the leaves curl a bit, turn a golden tan, and remain on the shrub through January. These qualities combined with its coarse, serpentine, and strongly oriental branching character and its heavily checkered bark give it a distinctively beautiful winter aspect.

Many shrubs that are definitely deciduous also offer four seasons of pleasure. Consider a planting of Black Chokeberry (*Aronia melanocarpa*) for example. This shrub inaugurates spring with a filigree of white blossoms in 2 in. clusters. Not a boisterous shout, just a quietly assertive presence. The blossoms give way to healthy, shiny foliage. The chill of autumn brings the shrub to its hottest colors; a fiery, copper-red, studded with large, blue-black berries. Even weeks after the last embers are shed, the berries will decorate the shrub. And in the winter, after a light snow, lace is piled on lace through the depth of the shrub. A February ice storm replaces the lace by a crystalline tracery that concentrates the dull light and reflects it with a frigid sparkle.

There are many other shrubs that play the same four movements but each with its own variations. Deciduous hollies like *Ilex verticillata*, crabs like *Malus sargentii*, barberries, shrubby dogwoods, cotoneasters of all sorts, and viburnums such as *Viburnum tomentosum* 'Mariesii' and *V. trilobum* (none finer than these two) all maintain a color high during some of the dreariest months.

One-season Shrubs

Besides these four-season performers there are those that provide a stunning show during only one season and then become unobtrusive bit actors for the others. Among these there are some that won't embarrass the garden even in their off-season.

Several shrubs are grown primarily for their scent. Nothing will draw me into the garden as quickly as a breeze through an open window full of the scent of Mock Orange or Spice Viburnum. I can't get enough of it. Even though a warm day and a slight breeze will fill the garden with the scent, I have to track down the source and bury my face in it. Viburnums like *Viburnum burkwoodii*, *V. carlesii*, *V. caricephalum*, Sweet Pepperbush (*Clethra alnifola*), Carolina Allspice (*Calycanthus floridas*), and Mock Orange (*Philadelphus* varieties) are among the best and most popular scent shrubs. One should also mention Clove Currant (*Ribes oderatum*), lilac (*Syringe* sp. and varieties) and some of the shrub roses. The scent of daphne is legendary, but these are more than one-season performers. The evergreen ones like *Daphne* × *Burkwoodii*, *D. odora* (for warmer climates) are more than fair when out of bloom, and the deciduous *D. mezereum* contributes its scarlet berries to the winter scene. There are delightfully fragrant honeysuckles, but most are too rank and coarse to make a positive contribution to the garden in their off-season.

There are others that are grown primarily for their flowering proclivity. Some of the spireas, the forsythias, Beauty Bush (*Kolkwitzia amabilis*) are essentially one-season shrubs. However, in their season there are few that surpass them. And if a chill and dreary April morning has you doubting if the sun will ever shine again, step outside to see a forsythia in full bloom and you'll be reassured.

But still, for the space and effort, it is usually possible to find a four-season shrub that will clearly better these in the off-seasons and make a good showing against them in their season. And if the one-season shrub blooms for only a few weeks, as is usually the case, the tradeoff is more than justified.

[2.6] PERENNIALS

My view is that the trees and shrubs are the main design components of the garden, and the perennials play a subsidiary role, presenting a highlight here and there—corners of more or less temporary interest. This view is more in keeping with the Japanese concepts of garden design than, say, that of the English, who have favored extensive plantings of perennials in overly elaborate borders and islands.

Shifting the emphasis to perennial beds will certainly cut down the problems of design and the labor and cost involved in establishing the garden, at least initially. Perennials are relatively inexpensive and most are easily moved, so mistakes in design can be readily corrected by a couple of deft strokes of the shovel. And perennials reach maturity much more quickly than woody plants, an important consideration when time is a factor. But such a design does not provide the kind of embracing surround, the sense of privacy and seclusion that is offered by a planting based on trees and larger shrubs.

The perennials I prefer are those having more than one season of interest. Hostas, Siberian Iris, rodgersias, and lupines have interesting foliage throughout the growing season. Better yet hellebores, sun roses, some dianthus, some grasses, some ferns and many others have attractive foliage throughout the entire year. I demand that the plant be able to support itself without staking, not appear sloppy or rank at any time, and not require extensive management like spraying, pinching, or pruning. Tasks like deadheading will produce only dead heads.

As with all the other components of the garden, the nod should go to those perennials which will blend amicably into the landscape, and not steal the show or strike some eye-wrenching, clangorous discord. Usually it's the more subtle colors and shapes that hold the interest longest.

It is true that a large planting of zinnias, or mums, or rudibekias can offer a rousing visual kick, a joyous, raucous, shout of color. I have to fight the impulse to run naked through the fields, hot in pursuit of some real or imagined Diana. But there isn't enough structure or variety. It's good for a ten-minute high, and then the eye is sated to exhaustion, and the mind is stoned to apathy. It's all cayenne and tabasco, and the more delicate nuances and interesting subtleties of the garden are overwhelmed by the fire.

Go for the instant shocker. This will knock your socks off. A field of day-glow color. Such effects are so commonplace and so easy to obtain that it seems silly to break one's back in the garden to repeat them.

I don't want to be shouted at when walking through the garden and this kind of planting will outshout an entire arboretum.

Perhaps the eye's sensitivity can be eroded by overstimulation just as the other senses can. It is well known that hot foods taken in excess over a long period of time will permanently desensitize the taste buds, making subtle flavors difficult to discern and moderately hot foods seem bland and flavorless. The heavy-metal drummer so screws up his cochlea that he hears, or perhaps more accurately feels, little else than his own drum beat. Gone forever is his ability to appreciate a Beethoven quartet. Maybe the eye is like that. Bash it around a bit too much and it becomes calloused. It doesn't respond as well as it once did. Then one has to bash it harder and harder in order to raise any response. On the other hand if one nourishes it on more subtle fare its capacity to appreciate subtlety is increased. Satiate it over and over and only the heavy-metal views will illicit any attention, a shortsighted choice for the long run.

Sometimes nature paints a bold and unforgettable landscape by seemingly using a single perennial. An endless field of Blackeyed Susans, or a vast marshland of Purple Loosestrife once seen will stick in the mind forever. And how about a color fix in a field of poppies? But for such a scene

te columbines
k the Japanese Iris
in the author's
len. Often a peren-
is displayed to its
ing best in an iso-
d clump rather
massed and
ed among a
der full of other
ia donnas.

73

to be effective the scale has to be as grand as the design is simple, so it is unlikely that it can be convincingly realized in the garden. Even among those with an acre or two to lavish on such a display, few would choose 50 weeks of monotony for a two-week color blast, which itself becomes boring after a couple of days. A garden should be capable of much more than that.

Let me quickly add that I have a great fondness for certain perennials and ferret out every possible excuse to use them. Sometimes I develop an urge to rip out a tree in order to make room for some more Siberian Irises. But used with restraint, a clump here and there in a natural setting, not only displays their beauty much more tellingly than when placed standard-to-fall in an extensive bed, but enhances the garden rather than being its excuse.

[2.7] ROCKS

Boulders and rockwork have always been major design components in the oriental gardens. Indeed, there are modern and traditional gardens in which these are the dominant elements. In our gardens boulders provide sculptural interest and a sense of permanence. Their powerful forms and muted colors are the perfect foil to set off the beauty of the plants. No fern is as delicate and graceful as when placed against a large rock. Aspen and birch are never so white and elegant as when juxtaposed against massive, gray boulders.

It's a blessing to live, as I do, in a part of the country where decent garden rock is plentiful and inexpensive, and it would be a shame not to avail oneself of the opportunity to bring more rock into the garden. So every March my family and I go up to Loukonen's stoneyard to find some new material for the garden whether we need it or not. It's an annual rite of spring.

Moreover, I enjoy talking with the Loukonen brothers as much as I enjoy auditioning the rocks. Rino and Leonard by name, but Rhino and Dino by look and demeanor, they are second generation Norwegians, no doubt direct descendants of giant Norseman. Slow, lumbering, and built to match the boulders they haul from the mountains, either could stand at center in the Bronco lineup and force any lineman to take a great circle route to the quarterback.

They talk politics and weather and describe how the climate has changed since their youth. They take no interest at all in the boulders they sell; all are priced by weight. It makes me feel like I'm searching for a Rembrandt in a pawn shop. A bit of patience and I am sure I'll find that priceless piece of natural sculpture for which the brothers charge a mere 65 bucks a ton. The most exciting game in town.

I could collect boulders as readily as I collect plants. My self-control is sorely tested every time I visit the stoneyard. The largest rocks catch my mind and eye first, those that have been sitting there since the Pleistocene and will still be there when the polar icecaps melt. Realizing that I don't have a prayer of moving them at all, I focus on the next largest, those that can be moved only at the expense of a ruptured wallet and disc. Usually common sense in the person of Susie or one of my sons masters the urge, and I turn my attention to the next size, and search out those that are the most bizarrely and elaborately carved by the elements. I would take them all home, set them up and display them as the pieces of found art that they are. But I'm always reminded that we're working on a garden and not a sculpture court so I turn my attention to less individualistic boulders, ones that will condescend to interact amicably with each other, blend with the garden in a natural way, and not present a contrived pasticcio of isolated weirdos and misfits.

Limestone, Sandstone, and Granite

Usually the choice of rock is dictated by local availability, and will be granite, sandstone, or limestone. Each has its own character and uses in the garden.

Granite is the most dramatic in color and form. Usually a dark gray and of a simple shape showing little weathering, this is a stone for bold effects, featuring a few large boulders set off in small groups. The contours are often such that stacking the boulders, or even abutting them results in an unnatural looking mess.

On the other hand, sandstone tends to fracture in planes, so there are many beautiful formations to be found in nature in which distinct slabs of rock are stacked. This quality recommends it for the wide use of sandstone in rock gardens, as specimen groups, for terraces, paths and more. The color varies between light gray to a rather strident red-brown, although weathering, mosses, and lichens combine to give those rocks found on the surface a rich and varied color and texture that has considerable interest in its own right and blends easily and effectively with the other elements of the landscape. However, rocks of extraordinary individual interest are fairly common since sandstone weathers rather quickly and unevenly compared to granite. Sometimes these rocks are cratered into giant bowls, or split into weakly adhering layers, or even display delicate flanges. The stone dealers refer to such pieces as "rotten", a comment on their fragility and not their aesthetic appeal. But what these stones possess in individuality they lose in power and calm presence, and they are often too curious to meld into the design.

Naked limestone is usually the color of pale, raw umber, a lifeless, greenish tan. It's a color more suited to hot, deserty, wastelands than the mountains. The surface may be pock-marked and cratered, but the interesting striations of sandstone are largely absent, and the light color and cubical shape of limestone communicates none of the power or granite. Therefore, I was quite surprised and disappointed when the Denver Botanic Gardens constructed their rock gardens from limestone. Moreover, the individual stones looked anything but natural, and appeared to have been cut at the quarry on the very day of their installation, although the arrangement of the rocks is superb. But limestone was chosen primarily for horticultural reasons, its porosity and resultant water-holding capacity, and its heat-reflecting capacity. The plants took to these rocks as though they had evolved specifically for this site, and in a few years the plants embraced the rocks, enfolded them, scrambled over and between them, until now it seems so natural that one can not imagine a more appropriate kind of rock being used. However, in a situation where the rocks themselves are to be given more prominence, pale gray limestone is not likely to be the first choice.

Rock Stepping Stones

Flat rocks are often used to make a path and form a conspicuous and powerful design element. The general layout and the shapes of the individual stones do much to establish the mood and theme of the garden. Cut hard-edge into strict rectangular pavers and well matched into a straight and narrow path allows one to make a bee-line through the rose garden or annual bed. A reasonably brisk clip should take you through the garden in about five minutes. Such a layout also makes a suitable path to the public library or courthouse, and is unarguably the best route to an outhouse.

To create a more natural setting, something less severe and antiseptic is called for. A meandering path of irregular stones set on moss or gravel establishes a completely different mood. Rather than emphasizing the shortness of the distance between two points, such a path not only leads the viewer on a tour of all the garden's interesting niches but also augments the sense of the size of the garden. It may be designed to remind one of a late summer stroll through a dry stream bed or, alternatively, along a rocky footpath through a forest. Such a design does not take its cue from the fifty-yard dash but rather leads the viewer to pick his footsteps with some care assuring that he take time to enjoy the garden. The Japanese traditionally intersperse small stepping stones that are only large enough to easily accommodate one foot with an occasional larger stone that permits and encourages the stroller to stand on it with both feet, pause, and take in the beauty of the scene. So the very rhythm and pace of the walk can be controlled by the designer, with a significant effect on the mood of the stroller.

Boulders of moderate size can be used to edge a stream or pond or line the boundary of a path. In such cases they serve the dual purposes of design and utility—delineating the boundaries and physically keeping the elements on each side separate from each other.

Stonewalls, Terraces, etc.

Another time-honored use of stone is in the construction of terraces and walls.

Stone walls have a great deal of rustic charm but are a rather heavy-handed way of delineating boundaries. A 5 ft. high, gray, stone wall can be a rather oppressive backdrop for a small garden. Both its color and form seem to cramp the space and confine the area. The Japanese favor fences that are light and open, like those made of a lattice of bamboo. Such fences delineate an area gently, and seem to expand the space by permitting glimpses of what lies beyond. In short, the material is important; a chain-link fence is also light and open, but our associations with this material are not as friendly nor as inviting as with bamboo. There is a certain incompatibility between the metal and the garden.

On the other hand, there are few barriers as interesting as a dry stone wall when its chinks are chock full of alpine plants from around the world.

Formal rock terraces can also provide a horticulturally appropriate area for the cultivation of alpines but are not easily incorporated into a naturalistic plan featuring groves of trees and shrubs. Moreover, with a bit more thought and creativity, the rocks can be laid out in a more natural way to resemble an alpine boulder field or moraine. The plants will certainly be just as happy and even appear more content.

[2.8] GROUND COVERS

Ground covers can do much to establish the mood of a garden. A garden using mosses as its principal ground cover possesses a completely different character than one using 'Pfitzer' junipers. A moss garden, as the one on the grounds of the Saiko-ji Temple in Kyoto, evokes the soft gentle feel of the rain forest. Juniper, with its strength and character, conjures up the more rugged terrain of the foothills. These associations are not only the result of an awareness of the natural habitat of each plant—the differences in texture, color and form between the two are also factors. However, for most of us the comparison is specious since moss will not grow well in our gardens.

Living Ground Covers

For those wanting a mossy look in climates with little atmospheric humidity there are several choices. Among my favorites are *Sedum acre* 'Green acre' and *S. acre* 'Green Acre Minima' brightly evergreen through any winter, Scotch Moss and Irish Moss, both *Sagina subulata* varieties. The last two could stand to be toughened up; a severe Zone 4 winter won't kill them but will pretty much trash them out. Scotch Moss is a golden beauty while Irish Moss is a brilliant green. Both tend to mound up a bit which looks natural in my view, but if it becomes exaggerated a correction can be made with a heavy stamp of a foot.

Irish and Scotch mosses favor some shade, whereas the sedums prefer full sun although they will tolerate half shade. The sedums belie their mossy look when in early summer they cover themselves with starry, yellow flowers, but the sight of this gleaming yellow carpet excuses the deception.

In the great rain forests of the Northwest the mosses are studded with deer ferns and sorrel, each a complement to the other in color and texture. This effect can easily be duplicated over much of the country, using Scotch Moss or Irish Moss rather than true moss, providing the shade is not too dense.

Another plant that conjures up images of the floor of a rain forest is the delightful *Veronica repens*. This is a ½ in. high, dense, semi-evergreen mat of ¼ in. scalloped leaves studded with blue flowers from spring to summer, having a texture that roughly approximates that of Baby Tears (*Soleirolia helxine*). But this is Zone 4 tough in sun or partial shade and any soil. Any encouragement whatsoever may cause it to become too rampant but it's never threatening.

Rupturewort (*Herniaria glabra*) is considerably more attractive than its name. This is another tough, hardy, somewhat rampant plant having somewhat the appearance of moss.

Thymus serpyllum, and several creeping penstemons also offer a rough approximation to moss when not in flower but can be a major attraction in flower. They do not appreciate excessive foot traffic but otherwise are tough, hardy, and evergreen.

Native gingers (*Asarum caudatum*) are also frequent carpeters in the Northwest. They have an almost tropical look, with thick, green, heavily textured, and strikingly mottled leaves. The unmottled but hardier (Zone 4),

European ginger (*Asarum europeaum*) gives the same effect in a shady spot with woodsy soil. *Pachysandra terminalis,* an evergreen shrub to 12 in., needs the same conditions. Although different in appearance from ginger, it conjures up the same image of a forest floor of a temperate rain forest. Ivies have been used for the same effect under the same conditions, but I find the effect less pleasing and less convincing.

Foam Flower (*Tiarella cordifolia*), another choice plant for a moist woodland setting, is a 2 in. tall perennial with bright green, horizontally held, 2 in. wide, maple-shaped leaves. An easily controlled stoloneferous habit recommends its use in small patches. In the spring it bears 6 in. tall panicles of fluffy, white flowers that justify its common name. After showing a bit of fall color, it may go dormant for a month or so in a Zone 4 winter; not a major detraction from a plant that offers so much charm the rest of the year.

If you prefer the look of a mountain meadow, there are a vast number of choices that will give such an effect. Brooms, heaths, heathers and some of the low-growing junipers set the stage, and there are all sorts of rugged alpines to heighten the effect such as sages, Blue Fesque and other grasses, dianthus, Moss Phlox, Bearberry, arenarias, antennarias and many more. All will blanket an area with a patchwork of many textures and colors that honor each season with a dramatic change of appearance. But these plants require full sun for the most part, which means that large, shade-giving trees and shrubs will have to be dispensed with, a trade-off that many find unacceptable.

In the central Rockies, where there is more sun and cold, and the climate is much drier, mosses and moss-like plants are rare, but Bearberry (*Arctostaphalus uva-ursi*), one of my favorite ground covers, is abundant. This is a ground-hugging, dense, dark green, small-leaved evergreen shrublet, that is much easier to grow and is much more widely adapted to garden culture than previously thought. Its inherent variability has given rise to a dozen or so clones, differing in size of leaf density, winter color, and shade tolerance. Bearberry associates naturally with Creeping Mahonia and Rocky Mountain Juniper. This is a superb combination for a garden (but substitute either of the junipers 'Arcadia', 'Scandia', or 'San Jose' for the Rocky Mountain Juniper) and is an ideal foundation for a planting of Aspen, pine, or spruce in the spirit of the Rockies.

But the most commonly used ground cover is still grass in spite of its glaring shortcomings. A grass lawn has to be watered and fed, mowed regularly, thatched occasionally, and aerated once in a while. Turn your back on it, and insects will chew it down from above, grubs will devour the roots from below, and Fairy-ring fungus will spread its unsightly halo overall. Even in Japan, where so much praise has been lavished on moss, grass is the predominant ground cover.

There are many reasons for its continued, world-wide popularity. It is adaptable to a wide range of conditions, has superb color over a long season and a fairly pleasant off-season color, and is highly tolerant of foot-traffic. No other ground cover forms such a plush, springy carpet or one that is so pleasant to walk on. So until the reality of the looming water crises is upon us, and research provides us with alternatives, grass will remain our most widely used ground cover.

Stone stairway in
author's garden w
Sedum 'Green Ac
providing a mo
ground cover. 1
flowering shrul
Viburnum lentago w
three seasons
beauty—in sumr
when in full leaf, in
fall when its cluster
black berries are set
against coppery
foliage, and as
tured when flower
in the spri

Inert Ground Covers

There are all sorts of nonliving plant materials used as ground covers, such as grass clippings, saw dust, coffee grounds, chipper chips, and tree bark. Some, like the first two, are used primarily as weed suppressants, soil amendments, and to provide a cool, shaded root run for plants like rhododendrons; their visual effect is not considered an asset. On the other hand, bark, chips, and coffee grounds provide ground covers that are quite natural in a forest setting and serve the same purposes as saw dust and grass clippings. They all decompose, enriching the soil, and so need to be topped by new material every few years.

The use of gravel as a ground cover has a noteworthy precedent in the history of the Japanese garden. Indeed, in the gardens of Ryoan-ji, and Daitoku-ji in Kyoto it is one of the most dominant elements. Raked into abstract patterns to suggest water in motion, as a flowing river or waves rolling onto a beach, it sets the mood of the entire composition. In our gardens raking the gravel in this fashion would not only be a chore but a bit of contrived artificiality. However, a bed of unraked gravel also suggests a dry river bed, or river bank, or gravel washed down a mountain side.

Gray river gravel sets off the greenery of plants beautifully but not garishly, and is close to being maintenance-free. We are not talking about that black or red lava rock, disgorged by gassy volcanos and with good reason. I have never seen the stuff employed to good effect except as an additive to the soil mixes used by orchidists for their cymbidiums and paphs. In the garden, after it collects a bit of wind-blown dirt, it becomes a soggy, spongy mass, that seems the ideal planting mix for every possible weed. Further, its appearance is atrocious.

White quartz and pulverized marble chips are equally grotesque in any setting modeled along natural lines. And surely the marble chips must leech alkaline or something else that's poisonous. The plants must know it, for they appear to be uncomfortably perched on top of the gravel, afraid to let any important piece of themselves touch the hideous stuff.

[2.9] GARDEN ART, ORNAMENTS, AND OTHER DOOHICKEYS

Lanterns are traditional elements in the Japanese garden. Now they are used primarily as ornaments and to provide light, but previously they had some religious significance. Even modest-sized stone lanterns of the Japanese style are damned costly. For example, $350 is commonly paid for a wimpy, eighteen-incher carved out of granite. Lit by oil, these lamps yield a soft flickering light that responds to every breeze, not the dead, even light of our electric lamps. But, for the most part, electric garden lamps are well designed, efficient, and economical. These lamps may not be objects of great distinction, but I find them unobtrusive and rather pleasant. Moreover, when breezes animate the trees and shrubs the light gives play to the shadows and forms created. So even under electric light, there is enough movement in the garden to make evening a mysterious and romantic time in which the garden can still be enjoyed.

There is little call these days for teahouses or maple watching stands. A gazebo? That's a Hungarian sausage, isn't it? Or is it a sexy Hungarian film star. It's a Hungarian something or other, for sure. Tastes have changed. And what may have been in vogue in a 19th Century English garden is now too space-consuming, too expensive, or just too crass and ostentatious by today's standards.

What we need now is a storage shed for the lawn mower and the bags of sheep manure. Fido needs a doghouse and maybe a run. But these features are usually not considered garden assets, and so are tucked into some obscure corner. Other contraptions like the satellite dish, the hot tub, the tennis court, and the greenhouse, are no more sightly, but are given the prominence their price tags call for. Some of the lesser garden accouterments can be assets if well designed. But the ornamental birdbath with or without fountain, the wrought-iron lawn furniture with the overwrought curlicues, the marble cupid with all four cheeks abillowing in the wind, seem strangely out of place. A fake stone Leda assaulted by her swan, the centerpiece of a garden 50 years ago, is now a princess of kitsch, a bit of nostalgia served ice cold and belly up.

Three winter gardens. Yellowstone
National Park, Wyoming.

Photo by Seth Malitz

83

Valley of wildflowers backed by the
Grand Tetons, Wyoming.

Above. A snazzy annual border in Longwood Gardens, Kennett Square, Pennsylvania. Photo by Susan Malitz

Left. *Rudbeckia* 'Goldsturm'.

Natural rockwork provides a
wealth of landscape models.
Above. Precisely fitted and
smoothed boulders contain a
stream. Mount Rainier National
Park, Washington.
Left. A superb boulder grouping
about 30" high, Ruby Beach,
Olympic Penninsula,
Washington.

"Moss gardens" with true
mosses, sedums, and
selaginellas, near Box Canyon,
Mount Rainier National Park,
Washington.

Photo by Seth Malitz

CHAPTER 3 *Favorites—Real and Imagined*

[3.1] MADE FOR LANDSCAPING

Every plant has its perfect site—one that it enhances and is enhanced by. But some plants seem to have been created for the primary purpose of gracing our personal landscapes. With a planet of plants to choose from, landscape architects through the centuries have come to rely on relatively few as major components of their designs. What factors influenced the selection? Availability and adaptability certainly played a role. In some cases, even religious symbolism and particular cultural values and mores influenced the choice. But primarily it is a plant's ability to contribute to a variety of designs in combination with other plants and as a specimen, and its ability to enhance architecture and garden features such as paths and fences while maintaining its own individual beauty and personality that determines its usefulness in landscape architecture.

Among these plants I have my own favorites, and a few of these are mentioned here. For the most part, the selections are well known and widely available. Most are widely adaptable, but restricting the choice to plants that are universally adaptable would limit the discussion to dandelion and thistle. In particular, several of my favorites are but a zone or two out of reach of my current garden, causing me no end of frustration and green envy. So the last section was written in the hopes that the catharsis would bring some therapeutic relief, and that out of sympathy some plant breeders would be marshalled to address these oversights and injustices of nature.

[3.2] FAVORITE TREES—MAPLES

The genus *Acer* gathers together an extraordinary diversity of grand trees, many of which are treasured garden subjects. There are some of such noble proportions that at maturity a single specimen will subjugate the average suburban plot, allowing no room visually or horticulturally for much else. The Big Leaf Maple and the Sugar Maple are among them, but on the other hand no others can take their place in a park setting or a public square.

It is true that a few maples are weedy, buggy, or weak wooded. Included among these black sheep are Box Elder (*Acer negundo*), Silver Maple (*A. saccharinum*), and under some situations, the Norway Maple (*A. platanoides*). But even these have considerable beauty and usefulness under conditions too harsh for their more delicately constituted relatives. True, the Box Elder is buggy, suckers, and is short lived, but it offers a natural copice by a stream, which is both graceful and individualistic. The Norway Maple is frequently a host to hoards of aphids, and its dense shade and heavy surface roots will outcompete most other plants, but the shape of its leaf is superb and often colors to a beautiful golden yellow for autumn. The popular purple-red-leaved varieties, like 'Schwedleri' and 'Crimson King' tarnish to rusty-greens and greenish reds by summer in cyanic shades that I find depressingly heavy. There is a variegated form 'Drummondii' that is difficult to place and looks sickly wherever placed. On the other hand, selections have been made for size, habit, growth rate, and foliage that are sun and wind tolerant, and some of these trees are reasonable garden candidates.

At maturity the Silver Maple is too large for most gardens, and its weak-woodedness poses considerable problems. But this tree can be grown as a multistemmed 15 ft. shrub, and this ameliorates most of the shortcomings and produces a sturdy, long-lived specimen that is quite appropriate near a stream or lake.

The Red Maple (*A. rubrum*) is never disparaged where it can be grown well. Conspicuously red in flower, pink in new leaf, and stunningly scarlet in fall color—all this against a black framework of moderate size (40 ft.)—makes it eminently worthy for use in the private landscape. There are some climatic restrictions that limit its full potential in some areas—restrictions that curtail its autumn display or even its growth—but new clones are being introduced which address these problems. Forms are now available that are strongly fastigate, wide-spreading, color early or late, and are reliably hardy and colorful in Minnesota. In the garden the tree can be used wherever a deciduous, moderately large, all-season performer is needed, either as an isolated specimen, or in a grove. Its latter use is as rare as it is stunning—for the tree is well-adapted for growth in this way and forms a high branched canopy supported on relatively straight boles whose black color gives extraordinary contrast to the coppery-red, autumn foliage and a no-less striking pattern against snow.

Each of these maples is a grand tree, and each has its places where no other is as suitable. But there is a maple that is more cherished than any of the above for the making of gardens—the Japanese Maple (*A. palmatum*). Speaking of it as a single species may be taxonimetrically correct, but masks the enormous diversity of size, habit, leaf color and shape, bark color and texture that is expressed in this taxon.

There are many maples indigenous to Japan, but only one is called the Japanese Maple. *A. palmatum* has been a revered and treasured garden tree for centuries, and its use in Japanese gardens has been so extensive that the character of many of these gardens is inextricably associated with this tree. It is said of this tree more than any other that it has a Japanese character. How can one speak of the character of a species that shows such a wide diversity of variation? In the traditional gardens the more exotic variants are usually not entertained. The strongly colored forms, weeping forms, and dwarf forms if used at all, play a fairly minor role as shrubs, or may appear as potted plants or bonsai. Those that are used are usually small trees to 15 or 20 ft., with a fairly delicate framework and horizontal branching which gives the canopy a distinctly layered look. The palmate leaves with fingers drawn-out and finely

A small hint of the diversity and delicate grace offered by the hundreds of available cultivars of *Acer palmatum,* the Japanese Maple.

To the right, a Japanese Maple. Below. A Vine Maple, *Acer circinnatum*, overhangs a stream in the Quinault Rain Forest, Olympic Penninsula, Washington.

91

pointed, impart a fine texture to the crown that contributes to the over-all appearance of grace and elegance. And the tree lends itself to thinning and shaping which when skillfully done accentuates its flowing lines and airy grace. Its autumn colors of reds and yellows are unsurpassed, and its denuded winter line again speaks of elegance but in the sparest terms. Although the shrub forms and weeping forms have a place, and though the more exotic varieties are eminently collectible, it's the less-elaborate forms that capture and distill the essence of the Japanese garden aesthetic.

A. palmatum alone should constitute a country's full allocation of maples, but Japan boasts many others that are singularly beautiful and distinctive. Snake bark maples like Herr's and Father David's (*A. herssii* and *A. davidii*) have dark trunks lined vertically with silver-green ridges giving an extraordinary effect when grown in groups. Autumn color is more subdued—mostly mild yellows—and the leaves are not "maple-like" but ovate to about 6 in. long. These trees mature at 30 ft. or so, quite a usable size for the average private garden.

North America has its snake bark maple, *A. pennsylvanicum*, with an equally beautiful striated bark, but its leaves are 9 in. wide, with three obtusely pointed, stubby lobes, giving it a delightfully coarse and informal aspect when in leaf, as befits its moniker "Moosewood". Its usefulness is furthered by its Zone 4 hardiness and its shade tolerance.

The Paperbark Maple (*A. griseum*) is another extraordinary maple from Japan. The top layers of its bark are russet colored and shreds off in strips, baring the satiny-smooth, auburn inner layers, presenting an appearance like that of the Black River Birch (*Betula nigra*), but showing more color. The leaves are divided into three leaflets 1½ in.–2½ in., not "maple-like" at all, but quite elegant, nevertheless, and they color superbly in the fall to shades of yellow, orange, and red.

One other Japanese maple must be mentioned—the glorious Full-moon Maple (*A. japonicum*). This is generally a stubbier tree than *A. palmatum*, and has 7–11 pointed leaves approximating a disc if the points are joined by straight line segments. Autumn color is spectacular in yellow, orange, and red depending on the clone, and to some extent, the method of cultivation, and the site. There are golden cultivars ('Aureum'), cultivars with dissected leaves and semi-weeping habit ('Aconitifolium'), forms with particularly bold leaves ('Vitifolium'), and small-leaved forms ('Junihitoye'). In Denver the type tree is much hardier than *A. palmatum*, but is not something to plant on an exposed site.

North America has an approximation for this tree also—the Vine Maple (*A. circinatum*). There is evidence that this tree is both hardier and more adaptable than the Fullmoon Maple and so may be the one to try in locations where its Japanese counterpart is only marginally suited.

The Siberian Maple (*A. ginnala*) is often suggested as a standin for the Japanese Maple where the latter is not hardy. Not only is the Siberian hardy in Zone 1, but it will grow in fully exposed sites as well as in fairly shady ones, and on any soil short of a slag heap. It's a splendid little tree to about 15 ft., with a tendency toward multistemmed, bushy growth, and I like them this way, although the doggedly persistent can train them to a single stem. There are dwarf selections that are particularly shrubby and mature to about 6 ft. ('Compacta'), and selections that guarantee a splendid, ruby-red fall color

('Flame'). The leaf is narrow, sharply three-pointed, and held in a lax position; the branching is not horizontal, but erratically ascends at a 45-degree angle so that the foliage is simply massed rather than layered. These traits are not at all characteristic of the Japanese Maple, and as a substitute for it the Siberian is second best at best. In fact it's much more analogous to the Trident Maple (*A. buergeranum*), yet another maple of Japan.

A. truncatum hails from China and is Zone 4 hardy. It looks like a much refined Norway Maple, with leaves half the width of the latter, finer twigs and branches, and a mature height of only 25 ft. New leaves and fall color show strong, purple tints, and the leaves are held horizontally even in the summer heat. This is a choice but seldomly seen tree which should be considered wherever a Norway Maple would be useful were it not for its size and coarseness.

Two of my favorite maples are native to the Rockies: the Big-Tooth Maple (*A. grandidentatum*), and the Rocky Mountain Maple (*A. glabrum*). The first is sometimes considered a variety of the Sugar Maple, but its appearance is quite different—a much smaller tree with a propensity for shrubbiness, leaves half the width of its relative and more deeply indented but squared off (the big teeth of its common name). It is usually found in rather "cushy" surroundings on cliff sides bordering a stream, and so is not much hardier than the Sugar Maple and only slightly more tolerant of Midwestern soils. But it is so distinctive in leaf shape and habit, and so splendid in fall color that it deserves much more attention. This is an ideal maple to grow in thickets on a hillside or in groups in a not-too-shady understory.

The Rocky Mountain Maple (*A. glabrum*) is quite different. Invariably it is a shrub in nature, often with 100 or more stems, and its leaves are like those of the Norway Maple but much more delicate in texture and size (to 3 in.). The contrast between its blocky massiveness and the delicate overlay of its fine twigs and elegant leaves makes it unique. The autumn color is a buttery yellow—pleasing but not startling. In winter its massive glut of stems is unusual enough to be interesting, while its red buds provide a modest bit of color. This is a slow grower but is hardy to at least Zone 4 and is quite adaptable. This is a very distinctive maple—too little known and far too little used.

Overleaf. Rocky Mountain Maple (*Acer glabrum*) in full autumn color along Fern Lake Trail, Rocky Mountain National Park, Colorado. A very hardy adaptable shrub to 12 ft. in height, tolerating a diversity of soils, exposures, temperatures, and light conditions. The habit of this specimen is typical—a hundred stems or so packed together to give the tree a massive, blocky appearance. In moister sites this tree is often allied with the Red River Birch (*Betula fontinalis*) which also forms many stems but not as many as the maple. It offers the bonus of a shiny, red, cherry-like bark and also has golden fall color. Neither of these trees is common in the garden.

Trees flower—that's not a novelty. Maples, oaks, elms, pines, spruce all flower, but none are called flowering trees. That appellation is reserved for those few that flower so prodigiously and gorgeously that the trait takes precedence over all their other attributes and all their shortcomings. Some of the larger flowering cherries cast considerable shade, but no one refers to them as shade trees. And if you accuse a flowering peach of being buggy, someone will probably sue you for libel, particularly in the U.S.

Flowering trees are among the most popular and most overused garden adornments. Seeing them in flower when one is planning a landscape may ignite such a passionate desire for them that the ensuing design excludes all else with no thought of the off-season effect. However, there are a few flowering trees that are extraordinary in bloom and also a credit to the garden when not in bloom. From this favored, select few I have selected a few of my favorites.

The flowering crabs and cherries have been popular garden show-pieces for centuries and present as gorgeous a spectacle in bloom as any other tree. They range in size from 6 ft. dwarfs like Sargent's Crab (*Malus sargentii*) to the glorious 50 ft. Sargent's Cherry (*Prunus sargentii*).

Available shapes cover all possible tree forms—fastigate, columnar, spreading, weeping, and everything else. Some of the crabs have a jaggedly, informal "picturesque" shape—a complimentary term in certain situations and perjoritive in others. Many of the cherries offer a satiny-smooth, auburn or mahogany-red bark to enliven the winter landscape. And a few, a very few, of the crabs and cherries offer some fall color worthy of note.

Frequently, the crabs and cherries are planted in groves the flowering of which can shove the senses into overload. But such a design seldom sustains interest throughout the year. Although the extensive plantings of *P. yedoensis* 'Yoshino' cherries in Washington D.C. draws tens of thousands of springtime visitors, I know of no one who went at any other season in order to enjoy these trees. For most private gardens crabs and cherries are best used sparingly, as isolated specimens. In a complimentary setting, say against a backdrop of evergreen trees, a single crab can present as memorable a show as an entire hillside of them.

There are enough crabapples and cherries to fill a lifetime of gardens, and since these trees are so familiar and so overused I won't single out my favorite varieties. But a word of caution might be in order. Some of the crabs are alternate bloomers—giving a heavy display one year and a weak one the next. Some of the crabs and cherries are much more prone to insect attack than others, and some are much more prone to disease than others. Diseases like fireblight can be disfiguring, and not infrequently deadly. But there are annual bloomers and disease-resistant clones that are as ornamental as any, and it's worth the effort to seek them out.

The dogwoods include two of the finest flowering trees—the Kousa or Chinese Dogwood (*Cornus kousa* and *C. k. chinensis*), and our Eastern Dogwood (*C. florida*). Each has something to offer in every season. Our native gives us white, pink, or rose-red, blossom-like bracts in May on naked branches; its oriental cousin waits a month and then layers blossoms of white or pink on top of its fresh, new leaves. Both have superb autumn colors—setting red berries against the red foliage. The berries of the kousa are quite palatable, but I do not advocate planting it for its fruit. And the bark of the kousa—crisply mottled in splashes of tan, cream, and mahogany—is as striking as any in the winter landscape. These are trees for all seasons but, unfortunately, not for all climates and soils even within their range of hardiness. Where they can be grown well, they are as highly regarded as any flowering tree. These dogwoods are superb as isolated showpieces or in small groups, and planting a pink in association with a white or two gives an unbeatable combination.

There are other dogwoods notable for their flowering. The Pacific Coast Dogwood (*C. nuttallii*) is extraordinarily showy with bracts spanning 3 in., but it has a narrow range of adaptability. The Cornelian Dogwood (*C. mas*) and the Pagoda Dogwood (*C. alternifolia*) are both superb—the first with small yellow flowers in late winter, the second with a strongly layered habit and cymes of small white blossoms—but both are more shrubby than tree-like. Wonderful as they are, they take second place to *C. florida* and *C. kousa* as do most flowering trees.

Less commonly used but potentially more useful are the hawthorns. There are many fine species and many fine clones, but I'll champion only 2 of them—the Washington Thorn (*Crataegus phaenopyrum*) and Cockspur Thorn (*C. crus-galli*). Both have a profusion of flat cymes of ½ in. blossoms in spring—a display easily qualifying them as flowering trees. Both kindle an autumn display of scarlet that is unmatched, and after leaf fall the scarlet is retained in masses of berries that decorate the tree until winter. Both have an interesting winter aspect, especially the Cockspur with its dense twiginess and pizzicato spikiness.

In a genus beset by leaf spot diseases and fireblight, these two are quite disease resistant. Both are Zone 4 hardy, highly drought tolerant, and unconcerned about soil type although they prefer good drainage. It is said that they require full sun, but several of each are thriving in nearly full shade on the campus of the University of Colorado at Boulder. It's difficult to choose between them but the Washington Thorn is my favorite among favorites. The leaf is lobed like that of a diminutive Red Maple and the habit of the tree approaches the grace of a Japanese Maple. The Cockspur is squatter, more bush-like, and its leaves are elliptical. Each has its places but the Washington Thorn has more of them. Few flowering trees, certainly none of the *Prunus* or *Malus*, can match its airy grace. Indeed, in many places where a Japanese Maple might be suitable a Washington Thorn could be used—it is superb as a specimen or in a small grove, grown to a single stem or multiple stemmed. On the other hand, planted on a hillside in small, close-packed groups, grown as shrubby trees with many stems and branches near ground level, nothing surpasses the Cockspur.

I have other favorites, perhaps not as useful or as adaptable as the above, but nonetheless glorious. The Japanese Snowbell (*Styrax japonicus*), the Carolina Silverbell (*Halesia carolina*), and *Franklinia alatamaha* are superb little trees with multiseason interest, but with a strong tendency toward shrubbiness. I don't mind since I like them best when grown as shrubs. The stewartias comprise another genus of four-season trees, some are shrubby, others more tree-like, most are magnificent. More steadfastly tree-like is the

98

Photo by Seth Malitz

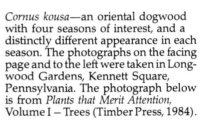

Cornus kousa—an oriental dogwood with four seasons of interest, and a distinctly different appearance in each season. The photographs on the facing page and to the left were taken in Longwood Gardens, Kennett Square, Pennsylvania. The photograph below is from *Plants that Merit Attention,* Volume I – Trees (Timber Press, 1984).

Photo by M. Dirr

Sourwood (*Oxydendrum arboreum*) with peach-like foliage and drooping pannicles of white blossoms like the Japanese Pieris but displayed in autumn against scarlet foliage. It's a superb tree through at least three seasons, but a bit more tender and finicky then some of the others, and distinctive enough to hamper assimilation in many designs.

The American Redbud (*Cercis canadensis*) is another gem that can be grown as a tree or a shrub. I prefer it as a shrub. It is as notable for its bold, relatively stiff, cordate foliage, buttery fall color, and sprightly framework as it is for its abundance of small, pea-like, sharp, violet-pink blossoms that encase every twig and minor branch in early spring. There are rare, white-flowering clones which are at least as striking. The redbuds go well with birch and conifers and are quite adaptable, tolerating considerable shade contrary to some advice.

There are other glorious trees which, for this reason or that, I consider far less useful in the setting of a personal landscape. The Yellowwood (*Cladrastis lutea*), the Tulip Tree (*Liriodendron tulipifera*), some of the horsechestnuts, and most of the larger magnolias are either too large or too coarse for a private landscape. Moreover, they may not flower until 10–20 years old, and then not reliably. Some produce enormous and gorgeous blossoms but so sparsely or so hidden by their foliage that the effect is unremarkable to the point of being unnoticeable. These are worthy trees for parks and arboretums but there are much better choices for the private garden.

[3.4] FAVORITE BIRCHES

I grew up in Connecticut not far from its namesake river at a time when here and there along its shores one could still find a few sizable stands of Paper Birch (*Betula papyrifera*), and this is where my love for these trees began and was nurtured. My buddies and I would often go down to the river and bivouac for an afternoon to fight Indian wars, or to soak a worm in hopes of catching crappie or sunfish, or just to loaf around.

The fishing was a brain-bruising bore, and I was convinced that the fish took the bait only to relieve their own boredom. But a birch forest offers many entertainments to delight a ten-year-old boy. We were well steeped in Indian lore and crafts, and unfortunately a tree or two suffered because of this knowledge. They stoically endured our mischief in other ways too. Young birch make worthy wrestling opponents, and even when taken down for a count of three they don't seem to mind much and are able to more or less right themselves in a couple of weeks. In addition to these diversions there were all sorts of creatures to hunt and observe—crawlers and climbers and flyers and slimers, and everywhere there was an abundance of wildflowers. Of course, a boy of ten pretends not to notice the flowers. In fact it was the forest itself and its birches that I enjoyed most, but this too is something that a north-end kid does not admit for fear of being thought strange.

After a few years the excuse of fishing was no longer necessary and I came to visit this forest more and more frequently. It was the instrument by which I followed the seasons—each caused it to resonate in a unique way and no forest does so with greater harmony or responsiveness.

Birch leaf out in early spring in translucent shades of yellow-green with the evanescent sparkle of a shallow stream. With the approach of summer the leaves enlarge, turning a deep green on the upper surface and a glaucous green below, making the entire composition seem more substantial and bolder. The green is played out by late September, but the boldness remains, now expressed in tawny golds—not stridently polished but quietly assertive. Later, they shed their leaves and stand white-skinned and naked on their golden robes, seeming too frail and delicate to bare the brunt of the next season. But when autumn hardens into winter, they too seem to harden, and what could pass as skin earlier in the season now seems more like lifeless bone—fully calcined to endure the cold. Then with the snows, white against white against a pearlescent sky, they dissolve into the most ethereal of landscapes, a landscape barely there, an apparition of a forest.

Birch and Aspen are as glorious in the garden as in the wild, and domestication in no way curbs their interplay with the seasons. Winter still picks them clean to skeletal spareness. Spring still brings out the emerald flush, and every autumn will newly mint its gold. And always the birch and Aspen have a sophisticated elegance that harmonizes with all sorts of plants from evergreen trees to the spring bulbs. Their dignified but delicate line, light branching and foliage soften the harsh formality of architecture while architecture in turn accentuates their easy grace—each the ideal compliment for the other. They can be arranged in so many ways—in isolated clusters or groups of clusters—and in so many mutually flattering combinations with other landscape components, that they must be considered one of the primary resources for the design of gardens and certainly one of the most distinctively beautiful.

The European Birch (*B. pendula*) offers many of the same effects as our eastern native although the European tree is denser and the branches more pendulous. This makes them more impressive as individual specimens or in isolated clumps but less suitable for grove plantings.

The Orient, too, has its own white-barked birch (*B. platyphylla japonica*). This is more than a fair substitute for the above two since it is available in clones that are strongly resistant to attack by the bronze birch borer—a creature that tunnels into the cambium layer and often kills a tree by ringing it. Strangely, this striking, elegant birch is seldom used in contemporary Japanese landscapes and is virtually absent from the classic gardens. Instead, where a graceful, vertical motif is desired the Japanese favor bamboo. I find this inexplicable since birch have an ample measure of many of the attributes cherished by the Japanese—grace, elegance, and a striking but not brazen beauty that blends with a diversity of other plants. Surely this tree will not be overlooked by gardeners outside of the Orient since it has all of the desirable features of the Paper Birch but is far more adaptable and reliable.

There are several other birch such as the Russian Rock Birch (*B. ermanii*) and the Chinese Birch (*B. albo sinensis septentrionalis*) that have excellent foliage, and strikingly colored, smooth bark, and a growth habit suited to group planting, but none surpass Paper Birch in its radiant elegance.

A much different tree is the Black River Birch (*B. nigra*). The bark is singular in color and texture—a dark mahogany, chiseled into clinging curls to expose a new, satiny smooth, auburn surface. Like most birch, fall color is reliable and pleasant in warm yellows. The over-all aspect of this tree is more massive and less graceful than the above, but still it works well in clumps and in groups, particularly the selection 'Heritage' which is more fastigate and less pendulous than the type.

Aspen (*Populus tremuloides*) offer many of the same perks as birch—a slender, easy elegance, striking bark color (white tinted, greenish ivory), and golden-yellow, autumn colors that outshine those of any birch. I don't favor one over the other—I love them both, but climatic restrictions often dictate which can be used.

Certainly, exquisite and simple designs can be created using no other trees than these. But I've seen equally unforgettable landscapes in which birch (or Aspen) is planted in association with Red Maple, Japanese Maple, Eastern Dogwood, pine, or spruce—combinations which are hard to match.

[3.5] FAVORITE PINES

By its noble bearing and ancient garden heritage, the pine commands as much respect as any other tree. Even a single specimen makes a significant impact on the landscape, and a group can completely dominate and determine its character. Yet pines blend easily and naturally with many other components of the garden.

Even though they are evergreens their contribution to the garden varies dramatically with the seasons. Pines in spring, punctuating each branch tip with exclamation points of 8 in., ivory candles, have a spikey, perky appearance fully appropriate and complimentary to the season and in sharp contrast to their more restrained aspect later in the year. In winter, wearing ermine and set against a white backdrop, their color appears black which enhances their majestic quality as they reign unchallenged over the dormant landscape, giving protection to the naked trees and shrubs while providing the perfect foil for them. Evergreen does not mean ever-the-same.

Since larger specimens are such dominant features, occupy so much space, cast such dense shade, and have such a profound effect on the soil (acidifying it with their fallen needles and drying it through their roots), some restraint in their use is probably advisable; although I have not been able to follow this advice. Their visual impact, too, is proportional to their size, and specimens can grow to a size that will trivialize almost any man-made rock arrangement, pond, or path, and this makes it difficult to design a plan incorporating pines that will be satisfactory over the long run.

Among the coterie of candidates suited to grace a garden, which are my favorites? There are a great many that I like but none more so than the Austrian Black Pine (*Pinus nigra*), and none exemplifies the bold character and massive strength of pines more than this one.

To me, the Austrian Black Pine is the quintessential pine. Its structure and needle length seem more like those classic images of pines rendered in jade or sumi ink paintings than the Japanese Black Pine which provided the model for these images. It's a rugged tree, capable of assuming many forms. It can be grown as a majestic upright specimen to 50 ft. or maintained as a multi-stemmed and twisted tree at 15 ft. But always it is a powerful presence in the landscape, picturesque and full of character. In spite of its dramatic form, it associates easily and naturally with many other trees and shrubs. Its dark color and massiveness make the perfect setting for a stand of delicate birch or

Japanese maples—accentuating their grace, their bright, spring and fall colors, and their winter form. Larger trees too, like the Honey Locust or Katsura Tree combine well with pines—each complimenting the other. Flowering shrubs, particularly those with white blossoms, are stunning when interplanted among pines, while low-growing, broad-leaved evergreens like the grape hollies, pieris, rhododendrons, and kalmia seem to have been created especially to serve in the understory.

The Ponderosa Pine (*P. ponderosa*), particularly the variety found in the Rockies, is a close counterpart of the Austrian in size as well as habit to all except needle counters (the Ponderosa is three needled while the Austrian is two needled). Some say the Ponderosa is tougher and has longer needles and view both properties as perks. Some say the Ponderosa's color leans more to a yellow-green and certainly the bark of mature specimens is more interesting in its scaly texture and auburn color under dark gray reticulations. Unfortunately it is susceptible to periodic attack by a trunk-mining beetle which carries a lethal fungus, whereas the Austrian is nearly immune, and for me this decides the issue.

Japanese Black Pine gives another approximation, but is lankier, a bit gawkier, and less hardy. On the other hand, it is available in dozens of clones selected for needle length and shape (1 in. to 4½ in., wavy or straight); needle color (yellowish, bluish, or emerald green); bark character (checkered, lumpy, or heavily corked); and height (from 6 ft. dwarfs to the standard height of 100 ft.). The result is an extraordinarily diverse collection of garden subjects useful for an equally diverse set of garden designs. But as a full grown tree I still prefer the Ponderosa.

The Japanese Red Pine (*P. densiflora*) is another popular garden tree particularly in some of its distinctive clones like the 'Table Top' (flat topped as though hedge-sheared to a height of 9 ft.) and the 'Dragon Eye' (*P. d.* 'Oculusdraconis'). The texture of this pine is distinctive—longish, slender needles of a more glaucous cast give it a softer look. The type tree matures at 50 ft. with a looser and a more casual habit than the above and a tendency to form multiple stems. With age the casual look is accentuated to the point of sloppiness. So while it has its place, I prefer the Ponderosa. Scotch pine (*P. sylvestris*) is another common garden pine. It has rather short needles (1½–3 in.), a cinnamon-colored bark, and a much more open habit than the Ponderosa that becomes extremely picturesque in age. However, this picturesque openess can all to often pass as scraggly, unkempt, or even shabby. It too is available in all sorts of selected clones—dwarfs, fastigate, glaucous, and so on, some of which age more gracefully and more controllably than the type, making them more reliable design components.

Our native Eastern White Pine (*P. strobus*) is another large (to 100 ft.) tree, well represented in gardens. It is a five-needle pine with slender needles to 2–4 in., giving young trees an aura of casual grace compared to the stiffer aspect of the Ponderosa. But to my eye the young tree has a weak and almost flimsy appearance with little character. The adult tree, however, presents a different picture—its lower branches gone, its trunk bifurcating near the top to make a broadly layered flat-topped crown, the tree assumes the appearance of a tall and stately Lebanon Cedar and is superb. But the length of time needed to acquire this character, and the radical change in its appearance over time argues against its usefulness in the personal landscape.

Japan has its own five-needle pine, the Japanese White Pine (*P. parvifolia*). This is a highly variable species, varying in response to growing conditions and its genetic makeup. The type may be multistemmed and shrubby from 20–50 ft., single stemmed to 60 ft. or anything imaginable in between. The needles are 1½–2½ in. in length, a good green, and densely borne, giving the tree a bushy appearance and facilitating pruning. Its genetic variability has given rise to hundreds of cultivars selected for dwarfness (as short as 3 ft.); needle color (blue, yellow or green); needle length (some less than 1 in.); needle shape (bent or curved); bark texture (finely checkered, corticate etc.); and other qualities. These trees are the most frequently used conifers for bonsai, and some make distinctive garden ornaments— invaluable in small, Japanese-style stroll gardens. As a full size garden tree it is not as impressive as the above and is not as frequently seen.

There are many other superb pines eminently suited for garden use. Some like the Lacebark (*P. bungeana*), Bristlecone (*P. aristata*), and Italian Stone Pine (*P. pinea*) are distinctive enough to be best displayed as individual specimens; some like the Mugho (*P. mugo mugo*) are more shrubby than tree-like. Others like the Monterrey Pine (*P radiata*) and Montezuma's Pine (*Pinus montezumae*), have a more restricted range of adaptability.

There are also many not-so-superb pines—"collector's conifers" selected for their strangeness and not for their design worthiness. Most of these cripples, misfits, and grotesqueries are best placed in a zoo of their own or in zones in which they are not hardy. These plants are among the few that appear most natural and look best when displayed next to very prominent signs giving their name in full, such as: *Pinus interruptus* var *contortus grotesques*. I find these trees amusing and interesting but prefer to see them in arboretum sideshows rather than in the private landscape. For garden use I prefer the unalloyed, unadulterated pines of noble mien like the Austrian Black and the Ponderosa.

[3.6] OTHER FAVORITE TREES

Here my choices are quite restricted since I want to avoid those megatrees like most of the beech, catalpas, white oaks, and cottonwoods— trees so large that a single specimen usurps the entire garden dismissing the question of a landscape plan. Others, like weeping willows, phellodendrons, and maackia are considerably shorter, but these too will be slighted because their low-branching, wide-spreading habit is just as space consuming.

Among those that remain, the Honey Locust (*Gleditsia triacanthos*) is a top contender. This tree is often suggested as a substitute for the beleaguered American Elm, and there are similarities—both have chlorophyll. But the analogy does not extend much further than this. Whereas the elm erupts in a cluster of huge branches that reach upward, splay, arch, bifurcate, and then turn back downward like a giant fountain, the Honey Locust sends up one or several trunks that remain more or less vertical and give rise to lateral branches. These horizontal branches are layered and the foliage is held in flat sprays—not at all like the massed foliage of the elm. Nor do the leaves compare—those of the elm being simple ovate-oblong in shape to 6 in. and rather coarse, while those of the Honey Locust are pinnate with small leaflets giving an effect that is almost fern-like in its delicateness. Moreover, the Honey Locust's leaves are a much darker green and the fall color is a brighter gold than the elms.

Unlike the American Elm, the Honey Locust is well suited for planting in groups, and the tree combines well with companions of all sorts. On the other hand the heavy shape and shade of the elm severely restricts the number of suitable companions. In fact, in its airy grace, its horizontally, layered branches, its delicate foliage and light shade, the Honey Locust is more aptly compared to a Japanese Maple than an American Elm, although this analogy is also farfetched.

The tree has a tendency to form multiple trunks and is superb when grown this way. The wild type is fiercely armed with 4 in. spines in clusters on the trunk and branches; mercifully, the commercial clones are stripped of these spectacular but dangerous adornments. Also gone are the decorative but messy, foot-long seed pods that look like giant, leathery, Chinese pea pods—belying the trees membership in the Leguminosae. This is a tough and hardy species, but lately a tiny fly (the locust pod midge) is making life miserable for the tree and for those of us that love it, and it should not be planted where this despicable Diptera is prevalent.

The true locusts (Robinia) and the Chinese Scholar Tree (*Sophora japonica*) have some resemblance to the Honey Locust in foliage or habit, and both offer a bonus by way of flowers. But the first is brittle, buggy, and beset by borers, while the second is less hardy, and its more lax and spreading habit combined with a short stature lessens its usefulness in groups of its own kind or with other trees.

The Lace-bark Elm (*Ulmus parvifolia*) is another recommended substitute for the American Elm, but it too is not a close approximation and the differences favor Lace-bark for use in private landscapes. It is not as tall (mature height 50 ft.) as its American counterpart; the leaves are much smaller (to 2 in.); its scaffolding more delicate, and airier; in many ways it resembles the Honey Locust more than the American Elm. On the other hand, its bark—gray chips flaking away to expose a smooth, rich auburn new surface—is unlike anything else.

In the case of the Zelkova (*Zelkova serrata*) the analogy to the American Elm is less farfetched—the height is the same, the structure is similar, and the leaves are similar both in size and shape, although at the end of the season those of Zelkova veer more toward red than yellow. However, the Zelkova is not as pendulous—a feature which weighs in its favor for garden use.

The Common Hackberry (*Celtis occidentalis*) is also a reasonable stand-in for the American Elm, fairly similar in height, reach, leaf shape, texture and habit, although the elm is more pendulous and considerably more graceful. The Hackberry offers small, red berries in the fall—not very ornamental but nevertheless appreciated by the birds. Tough and hardy, and maturing at 40 ft., it is a reliable and usable garden tree, but there is a certain coarse and disorganized commonness to the Common Hackberry that I do not appreciate.

In fact each of the trees mentioned above is better suited to personal gardens than the American Elm, but nothing can replace the majesty of the latter as a park and avenue tree, and only a tiny beetle and the nearly microscopic fungus it carries can curtail its reign.

The overgrown, full-blown, big-buck buckeyes like the Common Horeschestnut (*Aesculus hippocastanum*) and the Yellow Buckeye (*A. octandra*) are too much tree and too much litter for a private landscape, although I love them in an estate or park setting. A better bet for a buckeye befitting the garden is *A. glabra*, the Ohio Buckeye. This is a smaller tree maturing at 35 ft., is less buggy, less susceptible to wind burn, Zone 3 hardy, flowers nicely but not as spectacularly as some of the other horeschestnuts, and has bold, palmately compound leaves typical of the genus but atypically coloring a brilliant orange in the fall. Overall, this is the superior horsechestnut for the private garden.

The Katsura Tree (*Cercidiphyllum japonicum*) is also quite distinctive enough to parry comparison with any other. The over-all shape varies from tree to tree, but most form a columnar outline with several slender, straight trunks and short lateral branches. The 2—4 in. leaves are flat and broadly cordate, emerge a rose-pink, then turn green with a slight glaucous tint particularly on the under surface, and finally color yellow with occasional hints of purple or red—an exquisite tree with the elegance and grace approaching that of birch or Aspen but not as hardy and more prone to wind and sun damage. Strangely, as in the case of the Japanese Birch, this tree is seldom seen in the traditional gardens of its native land although it possesses many of the attributes which the Japanese hold in high esteem.

There are several other trees that are part-time favorites, trees that feature some superb seasonal attraction along with some not-so-superb detractions. Take lindens for example. If my olfactory sense ruled, I would plant them everywhere. Each June I'm led by the nose along every linden-lined path in Boulder. At that time even the parking lot of the Engineering Center at the University of Colorado has the scent of heaven as dozens of these trees flower in their planters amidst the searing blacktop. One has to wait until the flowering is finished before an unbiased assessment can be made of the tree's potential for the private landscape. The mind has to clear and the intoxication subside before one can admit that the American Linden (*Tilia americana*) is much too big and much too coarse. And the smaller and finer textured Littleleaf Linden and its cultivars like 'Greenspire' are so up-tight pyramidal or fastigate that they are best suited as highway sentries. Theirs is a stiff formality that runs counter to the canons of natural design which I prefer in the garden.

Even the glorious Pin Oak (*Quercus palustris*) is difficult to accommodate in the private landscape, both because of its strict pyramidal shape and its ground-sweeping lower branches. Too bad, for the intricately cut leaf and the scarlet fall color are magnificent. Much the same criticism and praise can be leveled at the Sweetgum (*Liquidambar styraciflua*) which has other credits and debits depending on where it's grown. Here in Boulder, Colorado it is lucky to reach a tight 16 ft. with 3 in. maple-like, palmate leaves. But on the West Coast, near the Bay Area, it can reach a sloppy-floppy 60 ft. I like it best where it likes it least.

Another part-time favorite is the Kentucky Coffee Tree (*Gymnocladus dioica*), so called because the early settlers extracted a coffee substitute from the beans in its foot-long, brown pods. It is a superb tree in the summer, but its winter aspect leaves me cold. It matures at a garden-usable height of 50 ft. and bears enormous 3 ft. long, bipinnate leaves with 3 in. leaflets. From late spring to early fall it has the luxuriant tropical look of a giant Staghorn Sumac except that the leaves of the sumac are pinnate and that the Coffee Tree favors one trunk and has no fall color worthy of note. It also resembles the sumac when defoliated, but its form is even more gaunt and angular, more like a snag in the Serengeti rather than a tree for the private landscape, and this is what makes it a only a part-time favorite.

There are many other trees which are wonderful now and then, but a nonfickle favorite has to be wonderful always, and such trees are not easy to come by.

[3.7] FAVORITE SHRUBS

Without beating around the bush, let me say straight away that I find many of the most popular shrubs not to my taste, or at least unsuited to those kinds of landscapes that I prefer. For example, I take no fancy to fancy roses with all their high-blown, highfaluten, snobbish beauty—certainly not in the garden atop nondescript, shabby shrubs that no one would cultivate were it not for the blossoms. I prefer them on long stems in crystal vases on the dining-room table where their ostentatious pulchritude won't detract from the more modestly adorned garden plants. In the landscape the single varieties, on short, neat bushes with vibrant fall color and scarlet rose hips until November are far more acceptable.

I have no love for lilacs that grow to 20 ft., with coarse, unremarkable foliage and branch structure. But I do like the dwarf Korean Lilac (*Syringa Patula*) and its variety 'Miss Kim' growing to 9 ft. and 5 ft. respectively, flowering several weeks later than the Common Lilac, densely suckering, and with neat, small leaves that turn reddish purple in the fall—uncommon in the genus. However, my schnozz does not agree with those that find the scent of their blossoms unreproachfully pleasant. After a few days with the pannicle still in prime condition, I find the scent sickeningly pungent.

Tree Peonies have their place but not in my garden. It is true that the modern wonders had their origins in the Orient, and certainly many fit in beautifully with the red and gold enameled architecture that is so much a part of the classic Chinese garden. They are far less used in the traditional gardens of Japan, probably for the same reasons for which I avoid them. In spite of an attractive leaf shape the habit of the plant is klutzy, and its deciduated aspect is ungainly. The flowers are undeniably gorgeous—huge and with the silken texture of a rumpled kimono. But they blend none too well with subtler plants (which includes all other plants), and after a few days they dishevel themselves into a shabby mess requiring immediate deadheading. In fact I find them much more attractive when clipped from the shrub upon opening and floated in a shallow glass bowl of water than when displayed in the garden.

I even have reservations about camellias, although they are anything but shabby providing spent blossoms are promptly removed—a non-trivial chore with such large plants. In fact what bothers me about them is that their design is too prissy-pure, too formal, too up tight for the kind of casual grace that I prefer in the personal garden. This is another plant that we associate with the Oriental garden tradition, although it too is rare in Chinese gardens, and almost never seen in the traditional gardens of Japan.

I must also be rude to rhodos—at least to those bearing enormous blossoms in enormous trusses featuring the hottest hues of searing scarlet, outrageous orange or passionate purple. Out of flower they can be a beautiful and bold asset to the landscape, but in flower their brash and brazen display is an embarrassment to the more demure plants. I do not mean to condemn the entire clan because of the outlandish display of some, for there are a vast number of satisfyingly less gorgeous rhododendrons that make a compatible, all-season contribution, and these are among the most desirable of all plants for the personal landscape providing one can accommodate their somewhat finicky needs. Even the deciduous azaleas offer a long season of interest—spring bloom, lovely summer foliage, superb fall color, and an unremarkable but acceptable winter aspect.

There are several other members of the Ericacea that must be numbered among the finest garden plants, and certainly among my favorites. The Red-veined Enkianthus (*Enkianthus campanulatus*) and its various varieties are particularly distinguished by their upright structure, horizontal branching, and leaves clustered at the twig ends. The bell-like, red-veined flowers hang beneath the emerging leaves in May, presenting a layered appearance somewhat like that of the Japanese Snowbell. The Japanese Pieris (*Pieris japonica*) is an evergreen, mounding shrub from 1—10 ft. depending on the clone, lovely in all seasons and particularly in the spring when displaying its tassel-like 5 in. flower pannicles in cascading clusters. An American species, *P. floribunda*, has upright clusters of pannicles and to my eye is equally lovely.

Next to the rhodos, the Mountain Laurel (*Kalmia latifolia*) may be the most popular ericacious shrub, or soon will be now that so many new clones are being made available through the technique of tissue culture. This one species shows a remarkable variation in over-all form (from 4 ft. to 8 ft. in the garden); leaf shape (like Myrtle in the 'myrtifolium' type leaf, but usually more like a peach leaf); and bud and flower color (white, pink, red, or banded purple-brown and white). For the most part, these are superb plants well suited to a diversity of garden designs, although some of the hot pinks affect me viscerally in the same way that the sight of cotton candy does.

I have already confessed my love for viburnums. There are evergreen ones that are decorative throughout the year, but even those that are deciduous have an exceptionally long season of interest, spanning spring flowering to fall fruiting. Some like the Korean Spice Viburnum (*Viburnum carlesii*), and the hybrids × burkwoodii, × carlicephalum, and × juddii are renown for their fragrance although they are quite attractive even out of blossom and several have splended autumn color—usually a red-purple. The Double File Viburnum (*V. plicatum* tomentosum 'Mariesii') is considered the king of them all with "lacecap" cymes of blossoms (a center cluster of pearl-like fertile blossoms surrounded by a ring of flat-open, sterile blossoms) set above the branches with the new leaves below in double file, just like its name says. The branching is strongly horizontal, emphasizing the alternation of blossoms and leaves. Fall colors the fruit blue-black and the leaves red-purple ending the main show for the year. In spite of all these attractions I like the American Cranberry Bush (*V. trilobum*) as much, for although it lacks the stunning, layered effect of 'Mariesii' it does feature the lacecap flower pattern, berries that ripen to a brilliant red, and bolder and more interesting leaves, which are shaped like those of a Red Maple and color as strongly. The habit of the American Cranberry Bush is loose and informal, and can reach a height of 14 ft. making it an ideal background plant for a naturalistic design. The European Cranberry Bush (*V. opulus*) is similar but it is far more susceptible to aphids, except in the delightful, densely-mounded, dwarf clone 'Nanum'. There are other superb viburnums like Arrowwood (*V. dentatum*), Nannyberry (*V. lentago*), and Wayfaring Tree (*V. lantana*) each with the pleasant blossoms, pleasant shape, decorative fruit, and fine fall color that we associate with this wonderful genus. I don't think I ever met a viburnum I didn't like or one unsuited to a landscape that I did like.

Heavenly Bamboo (*Nandina domestica*) is indeed heavenly, but the climate up there must be considerably more benign than in Boulder, Colorado. It survives here occasionally obviously wishing it were elsewhere, so I make use of substitutes that have some resemblance to Nandina and have considerable merit in their own right. My two favorite stand-ins are False Spiraea (*Sorbaria sorbifolia*) and Burning Bush (*Euonymus alata*). The first is delicately upright to 7 ft., bears creamy white, astilbe-like pannicles of blossoms in midsummer, and has a lovely soft-rose color in autumn. The second can reach 15 ft. but is easily kept at 8 ft. When pruned to emphasize its horizontal branching and stripped of its lower branches it is more than just a fair substitute. The common name bespeaks its fall color which is second to none. There are dwarf clones to about 6 ft. which are too dense and twiggy to convincingly mimic Nandina, although these too are deservedly popular garden subjects.

There are other euonymus that are evergreen, and they do heroic duty in climates where broad-leaved evergreens rarely succeed. For example, *E. kiautschovica* 'Manhattan' and various shrubby clones of *E. fortunei* like 'Sarcoxie' and 'Green Lane' may be held in contempt by those who think them too familiar, but they serve nicely as substitutes for Japanese Privet, evergreen barberries, or even rhododendrons (out of flower, of course) where these latter plants can not survive. To see the similarity between these plants it helps to be nearsighted, but euonymus foliage is thick, stiff, and glossy green, attractive in its own right until winter thrashes it about.

Daphnes are a delight, and those that are evergreen are a year-long delight. They range from 6 in. shrublets like *Daphne blagayana* to four-footers like *D.* 'burkwoodii'. Most noted for the intense perfume of their blossoms, their habit and foliage alone qualify them as garden-worthy. The 2 ft. *D. retusa* and the 3 ft. *D. tangutica* have roughly the appearance of *Paxistima canbyi*, but the daphnes are more attractive. They are quite adaptable, more so than the rhodos, and are quite suitable for many designs.

I am fond of chokeberries (the plant, not the berry) like the black-fruited *Aronia melanocarpa* and the scarlet-fruited *A. arbutifolia* 'Brilliantissima'. These are deciduous shrubs, unremarkable only during those few months when they are neither in bloom, leaf, or fruit, and when not covered by snow or encased in ice. In flower they are delicately lovely with loose cymes of ½ in. white blossoms; in leaf they embody a perky vitality that blends well with other plants and in the fall its their turn to shout as red berries or black are set against incandescent scarlet foliage. The leaves are shed in October but the berries remain until November if the creatures let them be.

Some of my favorite shrubs are really shrubby trees. Dwarf and shrubby clones of the Japanese Maple, Hedge Maple, Siberian Maple, and Vine Maple contribute an exquisite leaf shape and marvelous fall color. Dwarf and shrubby pines, firs, spruces, yews, hemlocks and other coniferous evergreens are delightful and useful if one avoids the show-offs and monstrosities. Shrubby trees grown as shrubs like Sargents Crab Apple (*Malus sargentii*), *Styrax japonicus*, *Franklinia alatamaha* and several of the hawthorns are all superb.

Finally let me mention the old, reliable, shrubby junipers. I tend to overuse them, but they are beautiful, hardy, and very adaptable. I suppose if evergreen azaleas could be reliably grown here in a variety of exposures and soils, I would get rid of some of my junipers. But then again, on a hillside, among pine and Aspen, few plants seem more suitable than juniper.

[3.8] FAVORITE GRASSES

Grass. Certainly one of the most humble words in the gardener's lexicon, on a par with "mulch" and "fertilizer". Some have suggested that the term "Ornamental Grass" is the world's shortest self-contradiction. The butt of so many jokes from frigid Maine to the sunny side of France, grass has been woven into baskets, braided into ropes, and thatched onto roofs. Grass flavors some undrinkable and unpronouncible Polish vodka, and gracelessly graces the dinner table as schav—although as an edible blade it is best reserved for ruminating ungulates, saving the grains for human consumption (bamboo shoots and sugar cane excepted). We scour with it, and sweep our floors with it. On occasion children stretch it tautly between their thumbs and make music with it. Some claim to smoke it—but I think it's a different kind of grass. Mostly we mow it and curse it.

However, the garden-worthy grasses encompass much more than homey ground covers. Captured under that catchall is a diversity of delightful subjects with wide adaptability and applicability. Here are plants of reserved beauty which when used appropriately contribute a sophisticated elegance to the design. There are many garden-worthy grasses, but I will only mention a few of my favorites, most of which are hardy to Zone 4 and are tolerant of a wide variety of soils.

Calamagrostis acutiflora stricta and *C. arundinacea* 'Karl Foerster' are both called Feather Reed Grass, and both feature perfectly perpendicular, densely packed, slender culms. It is this dense, spiked verticality that makes these grasses such striking garden features, and at a height of 4–7 ft., depending on the clone, a feature not easily overlooked. Moreover, their contribution to the design continues throughout the year. They are particularly striking at the end of summer when their green stems are tipped with tight, tan inflorescences that later splay somewhat as they ripen but with such spare elegance that the vertical aspect of the plant is counterpointed and enhanced. Nor is its effect diminished when cold colors the whole plant a sprightly beige, and it remains stalwartly upright even after heavy snows. Add to this a Zone 4 hardiness and a wide tolerance of soils and you have a very usable grass.

The genus *Miscanthus* includes several of the finest ornamental grasses—plants of noble proportions, individualistic and striking, but nonetheless easily incorporated into a variety of designs. Their reign of beauty nearly spans the seasons—from late spring when their new growth splays up fountain-like to a height of 3–10 ft. depending on the species and clone, to late summer and early autumn when they set their feathery pannicles, to late autumn and winter when the culms are still upright but the blades are more pendulous and the cold has wrung out the green to bare the tawny hues which are so effective against the snow and evergreens. Most are Zone 4 hardy and tolerant of many soil types—in fact they do well by water and can be a striking feature beside a stream or pond.

Let me single out two of my favorites from among the many superb *Miscanthus* varieties for the garden: Zebra Grass (*M. sinensis* 'Zebrinus'), and Striped Euralia Grass (*M. s.* 'Variegatus'). Both are boldly striped, the first with ½ in. transverse bands of white against a dark green background at intervals of about 6 in., an extraordinary pattern in a climate hostile to bromeliads; the second longitudinally with cream and green, the lighter color predominating so that the plant has a glowing translucence when backlit (see fig. 00). They reach a height of 7 ft. and 5 ft. respectively when not in flower, and as striking as they are, they give up nothing in terms of grace and elegance. Among the larger grasses none are finer than these.

The fesques are deservedly popular and most have a wide range of adaptability. I grow a 4 in. tall, green-colored, evergreen variety in a small, shade garden where its exceedingly fine blades create a contrasting but very companionable texture for ferns, hostas, and other woodlanders. But most of the garden varieties are silvery blue clones of *Fesque amethystina* and *F. ovina*, and form pincushion hummocks from 6 in. to 18 in. tall depending on the selection. Most of these prefer a sunny location and show their best color there, but considerable shade is also tolerated. Beautiful as they are, their color and habit impart a desert-like aspect to a planting and I find them hard to accommodate in a forest-like setting.

Among the many others that deserve a nod, let me at least mention the following few.

Pennisetum alopecuroides, called Rose Fountain Grass by its friends, is a softly splayed, mounding fountain of fine foliage to 3 ft., crowned in late autumn by 5 in. tan-rose pannicles that remain effective through mid-October. Supremely graceful and elegant until then, it offers no further interest until late spring of the following year. This is a very adaptable grass, superb by water it is also fairly drought resistant.

Glyceria maxima 'Variegata' is more suited to waterside planting, and will take considerable moisture at the roots. It is variegated in the usual way, longitudinally in white and green with the white predominant, but does not look at all unnatural by water. Its reputation for rampant growth may dissuade some from trying it, but in heavy soil and between boulders I have found it easy to control.

Blood Grass (*Imperata cylindrica rubra*) is more gorgeous than gory—growing to a height of 12 in. with the upper ⅔ of the blade a translucent bright red. A grass of no interest from late fall to mid-spring, it is nevertheless so striking in its season that it must be acknowledged. Not as hardy as those mentioned above, it needs some protection even in Zone 5. It will tolerate some shade, but is best in full sun and there the red color can be incandescent.

For a shady site in humus-rich soil there is no more decorative grass than *Hakonechloa macra* 'Aureola'. Although I usually avoid grasses whose name is longer than their height, an exception must be made in the case of this gold and green-striped beauty. The vivid striping runs longitudinally along the blades, and the plant has a relaxed, mounding habit to about 18 in. It is hardy to at least Zone 4, and although not evergreen, has a very long season of interest. No doubt this grass would be much more popular if people were not embarrassed to ask for it by name.

Switch Grass (*Panicum virgatum*) has upright culms to 6 ft. and horizontally held blades, giving it the look of bamboo. In late summer it sends up a stiletto-like inflorescence which gradually opens and splays into a delicate haze. The onset of autumn ornaments the leaf tips with a flush of red, and several clones have been selected which emphasize this feature. Its winter aspect is pleasant, but not remarkably so. This grass is happy in a variety of soils and quite tolerant of shade.

Chasmanthium latifolia (syn. *Uniola latifolia*) is somewhat similar to the above in its requirements and somewhat in its appearance—at least when it is not in flower. Its inflorescence is much different—the seed heads are like flattened pine cones, and are held at the ends of arching, wiry stems, more like that of the quaking grasses (*Briza media* and the annual *B. maxima*), except that the heads are quite flat. It is attractive in winter, but less so than Switch Grass, and prefers more shade.

Molinia caerulea and *M. c.* 'Variegata' should be mentioned. Tufted and arching to 3 ft., the first is gray-blue, and the second is longitudinally striped in cream and green with the lighter color predominant. Both are adaptable, thriving in all sorts of soils and preferring sun, but tolerant of some shade.

For the Zone 4 gardener the most imposing grass of all is Ravenna Grass (*Erianthus ravennae*). The plant reaches 10 ft., and then sends its flower stalks to a towering 14 ft. It has been compared to Pampas Grass (*Cortaderia selloana*) which needs a climate at least as benevolent as Zone 6. But Ravenna Grass does not form as massive a plant, and its inflorescence is smaller, sparser, more beige than white, and is carried higher. These differences do not make Ravenna Grass less imposing—its appearance is less squat which gives it a more noble mien. In fact, so imposing are these two plants that it is difficult to incorporate them into a landscape—a group of them is a landscape.

Certainly there are many other worthy grasses but continuing the discussion would stoke my enthusiasm to the flash point where I could not resist adding a few more to my own garden. As it is, every year I find myself pulling up some perennials here and there in order to make room for yet another grass. I like them for their elegance, their individuality, and their quiet grace, even though they mix with each other with haughty reluctance. I should abandon this collecting and plant them as isolated specimens or in broad, homogeneous swaths. One can easily imagine a landscape with grass as its only perennial and pine the only tree.

Fortunately, only a few bamboos can be grown in Colorado, and fewer still do well. Otherwise I would be tempted to give up all sorts of other plantings in order to grow my share of them. I like bamboos; I like grasses.

[3.9] FAVORITE FERNS

What mental images are conjured up at the mention of ferns—the smell of a damp forest, croziers unfurling in the quiet shade like the unfolding of a pursed hand offering some cherished gift, unrestrained growth but subtle beauty everywhere, and everywhere a gentle air, a gentle light, and solitude. Certainly there are alpine ferns and ferns living in near desert conditions, but ferns are primarily plants of the forest, and this is the environment that their presence is most likely to evoke.

There is something more to the appeal of ferns than just their associations with those quiet, calm places that are so important in keeping our city-battered perceptions in balance. It is their ancient design and their unique and wondrous geometry that makes them special. Theirs is a design that is both simple and sophisticated—presenting variations on a theme, fronds entire, pinnate, bipinnate, or even tripinnate—a design as modern as fractals, and as primitive as the Devonian.

Ferns are the premier perennials for the shady garden—they look right there, and most grow well there. They are perfect companions for other woodland plants like bold-leaved trilliums, hostas, and violas; they compliment and are complimented by astilbes, tiarellas, bergenias, helleborus, and all sorts of moss-like ground covers. Even if we restrict our attention to the hardy ferns suited to garden culture in regions of Zone 4 temperatures, the choice is extensive, and so again I will focus on a few personal favorites. But first I want to malign several that would be among my favorites were it not for one damnable fault—a short season of interest.

The Ostrich Fern (*Matteuccia pensylvanica*), Lady Fern (*Athyrium filex-femina*), and the Hay-scented Fern (*Dennstaedtia punctilobula*) are certainly very beautiful, but in this climate they all suffer an ignominious collapse by mid-summer and remain dormant until the following spring. These are not small ferns, so their absence is painfully apparent and their exit occurs at a time when it is too late for companion plants to overgrow the void. Even Clayton's Fern (*Osmunda claytoniana*) and its somewhat similar relative the Cinnamon Fern (*O. cinnamomea*) have a tendency to deciduate by mid-summer, but I am so fond of them that I reluctantly give them a place here and there in my garden in spite of their truncated season.

On the other hand, there are many which I can not fault at all—ferns which contribute a long season of extraordinary beauty to the garden and which are easy to grow and hardy too. None is finer than the Northern Maidenhair Fern—an exquisite piece of sculpture, a delicate Calderesque mobile in miniature, its black, arching, wiry stems offering lax hands of bright-green pinnae each a ¼ in. scalloped fan of considerable beauty in itself. In spite of its fragile appearance, this is a tough and hardy fern.

The Japanese Painted Fern is a gem of a different cut—a more canonical cut as far as frond shape is concerned. But the color is not at all canonical—in fact, for a fern it's positively flamboyant. The frond is a dull green with a broad, silver center, and the stipe is red. True, these are not Day Glo dahlia colors but this is a fern after all, and it may well be the most colorful fern of all. Its exquisite beauty contradicts its Zone 4 toughness and adaptability, and it will even take a modicum of sun if not pushed too hard. Although it is not evergreen it remains a showpiece until mid-September. It grows to about 18 in. and some suggest planting it in groups as a high ground cover, but this does not do it justice and I greatly prefer to see it planted alone so as to emphasize its exquisite and unique features.

The Autumn Fern (*Dryopteris erythrosora*) is almost as colorful, but its color is more seasonal. The peak display is offered in the spring when the new croziers unfold in colors reminiscent of autumn—red-copper, bronze, and gold burnished to a satiny gloss and displayed against the evergreen foliage of the previous year. By summer, green masks these metallic tints, but it remains a fern of considerable beauty. It grows in height to about 18 in. with a spread of 24 in., and will take a bit of sun and exposure.

Another favorite Dryopteris is the Leatherleaf Wood Fern (*D. marginalis*). This is a tough evergreen to 24 in., with deep-green, leathery foliage and a stricter adherence to radial symmetry than the last two mentioned. It rarely has offsets or runners and so by nature and appearance it's best seen alone and it certainly deserves to be displayed as something special.

The 48 in. Giant Wood Fern (*D. goldiana*) and the Toothed Wood Fern (*D. spinulosa*) are also superb, but neither is as persistently evergreen as *D. marginalis*.

Many other garden-worthy gems are to be found among the genera *Asplenium, Cheilanthes, Pellaea, Polypodium,* and *Woodsia*—but most are smaller plants and make a less significant contribution to the over-all design in spite of their outstanding individual beauty.

Even the other ferns mentioned will be bit players in most garden designs since they are plants of modest size. But in small spaces their contribution can be considerable and may do a great deal to establish a dominant mood of quiet repose. Their use in the courtyard gardens of Japan provides ample evidence of this and in that context their effect is out of all proportion to their stature. Indeed, wherever they can be used their effect is likely to far exceed their size.

[3.10] OTHER FAVORITE PERENNIALS

It is tempting to use perennials in quantities far exceeding their contribution to a coherent landscape plan of full-year interest. After all, perennials are readily available, relatively inexpensive, easily installed and moved, yield their full effect in a short time, and many have extraordinary beauty. Our European garden heritage provides us with a wealth of knowledge on how to grow perennials and constrains us with a wealth of examples illustrating their use in islands, borders, and rockeries. Most of the varieties choking our nurseries were developed abroad, particularly in England, and their overuse is guaranteed to create a convincingly Victorian, dotty aura in even the most contemporary surroundings.

A different aesthetic prevails in the Orient, particularly in Japan. There perennials are used sparingly, and many of the most renown gardens hardly use them at all. When they are used, it is as single specimens or in small groups—almost never in broad sweeps or a mixed border. This restrained use of perennials in no way reflects the abundance and diversity of Japan's indigenous species. Instead it is more of a reflection of a refined and ascetic canon of garden design, one which emphasizes subtle modulations of form and texture, rather than brash color compositions accompanied by wrenching seasonal changes. The latter scheme is antithetical to a sense of timeless repose that is so cherished in the gardens of the Orient.

This aesthetic has a great deal of appeal to me, and I try to honor it while at the same time making at least some concessions to my insatiable appetite for these plants. I have many favorites—too many for my own good. Many that were originally welcomed into my garden and given a choice and perspicuous spot, were later shoved to the back, and then to a corner, and finally ushered through the gate and onto the hill behind our neighbor's fence. I cannot bring myself to toss any no matter how disenchanted I become with them. Only a few have remained, and some of these I still number among my favorites.

What beside idiosyncratic taste dissuaded me from growing the others?

I have an aversion to plants that require excessive disbudding, dead-heading, tying, staking, or any other S & M technique in order to keep them presentable.

I have too little time and patience to deal with over-exuberant plants that strangle their neighbors, tangle the paths, invade the lawn, or climb the trees unless beaten back every so often.

I detest those sloppy-floppy plants that have to be stake-stiffened to stand at all, and those sorrowful flowers that hang their macrocephalic heads in a depressingly dejected manner. I would rather grow competition-sized pumpkins for their contribution to the landscape.

I have precious little room to suffer one-season performers that strut their stuff for a week or so and then revert to a shabby mess for the remainder of the year.

I can't countenance those that mildew at the slightest mist, droop at the slightest drought, and cringe at the first sign of cold.

So is there anything left? Fortunately, yes—more than enough to plant my garden in perennials from corner to corner if I so choose. Each is a plant of considerable individual beauty, but more importantly each is a plant that makes a positive contribution to the over-all garden design. Among these favorites, let me mention the following few.

Those that I grow for their foliage, habit, and flowers include: iris (Japanese, Siberian, and several smaller gems like *Iris cristata* and the lovely *I. gracilipes*); *Filipendula hexapetala* for its lovely, loose pannicles of creamy white flowers, but mostly for its nearly evergreen foliage that easily passes for that of a fern although this plant thrives in places that few ferns would fancy; *Lysimachia clethroides* and *Lythrum salicaria*, the first for its goosenecked pan-nicles of white blossoms, the second for its pannicles of pink, rose, or purple, and both for their pink-to-red, fall foliage; geraniums like *Geranium macro-rrhizum* and *G. endressii*, at least as much for their extraordinary foliage as for their blossoms; the bold and noble *Macleaya cordata* superb near a stream, even when not in flower, with its 10 in. scalloped leaves on ascending, stiff 7 ft. stems; various helleborus, in or out of bloom, with wonderful palm-like stems of evergreen foliage; and a garden full of lesser gems, no less beautiful, but of lesser size—some campanulas, gentians, achilleas, helianthemums, *Stachys macrantha*, and many others.

Since I have a special fondness for daisy-like blossoms I grow the following: shastas (the neat foliage is almost evergreen, and dwarf varieties with single flowers are available like 'Little Princess'); *Chrysanthemum weyrichii* (which has white or pink flowers in September and nearly evergreen foliage); gaillardias (like the dwarfs 'Goblin' and 'Golden Goblin'); some coreopsis (like the dwarfs 'Goldfink' and 'Zagreb', the first a clone of *Coreopsis lanceolata* and the second a cultivar of *C. verticillata*); *Rudbeckia* 'Goldsturm' (in spite of its unremarkable foliage); and the purple and white varieties of *Echinacea purpurea* also with unremarkable foliage but, like the rudbeckia, ornamental over a very long season.

Perennials that I grow primarily for their foliage include: *Bergenia cordifolia*, and an occasional hosta (like 'Ginkgo Craig', 'Golden Tiara', and some *H. takudama* cultivars, although these do not have an extended season). Had I more room by our stream I would grow rheums, ligularias, and some of the larger hostas.

Specialty firms supplying woodland plants or alpines usually offer many selections which have an ungilded beauty that blends very well into a variety of landscapes. The woodland specialist can supply all sorts of ferns. From the alpine specialist consider plants like *Aster alpinus*, all sorts of true geraniums and campanulas, all manner of phlox and dianthus (some needing a bit more dryness and better drainage than the usual garden site offers), arenarias, armerias, aubrietas, helianthemums, penstemons of all sorts, and much-too-many more to mention. All of these provide several seasons of beauty and will not turn the garden into a circus when in bloom.

This list may not be large, but for one garden of moderate size it's far too large. I'm certain that I'll order many more perennials for the coming season—just as certain that I'll hate myself in the morning for doing it and that sooner or later almost all of them will end up on the hill behind my neighbor's fence.

Wishbook

[3.11] DAYDREAMS AND RAMBLINGS

There has been marvelous progress in ornamental horticulture in this century. The introduction of new species, the increasing awareness of the garden potential of native plants, the discovery of superior clones, and the breeding of new hybrids have all made enormous contributions to the enjoyment of the garden. And the potential of genetic engineering can not be overstated.

But far from placating my desire for new plant material these contributions just serve to whet my imagination and pique my anticipation. My ignorance of chromosomal compatibility allows me to conjure up all sorts of marvels, some of which might even be possible.

[3.12] BULLDOGS

If it has chlorophyll, there will be a sincere and enthusiastic group of hobbyists devoted to its cultivation and popularization. But much of this activity is directed toward a few rather narrow and unpromising goals.

Something of the dog breeder's attitude permeates the hybridization of ornamental plants. This attitude is exemplified in the evolution of the English bulldog. The creature had been selected over several centuries for the purpose of bull baiting. In this "sport" several were pitted against a loosed bull. Relatively short, slightly bowed legs gave the dogs the mobility to move next to and under the bull while avoiding its hooves. A mildly pushed in snout and undershot jaw permitted the dogs to breathe while retaining a hold on the jowls or neck of the bull. And a massive chest housed under a broad back not only gave them the lung power for a prolonged battle, but also the body weight to bring the bull to exhaustion, even to its knees, or cause it to misstep and stumble. When bull baiting was abolished in 1835, a club of fanciers was formed to "preserve" the breed. In order to have the breed recognized by the English Kennel Club a standard had to be drawn up describing the ideal bulldog. The above-mentioned traits which allowed the dog to compete successfully were described in the standard. Once set down it dictated the conclusion that the "better" dog is the one that most conforms to the standard, and the breeders set about creating a caricature that exaggerated each of the described traits as much as possible. The snout was so pushed back that a rippled palate in need of surgical correction became common, almost as common as are breathing difficulties and symptoms of asthma. The shoulders and chest became so massive in comparison to the width of the hip that Caesarean delivery is now also common. The legs have been so bowed that surgical intervention is often necessary to allow the animal to move in something of a normal manner. A slow jaunt around the show ring leaves the dog gasping for breadth, with its tongue hanging out and its sides heaving. When the judge stops to give a particular dog a closer look, an expert handler, kneeling beside the panting beast, will yank up on its lead and simultaneously tickle its privates. For a brief moment the creature shakes off its exhaustion and apathy and appears to show some semblance of life. When the judge moves on, the handler eases up on the lead, stops the tickle, and the dog collapses. This cultivated bag of deformities could not cope with a bunny rabbit never mind a bull. The breeders have made a mockery of the creature's heritage. The capable bulldog has been sacrificed for a crippled caricature.

The bulldog-breeding syndrome plagues both breeders of plants and breeders of animals everywhere. They want to see how far they can go. The Chinese have their foo dogs—snorty, snotty mimics of lions, custom made to be stuffed into the sleeves of kimonos. The "bigger-the-better" bomb peonies are also a creation of the Chinese. The Japanese, too, have a long history of breeding for the grotesque. They are the proud originators of those weird goldfishes like the Celestial sporting huge goitrous sacs under upward staring eyes, and the Oranda and Lionhead wearing raspberry-like face masks which on occasion have to be surgically pruned in order to allow them to see and eat. Those acrid yellow and sickly pink cactus that you see in the supermarket, parasitically clinging to their hosts for want of chlorophyll, are also of Japanese making. The temptation is there. You have something a bit different, exaggerate its differences to make it clear that it's different.

Setting down the standards of a rose or an iris has much the same effect. Novel or distinguishing characteristics are emphasized and magnified without regard to harmony or use in the landscape; utility and beauty are sacrificed for exaggeration and caricature.

The "improvement" of iris, peonies, hemerocallis and a plethora of other plants has been fostered by active specialty clubs with large and devoted memberships. Over a thousand new bearded iris and a thousand new daylilies are registered every year. But to what end? To add yet another fuddy-duddy frill or ruffle to an already rococo creation? Is the contribution to gardening in any way commensurate with the time and effort expended? Just imagine the boon to horticulture that might result from shunting some of this time and energy toward the breeding of wildly different varieties of dogwoods, maples, oaks, cherries, mahonias and so on with the goal of extending hardiness and adaptability, disease resistance, and the creation of decidedly new plant forms. Think of the personal reward and satisfaction of introducing a new plant to gardeners living in a climate unsuitable for the cultivation of anything remotely like it.

Why aren't more garden enthusiasts interested in such projects? Perhaps what is lacking is a convenient means of organizing and institutionalizing such interests, of canonizing meritorious achievements so that individuals can be duly recognized and rewarded for their accomplishments. It seems to be a question of social politics and not of botanical constraints. Indeed the botanical possibilities seem unlimited. It's fairly trivial to concoct some standard of excellence for a single narrow group of plants like daylilies or roses, but how does one standardize an effort directed against standardization, an endeavor whose intent it is to create significant new plant material in as wide a variety as possible.

Where it is deemed to matter more, as in the development of new fruits and vegetables, plant hybridization and selection has been much more rapid. We now have tearless onions, burpless cucumbers, and tasteless strawberries the size of baseballs. There are Zone 4 hardy peaches, nectarines, and apricots; almonds hardy in Zone 6; blueberries that will withstand temperatures to −40° F; pears and apples immune to or at least highly resistant to fireblight; apple scab, and rust. One nursery offers over 250 varieties of apples—enough to keep the doctor away forever and maybe enough to impart immortality. No doubt commercial incentive has played some role in this rapid progress. For ornamentals, exploiting the plant patent process to a greater extent may provide the incentive for more substantive innovations. In the meantime, we patiently wait as thousands of deservedly nameless hemerocallis, iris, and lilies are registered and given names.

Wishbook – Trees

[3.13] MAPLES AND CHERRIES

No genus frustrates this gardener more or teases with more promise than the maples. There are some stoic hardies like the Siberian, Silver, Sugar, Norway, and Tartarian Maples, to name a few. But the delights of the hundreds of exquisite cultivars of Japanese Maple (*Acer palmatum*) are just out of the reach of many climates in the U.S. There are varieties realizing every conceivable leaf color (white with pink, rose, red, yellow, and green in various mixtures and patterns); every leaf shape (large, tiny, substantial, filigreed, flat, curled and crinkled); and every size and habit (tall upright vases to squat cascading mounds). It seems that every conceivable shape between the extremes is approximated by some existing form. But this only increases the frustration. Again, daydreaming, there seems to be unlimited potential for the production of trees and shrubs in a wonderous diversity of forms, leaf shapes, and colors that can withstand a substantial Zone 4 climate.

Is this too much to ask for? I am not dreaming about date palms cheerfully spreading their fronds to catch the Minnesota snow or banana trees with their fruit glowing yellow beneath the January ice. Some cultivars of the Japanese maples are already marginally hardy in favored locations in the Midwest, and specimens can be found growing wild in Japan in relatively harsh environments. Moreover, there may be the possibility of hybridizing the Japanese maples with other species of maples, in particular with *Acer ginnala, A. truncatum, A. circinatum, A. grandidentatum,* and *A. saccharinum.* It may turn out that verticillum wilt will remain a scourge even if general hardiness is increased, but perhaps a breeding program could give some attention to this matter also.

The Vine Maple (*Acer circinatum*) of the Pacific Northwest is a close look-alike of the Full Moon Maple (*A. japonicum*), at least the leaves are almost identical. But the form of the Vine Maple is difficult to characterize since it varies dramatically with its environment—tall and viney in the dense forest, and short and shrubby in the open. Moreover, its wide range and current garden use are evidence that it is hardier and more adaptable than the Full Moon Maple. A recent trip to Washington's Olympic Peninsula left me wondering about the genetic treasures that might be locked up inside circinatum's code. In early August, in open fields abutting dense forest, we saw trees of the clearest crimson of any maple at any season and others with leaves of pink or orange. There are several distinctive cultivars already on the market, such as the 3 ft. bushy dwarf 'Little Gem' and the superb, dissected-leaf variety 'Monroe'. Given the skill and patience lavished on the Japanese maples, the Vine Maple might yield a comparable diversity of forms and with greater hardiness and disease resistance.

There is a shortage of distinguished, large, bold-leaved shrubs for temperate climates. Globe Norway Maple (*A. platanoides* 'Globosum') would do nicely. Unfortunately, it is never offered as a multistemmed shrub; instead it is pruned to a globe and grafted high on a standard, giving it the appearance of a Van deGraff generator with an Afro, out of place everywhere except

Disneyland. How nice it would be to have the unalloyed version available—but it isn't.

The Big Leafed Maple (*Acer macrophyllum*) could also be grown as a multistemmed shrub. Few have a bolder leaf, or one more interestingly shaped. But this is a plant for climates wimpier than Zone 6, and even grown multistem it is much too large to be used as a shrub. Perhaps a cross between the Big Leaf and the 'Globe Norway Maple' might give an approximation that is smaller and hardier.

I would like to see the Big Toothed Maple (*Acer grandidentatum*) selected for shrubiness and fall color, Silver Maples hybridized to reduce size and increase sturdiness, Moosewood bred to other snake-barked maples to increase their hardiness, Siberian Maples hybridized to yield more interesting leaf shapes, and *A. truncatum* given the popularity it deserves.

I would like to see the University of Minnesota Arboretum succeed in finding new selections of Sugar Maple and Red Maple that are disease resistant and reliably colorful in the fall throughout Zones 3 through 5. (Their program also includes a search for disease-resistant, hardy, adaptable, and garden-worthy Red Oaks, Eastern Dogwoods, and many others.)

In short, I would like to see more maples. I like maples.

Some of the same cultural restrictions that plague those who covet maples also bedevil the admirer of Oriental cherries. The Japanese garden in Golden Gate Park features many marvelous cherries, but I remember one in particular with large bell-shaped blossoms held in clusters to face the viewer full open as he gazes up into the tree. And the color is an icy, pale yellow-green against the bronze emerging leaves. Again, there seems to be no lack of breeding partners. Exceedingly hardy and adaptable prunus species abound, as for example the sour cherries like 'Montmorency', but I have no idea if the possibility of such a cross exists. In addition there are Zone 2 hardy prunus like the Goldenbark Cherry (*Prunus maackii*) and a number of Zone 2 and Zone 3 shrubby cherries like the American Wild Plum (*P. americana*), the Western Sand Cherry (*P. besseyi*), the Dwarf Russian Almond (*P. tenella*), and the Nanking Cherry (*P. tomentosa*) that could provide a surprising and extraordinary range of forms of exceptional hardiness and adaptability.

[3.14] DOGWOODS

Widely regarded as one of the most beautiful assets of which a garden can boast, the Eastern Dogwood (*Cornus florida*) has something to offer every season of the year. But its adaptability is severely limited, and if it survives in the Midwest at all it seldom thrives. However, there are dogwoods such as the Pagoda Dogwood (*C. alternifolia*) and the Cornelian Cherry (*C. mas*) that do fairly well in many places inhospitable to the Eastern Dogwood. The Redtwig (*C. stolonifera*) is a weed under almost any situation—wet or dry, sunny or shady, acid or sweet. Could some fortuitous compromise be struck by combining any of these with *C. florida*? It would be my brown-thumb luck to have such a match produce a totally non-hardy misfit with no fall color and insignificant flowers. But then again who knows. 'Eddie's White Wonder' is a successful cross between the Eastern and Western Dogwood (*C. florida* and *C. nuttallii*). Maybe even a cross between the large-flowered, 6 in. tall Bunchberry (*C. canadensis*) and the Red Twig or Eastern Dogwood is possible. It could yield some pleasant surprises by way of large-flowered, shrubby or dwarf dogwoods. H. L. Foster suggests crossing the Bunchberry with other dogwoods as a way of ascertaining genetic relationships and thereby getting some information on the phylogeny of the genus, but the horticultural possibilities should not be overlooked.

The Chinese Dogwood (*C. kousa, C. k. chinensis*) is also a challenge to grow over much of the country. What a boon it would be to have a clone or look-alike hybrid as tough and hardy as the shrubby dogwoods. Here is a four-season shrub, with good foliage, superb autumn color and fruits, interesting winter silhouette, colorfully mottled bark, and extraordinarily beautiful flowers borne in June after the cherries, crabs, and magnolias.

The Pagoda Dogwood (*C. alternifolia*) of the eastern U.S. is a treasure store of horticultural delights. It can be grown as a single-stemmed tree, but I prefer it as a large multistemmed shrub. Horizontal tiers of branches give the plant its common name. The leaves are attractive in the spring and summer, and downright spectacular when in fall color. The creamy white flowers appear in mid-May in dense fuzzy cymes. Pleasant but not spectacular, they are neatly held above the foliage. Sometimes a bit recalcitrant to take up new quarters, it is generally tough, adaptable, and hardy in Zone 3. Is there room to gild this lily even more? What would a cross between it and *C. kousa* or *C. florida* yield? Any intermediate form with larger flowers than the Pagoda Dogwood but with an increase in adaptability and hardiness would be a most welcome gift to the gardening world.

[3.15] OTHER TREES

The hawthorns (Crataegus) are a promising lot that are receiving more attention these days. There are many species that are extraordinarily beautiful in flower, fruit, and habit with interestingly shaped leaves and striking fall color. They come in a variety of shapes and sizes. Some are fastigate, others are spreading. There are shrub forms and sizable trees. Most are tough, drought resistant, and cold hardy. But fireblight and leaf-spot disease are severe problems as is susceptibility to aphids and other insects. Their spines also pose a problem in many situations. On the other hand, there are some species that are resistant to these diseases and insects, and some thornless selections already exist. Opportunities seem at hand. Belonging to the family Roseacea it is conceivable that some intergeneric cross, say between *Malus* and *Cretaegus* might work, and that would be a different ball game. Although new hybrids are coming out every year, there is nowhere near the work being done on these trees that we see being done with the cherries and crabs.

I am very partial to Honey Locust (*Gleditsia triacanthos*). This large tree combines a powerful line with a delicacy of detail. There are several selections which vary with respect to ultimate height, over-all shape, and the size of the leaflets. Except for cultivars like 'Rubylace' and 'Sunburst', both extremely striking but chromatically antagonistic to any other plant within a 50 yd. radius, these selections are quite similar to each other and to the wild form, although both are devoid of pods and thorns. Unfortunately, a plague has now beset the Honey Locust in the form of a barely visible fly, the locust-pod-midge. The creature lays its eggs on the leaflets of the locust, and when the eggs hatch and the larvae begin to feed, the leaf curls up along the axis of its main vein to form a pod around the grub. The creature is now safe from all contact insecticides, and even systemics seem to have little effect. Once encapsulated, the larva feeds with impunity until ready for the metamorphoses that takes it to adulthood and the next generation. The cycle is repeated several times during one season and is asynchronous making it unlikely that a spraying with any contact poison will be effective even against the adults. At the moment no effective control is known, and although the tree is not killed outright, it is disfigured into a shabby-looking mess giving no usable shade. Horticultural agents are now advising against the use of this tree in many of the regions where it had been widely extolled and highly rated.

Here is a tree that might profit from a shot of polyploidy. This increase in chromosome number often causes gigantism and doubling of flowers, and is usually accompanied by increased vigor. If polyploidy could be induced in the Honey Locust, it might confer several advantages. The pod-midge is so host-specific that any change in the shape or texture of the leaflets might impart some resistance to it. In addition an increase in the size of the leaflets would give a denser tree offering more shade.

I also like the true Locust (*Robinia pseudoacacia*), a species in many ways similar to the Honey Locust. This tree is blessed with stout wisteria-like clusters of flowers and bolder leaves that I find more attractive than those of the Honey Locust. But something has to be done about the curses that beleaguer the tree—its brittleness, susceptibility to borers and rampant suckering.

I remember groves of sassafras (*Sassafras albidum*) on the East Coast ablaze with autumn color. Even the Red Maples and Sugar Maples were unable to outshine them. And the Sassafras is not as coarsely textured, large, or formal as these maples. At maturity it has a casual elegance and a somewhat unpredictable structure with a marked oriental character. Unfortunately, the tree does not transplant readily, is said to be finicky in its soil preference, and is somewhat brittle. But this is a worthy tree that has been ignored by plantsmen, and no attempt has been made to breed or select for better forms.

A large hybridization program for oaks is being carried out at the State Arboretum of Utah, University of Utah, and many viable interspecific crosses have been made. I do not believe that the highly variable Ground Scrub Oak (*Quercus gambelli*) has been used. Here is the possibility of introducing a more manageable size while retaining an interesting leaf shape and color into the species of oak available for the private garden. And the dwarf, fairly hardy evergreen species like *Q. sadleriana*, and *Q. vaccinifolia* might offer pleasant surprises if used in a breeding program.

Some trees would be popular ornamentals were they not difficult to grow or transplant. For example, the Shagbark Hickory (*Carya ovata*) is a stunning, large shade tree with splendid leaves, good fall color, highly unusual bark and a strong winter outline. But being tap rooted, it is generally unavailable in larger sizes. Here horticultural technique rather than breeding might do the trick, growing the tree in such a way as to encourage a finer rooting structure.

Wish I may, wish I might grow the Japanese Snowbell (*Styrax japonicus*), the stewartias like *Stewartia koreana, S. pseudocamellia,* and *Franklinia alatamaha.* I would be delighted with them exactly as they are. All I ask is that their hardiness rating be given a gentle shove northward by a zone or two.

Finally, there are a number of highly desirable trees that can be grown over a vast area of the U.S. but for some obscure reason are rarely available commercially. *Ptelea trifoliata, Maackia amurensis, M. chinensis, Corylus colurna, Phellodendron amurense, P. sachalinense,* and *Ostrya virgineana,* and many, many more are tough, hardy, distinctive and generally unobtainable.

Wishbook – Shrubs

The smaller the plant the smaller the demands on space and patience required to breed and raise it; consequently, much more effort is being devoted to the breeding of shrubs than to the breeding of trees. Yet in spite of the marvels that have been made available recently, I still daydream about others.

[3.16] VIBURNUMS

The viburnums constitute one of the most varied, beautiful, and useful groups of shrubs available to the gardener. They range in size from about 1–30 ft. Some are evergreen, others deciduous and all with usually superb fall color. Most bear domed cymes of white flowers, but in some the flowers are borne in showy clusters or in the exquisite "lacecap" pattern. Recently, pink-flowering forms have been introduced. Some of the viburnums feature blossoms renown for their delicious, powerful scent. Many offer a late summer or fall bonus of fruit; yellow, red, and black berrying forms are available and some forms yield berries changing from red to black, each berry in its own time, giving a sharp contrast within the same cluster. Branching habit and over-all form also differ widely as does leaf shape.

A start has been made in selecting clones of the American Cranberry Bush (*Viburnum trilobum*) for abundance of bloom and fruit, as well as size. The leaves are shaped somewhat like those of the Red Maple, and the shrub is handsome even without the flowers and fruit. One wonders what genetic variability is present. Conceivably, a cross between *V. trilobum* and *V. plicatum* 'Mariesii' is possible, and might yield a hybrid with greater adaptability and a more interesting leaf shape than the latter, but with 'Mariesii's' magnificent layered habit and floriferousness. A cross between 'Mariesii' and *V. opulus* 'Compactum' might give Mariesii-like hybrids in smaller packages. All would be welcome and useful additions to our gardens.

[3.17] DAPHNES

I am partial to daphnes and wish that as much skill and effort had been lavished on them as on the rhodos. What daphnes need is a mid-western Rotheschild, Gable, or Leach. The flowers are beautiful but not garish and usually of legendary fragrance. The foliage is neat and often evergreen. They are easy mixers blending well with a variety of other plants. Many tolerate fairly harsh conditions and unlike the rhodos do not require an acid soil. There is no spectacular diversity of leaf form, but there are some with variegated leaves and most have glossy, deep green, smallish, elliptical leaves that are attractive enough. In height the plants range from a couple of inches to several feet. The form may be creeping or stiffly erect. Flowers can be white, many shades of pink to a fair red, and green. There are several species and hybrids hardy into Zone 4, and many daphnes can be easily grown in areas that are treacherous to rhodos. I don't know quite what to ask for except more, more, more.

[3.18] RHODODENDRONS

Rhododendrons are favored by hordes of rabid devotees, and there is no lack of interest in the hybridizing of these plants. Over the years the genus has been favored by several diligent and insightful breeders who have sought the creation of hardier and more adaptable forms, and their efforts will surely increase the size of the following. Large-flowered, large-leaved rhodos hardy to −20° F are becoming more common, and recently, the University of Minnesota released several deciduous hybrids with bud hardiness to −40° F.

For the most part, the effort has been directed to the production of the spectacular, with emphasis on huge flowers held in enormous trusses. Many of these plants are best suited for specimen display and are either too big or too brash to be harmonious with a naturalistic landscape. The breeding of dwarf, hardy, evergreen azaleas has not been keeping pace with the development of these flashier plants. It is interesting to note that the large-flowered rhodos are not favored in Japanese gardens. Their size and boldness make them incongruous with the refined naturalism of these gardens. On the other hand the smaller azaleas have been used in Japan for centuries and are prized as much for their leaf texture and habit as for their flowers. Indeed, they are often clipped to accentuate their mounding growth habit even though this practice sharply curtails blooming.

[3.19] GROWING NATIVE

For centuries the Japanese have been content to use a select fragment of their native plants for their gardens, although many other plants, both native and exotic, were available and horticulturally suitable. This restriction helps focus the attention on the over-all design of the garden and away from individual plants; harmony is given more importance than novelty. A restricted palate with which one is familiar, a palate in which the colors blend readily with each other, is easier to master than one crammed full of all sorts of hues without any thought of their compatibility.

Our gardening tradition originated in Europe, particularly in England, and therefore much of our plant material is drawn from European stock, and reflects qualities suited to European tastes and growing conditions. Our own heritage of native plants is at least as rich and varied as Japan's, and this country's climates encompass a lip smacking, hair pulling diversity. In spite of this botanical treasure chest relatively little interest has been evident in exploiting our native plants for garden use, especially the shrubs, although there seems to be a wealth of promising material to use as is or for its breeding potential.

The Creeping Grape Holly, *Mahonia repens*, is a bold, evergreen ground cover, with shiny leaves shaped like the Japanese holly. Winter paints it a vivid maroon-red, and in the spring it bears clusters of yellow flowers followed by blue berries. It is extremely hardy, tolerant of sun and shade, draught, and moisture. As far as I know, there have been no selections made on the basis of height, shape, flowering, or fruiting characteristics. Nor has an attempt been made to cross it with other mahonias like the magnificent *M. lomariifolia* or *M. bealei* which are not hardy over much of the country.

Ceanothus velutinus is a large-leaved, evergreen shrub of the foothills. The leaves are interestingly veined and have very distinctive, sweet, but pungent scent. In the spring astilbe-like pannicles of creamy white are both delicate and very noticeable. Yet with all these attractive, and distinctive features, the shrub is little known to horticulturists.

Ceanothus intermedia is a lovely 4½ ft. high evergreen shrub with delicate leaves and spirea-like flowers. While Zone 4 hardy, it is not easy to propagate and grow. A storehouse of possibilities await if it can be crossed with any of the dozens of clones and hybrid ceanothus of the West Coast with their endless diversity of shapes, sizes, and flower color. There are other ceanothus that might impart hardiness such as *C. fendleri* and *C. velutinus* mentioned above.

Another evergreen of extraordinary promise as a ground cover is the Bearberry, *Arctostaphylos uva-ursi*. Although it has been accused of having finicky soil preferences (it's an acid lover according to some and an alkaline dweller according to others), and of being hard to transplant and propagate, it is now available in a variety of forms for almost every situation—from hot, dry, sun-baked and sandy to moist, shady and humus-rich soil. Selections have been made for height, compactness, fruiting and flowering, leaf size, and winter color, which may be green, bronze, or red.

However, this arcto has several big brothers that are as yet unsung and unnoticed.

Arctostaphylos patula is a hardy (Zone 4) evergreen capable of reaching 6 ft. with stiff, blue-green, nonbronzing foliage on a pleasingly stiff, fairly open shrub. *A. nevadensis* is another manzanita, evergreen and hardy to Zone 4 growing to about 14 in. in height. Shrubby evergreens this hardy and tolerant of alkalinity, sun, and drought are a scarce commodity, and these might nicely fit the bill. Although a few selections have been made, these species deserve much more attention.

Paxistima canbyi is a 12 in., evergreen shrub somewhat like the Korean Boxwood in effect. Although popular on the East Coast it does not do as well in the Midwest and intermountain states. However, it has a look-alike relative called the Mountain Lover (*P. myrsinites*) that is quite adaptable to various exposures and soils. Totally unspectacular this is a plant of simple, delicate beauty, right at home in all sorts of company.

The Boulder Raspberry, *Rubus deliciosus*, is a magnificent shrub, somewhat appreciated in Europe but largely ignored here. Of loose habit its 8 ft. branches arch gracefully displaying large, yellow-centered, white blossoms in the spring. The leaves are the size and shape of those of the edible currant. The winter aspect is informal. The shrub displays a great deal of natural variation in the size and abundance of its flowers and in its shape and height. Those who think it can be improved by increasing its floriferousness and flower size might consider crossing it with some garden rubus like *R. tridel* 'Benenden'.

There are several other rubus species which are charming in a woodland setting and might be considered as breeding partners for *R. deliciosus* such as the Flowering Raspberry (*R. odoratus*) and Thimbleberry (*R. parviflorus*). The first has lovely pink flowers, the second white, both sparsely produced. The leaves of the Thimbleberry are large, to 4 in. and shaped like those of a Norway Maple. These features and their tolerance of shade make them outstanding in the understory of a woodland planting.

Cliff Jamesia, (*Jamesia americana*), is another overlooked gem—an upright deciduous shrub to 4 ft. with thick, fuzzy, ovate leaves to 3 in. which reliably color a spectacular bronze-red for many weeks in the fall. In mid-spring it offers 2 in. clusters of pink-budded, white flowers. Hardy to at least Zone 4, tolerant of sun and shade and many soils, it's superb as it is, but I know of no selections or hybrids.

The over-domesticated, prim and pampered hybrid rose nearly defines its site as a formal garden. Looking totally out of place in anything but a rose bed, it epitomizes the breeder's skill in creating exquisitely beautiful flowers of extraordinary appeal that are visually antithetical to any setting that is even remotely based on natural canons. However, there are wild roses of considerable charm with single blossoms in white, pink or red set against fern-like foliage showing spectacular autumn tints such as *Rosa nitida*, and *R. virginiana*. While most look shabby in the winter, some at least stay close to the ground and sport scarlet rose hips. Many are exceedingly hardy, rarely bothered by pests and diseases, and require far less attention than the elaborate hybrids. Although there are some hybrid singles, very little has been done to select and hybridize them with the goal of obtaining the most usable combination of beauty of flower, foliage, hardiness, disease resistance and form.

There are many other little known or underused native trees and shrubs that hold promise for the garden by reason of their hardiness, beauty and distinctiveness. To name a few: Green's Mountain Ash (*Sorbus scopulina*), like a multistemmed shrubby European Mountain Ash; Red River Birch (*Betula fontinalis*), a multistemmed shrubby tree to 15 ft. with shiny, red bark like a cherry and amber autumn foliage; shrubby Choke Cherries (*Prunus virginiana* and *P. v. demissa*) with pleasant heads of small, creamy white flowers, followed by blue fruits in clusters and bronze-red autumn color; *Rhus glabra cismontana*, a thicket-forming dwarf, smooth sumac, something like a coarse fern, prefering hot and dry situations, and turning a brilliant scarlet in the fall; *Ptelea trifoliata*, the Hop Tree, a shrub to 15 ft. with bold distinctive foliage and nondescript flowers with a powerful scent that does not appeal to everyone. And there are many others.

[3.20] PERENNIALS

Much more effort has gone into the hybridization and the clonal selection of perennials than into the woody plants. No doubt this is because perennials take up less room and require less time to bring from seed to flowering.

The outcome of all this effort is a vast and rapidly increasing store of hybrids and cultivars of some two dozen or so old standbys. But most of these reflect the tastes of bygone times in England, perhaps with a mixture of the Texan's credo "more is more". High rise delphiniums stagger to a height of 6 ft., some of the Asiatic lily hybrids teeter to 8 ft., and giant dahlias sway like drunken sailors even with support, and nod their shaggy heads at you at eye level. None of these are free standing, and all have to be staked. Any telephone pole will do.

It took patience and skill to divest Japanese iris of their grace and beauty. Tetraploidy and other induced forms of gigantism have given us 4 ft. flower stalks unable to support the weight of 11 in. blooms that are fluted, ruffled, crimped, and colored in a variety of designer hues that thwart assimilation in any garden honoring nature's canons of design. Curiously, their size gives them a fragility that is not offset by their added substance—they wilt in a July scorcher, and a heavy thunderstorm will ruin them completely. Harper and McGourty suggest that no Japanese iris surpasses a single, small-flowered white. I agree, but try to find one. I have a passion for iris in general, but I relegate the taller Japanese iris and the even gaudier, tall German beardeds to the cutting bed where their coarse foliage, fading flowers, and brash color schemes will not detract from the rest of the garden.

Even when gigantism is not the main point and the goal of hybridization is the creation of a small, compact plant, the canon of beauty is not that of spare grace and elegance that will blend easily into the garden, but rather that of a congested, floriferous lump of color. As is the case with the cushion mums and asters, the flowers are usually double, and any remaining grace they might have retained individually is completely obscured by the dense pack.

Among the plants that are grown primarily for their foliage hostas hold first place. They can be delicately graceful or bold and lushly tropical. The leaves can be lance-, heart-, or almost disk-shaped; ribbed, puckered like searsucker, or satiny smooth. Colors include blues, yellows, and greens, either as selfs or in combined patterns, margined, feathered, or blotched. Many have noteworthy flowers—some with a scent, some blue, some white, quite attractive in their own right but considered merely an insignificant addenda to the plant's main attraction—the magnificent foliage. This is another group of plants that has attracted a hoard of zealous hobbyists committed to the creation of every conceivable permutation and combination of shape and color. Although there are some marvelous miniatures, the bulk of the breeding effort has been devoted to the creation of bigger, bolder, and

Above. The auburn beauty of wild grasses in autumn suggesting the use of a medium-height, unmowed grass as a garden ground cover. Cub Lake Trail, Rocky Mountain National Park, Colorado.

Left. Thyme, pentstemon, sedum, helianthemum, Moss Phlox, Creeping and Woolly Veronicas, and others make a carefree ground cover in the author's garden.

Left. *Peltophyllum peltatum.*
Below. *Petesites speciosa,* on the shore of Mora Beach, Olympic Penninsula, Washington. Might these be bold alternatives to hostas, and other perennials grown primarily for their foliage?

more brazen forms—plants of specimen status, prima donnas ill at ease unless given center stage.

However, there are some largely overlooked native plants with superb, bold foliage in completely different shapes. Three that I find particularly beautiful are the Vanilla Leaf (*Achleys triphylla*), Coltsfoot (*Petesites speciosa*), and *Peltiphyllum peltatum*. All of these offer bold leaf size combined with extraordinarily beautiful leaf-shapes like giant snowflakes or scalloped doilies. Coltsfoot, in particular, seems to possess an abundance of genetic variability in leaf size and pattern. Moreover it thrives in a wide range of habitats from sea level to 12,000 ft. from ocean side in sandy soil exposed to full western sun, to shady fir forests, and even fairly dry roadsides.

Alchemilla vulgaris has some similarity in shape to *Peltiphyllum peltatum* but on a much smaller scale, and some geraniums like *Geranium himalayense* and *G. macrorrhizum* have leaves bearing a superficial resemblance to Vanilla Leaf and Coltsfoot, but do not match their bold leaf size. Since I am particularly fond of geranium leaves, I would find varieties bred for low, sturdy growth and huge leaves both useful and beautiful. Such varieties would offer the same effect as these untamed natives. On the other hand maybe some of these three wild species can be domesticated or can be bred and selected for garden adaptability. Either alternative would present great possibilities for the woodland garden.

[3.21] GROUND COVERS

The ground covers comprise one of the most important and least romantic groups of plants, I don't think that there is a ground cover society, and great hybridizers devoted to the quest for better ones, are either unsung or nonexistent. But ground covers are a greatly varied lot which can do much to determine the character of the garden and much to determine the amount of upkeep devoted to weeding and mowing.

Plain old grass is the ground cover of choice for a wide diversity of situations. For the beauty of its colors, texture, long season, ability to withstand foot traffic, and its ease of maintenance, it's hard to beat.

In the U.S. bluegrass is the most widely planted, but fesques are coming into their own especially for use in heavy shade and there has been some breeding effort to improve these grasses. Drought-tolerant, dwarf grasses like Buffalo Grass have application in areas where maintenance must be kept low, but most of these are clumpy, and go dormant early in the season. Zoysia is popular in warmer regions and needs no mowing.

Gardeners and plantsmen everywhere dream of a tough, hardy grass with the appearance of bluegrass, that needs no mowing, but at the moment the dream is elusive. Maybe a Zoysia or fesque will be bred to fill the bill. Jan Weijer of the University of Alberta, Canada, is working with a highly promising group of grasses native to the eastern slope of the Canadian Rockies. These are long-season, drought-tolerant grasses, that are resistent to foot traffic, fungus, and disease. Moreover, they grow to a height of only 2–8 in. and so require little mowing. At least four years will be needed to produce enough seed for commercial distribution.

There are some ground covers that are popular in the East but need a bit of toughening up before they can be as successful in much of the rest of the country. Pachysandra, and English Ivy survive in the form of one clone or another, but their beauty and potential usefulness calls for much more effort by plantsmen.

Several tenacious, low-growing, dense plants that are usually reserved for the rockery hold promise as ground covers for more general purposes. For example thymes like *Thymus serpyllum*, and *T. lanaginosus*, the creeping veronicas, various dianthus, and many penstemons are suitable ground covers—all are tough, short, dense, and evergreen. The helianthemums and iberis also serve the purpose. *Arctostaphylos uva ursi* and *Mahonia repens* have already been discussed. The various Pussytoes, (*Antennaria* species) are tough, mat-forming plants made up of silvery rosettes. The flower heads resemble those of armeria and can be any color between cream and deep pink, but I would do without them if the sticky, feathered seed heads could be avoided.

The globularias like *Globularia cordifolia* and *G. bellidifolia* are much more attractive then their name and very promising as small-scale ground covers. They form dark evergreen mats of very dense rosettes. The powder-puff, blue flowers are a welcome bonus in the rockery, but do nothing for the plant when it is used as a ground cover. Never weedy, they spread slowly, densely, and consistently.

[3.22] TOMORROW

It is difficult to make predictions,
especially about the future.

Luigi Nervi

The creation of new plant forms and the selection of superior clones are as old as agriculture, but the rate at which new plants are being created is increasing dramatically. This is partly due to the wider understanding of the laws of heredity among a greater number of hybridizers, to chemically induced polyploidy, and to a greater market. New techniques, barely tapped, include gene splicing and the creation of chimeras at the cellular level—techniques that smack of black magic and have people talking about new life forms.

Shelley would be surprised to learn that human cells and mouse cells have been melded together into viable hybrid cells. Much more than a mere curiosity or a technical tour d'force, these chimeric cells are providing biologists with a means of constructing a human gene map. As the hybrid cells divide they shed some of the human chromosomes until only a few are left. Since the different human chromosomes can be identified under the microscope, and since the human genes continue to function in the chimera, assaying the cell products for human proteins and observing which human chromosomes are present in the chimera allows one to determine which genes are present on which chromosomes.

Genes from the lightening bug have been transferred to the tobacco plant causing its leaves to glow day and night. This could be a boon to people who feel compelled to take matches to Gas Plants at night.

131

More relevant to horticulture is the promise of isolating that bit of code that enables the legumes to fix atmospheric nitrogen and splicing it into plants that lack the capability. Curtailing the need for nitrogenous fertilizers would be an unparalleled boon to agriculture. Perhaps a fortuitous gene splice could bestow the capacity to utilize iron in non-acidic soils to ericaceous plants like Mountain Laurel and rhododendron.

Other possibilities include the transfer of genes that code for insecticides, fungicides, and insect repellents from plants that have them to plants that don't.

There has been no lack of progress in the low-tech side of horticulture either. Chemically induced polyploidy remains in vogue but is primarily used to induce gigantism and double flowers. Meristem cloning has been a blessing to gardeners, affording them genetic copies of all sorts of plants, including hems, hostas, kalmias, and orchids, without the expense and wait required by vegetative propagation. And the plant hybridizers continue to supply all sorts of new wonders. Not only do they effect crosses between different species but even between two or more different genera. Examples of man-made genera resulting from a cross of two or more different genera include × Solidaster = *Solidago* × *Aster*, × Mahoberberis = *Mahonia* × *Berberis*, and × Potinera which is a quatragenric orchid cross involving *Brassavola*, *Cattleya*, *Laelia*, and *Sophronitis*.

What else can we expect? The imagination leaps at other possibilities: × Canornus = *Canis* × *Cornus* adding bite to the dogwood's bark, × Platamnus = *Platycodon* × *Dictamnus* giving a lift to the sprawling Balloon Flower, and × Pacayote = *Payote* × *Cayote* producing a hairy cactus that howls at the moon and with good reason.

The possibilities seem limited only by human time and energy; and new, imagination-jarring wonders are destined to appear at an ever increasing rate.

CHAPTER 4 *Indulge*

[4.1] INTENT

A garden can offer so many pleasures that one is hard-pressed to decide which to cultivate. My own preference is for gardens that are environments, ones into which I can stroll and derive a sense of repose and sanctuary. I view them as idealized bits of scenery that excerpt and concentrate the beauty to be found in nature. But this is just one possibility. There are many others, some more practical and utilitarian, some more whimsical and eccentric. A garden might combine several of these in complete harmony, but other choices are incompatible either because of horticultural constraints or for aesthetic reasons. Here we take a glance at some of the possibilities, not in an attempt to praise or bury, but to evaluate, compare, and criticize. This is not meant to be a comprehensive encyclopedia of possibilities, but hopefully it includes enough examples to provide a basis for comparison.

[4.2] TREES AND SHRUBS FOR COLLECTORS

I'm a plant junkie, and have to be constantly on guard against the addiction. Every new nursery, every new catalog puts me on the edge of control. I develop an overwhelming desire to collect every species that might be hardy here or might survive given a heroic measure of life support and to hell with garden design. I know the feeling, and I sympathize. It's the addict's credo—one is too many, twenty is not enough.

Had I the time, the room, and the money, I would collect birch, viburnums, conifers of all sorts; not just the iddy-biddy ones but the giant firs, spruce, pines and cedars. Every new Siberian Iris would be welcome, every exotic grass, every alpine plant, and every known maple.

Yet I have nightmares about my Siberian Iris crowding out my pines and Aspens, or Susie's saxifrages heaping themselves up until all our rockwork vanishes, or Seth's fern garden enveloping the entire yard in a choking cloak of roots and croziers. If I turned my back on the garden for just one season, it could easily happen.

But most of all I want the garden to be an environment, a unified and convincing bit of walk-into scenery, and this desire tempers my collecting zeal.

Of course there is always room for a few unusual trees and shrubs and their addition only adds variety and interest to a planting without sacrificing its integrity. For the most part, the constraint of space is enough to curb the would-be collector's enthusiasm; there are just so many oaks that can be stuffed into a quarter-acre lot.

On the other hand, certain trees and shrubs simultaneously encourage the collector and landscape designer. One can plan an entire garden around a carefully chosen collection of Japanese maples. The maple garden at the Washington Park Arboretum in Seattle is a good example. The tree forms are elegant in leaf and structure, and when differences in leaf color or texture are not conspicuous several different varieties can be associated in a grove, providing variety within harmony. The dwarf and weeping forms are distinctive enough to provide a contrasting understory. However, incorporating the forms with highly colored summer foliage, like 'Bloodgood' into the garden scheme is not so easy.

A small collection of flowering dogwoods set against a backdrop of pines or spruce is a four-season delight, and fortunately the variety available is currently quite limited and so is not likely to overburden the garden.

On the other hand the flowering cherries and crabapples present an embarrassment of riches. Most are so spectacular in bloom or so idiosyncratic in form that attempting to blend more then a few is likely to lead to a discordant hodgepodge where the pleasure derived from the whole is much less than can be derived from a single specimen.

The same can be said of collecting camellias, and the larger rhodos. There are so many distinctive forms and colors that even a small collection comes off as an inharmonious jumble. Moreover, nothing frustrates the collector more than the realization that his collection is wimpy, poorly representative, and no longer expandable.

Azaleas and dwarf rhododendrons have fanatic bands of devotees worldwide. Again there is no lack of variety in either color, shape of blossom or habit of growth. These are plants that combine and mass superbly. They look and most grow well under the dappled shade of trees. They are visually and horticulturally compatible with a large variety of interesting and beautiful plants: kalmias, Enkianthus, Asarum, Japanese iris, and many ferns to name a few. Unfortunately, their use is severely limited by soil conditions, atmospheric humidity, and temperature.

Over much of the U.S. rhodos are rarely grown. Alkaline soils, piercing winter sun, extreme temperature fluctuations and dessicating winds make them a challenge. Of course the true aficionado will not be dissuaded by such adversities. So with misters, shade covers, and sometimes heating cables to assure a minimally satisfactory microclimate, the real aficionado cultivates them. In fact the very difficulty in growing them sharpens the collector's sense of accomplishment and stimulates his desire to grow more. Between their efforts and those of hybridizers like Leach, Galle, and Gable we may yet see rhododendrons being grown throughout most of North America.

Hybrid roses offer a particularly insidious threat. A casual flirtation with one or two is likely to kindle a fiery passion to collect all kinds,—teas, floribundas, and grandifloras, in all forms, dwarfs, climbers, standards, and the like. The result is a rose garden, a very special kind of garden calling for pergolas; white, curlicued, overwrought, lawn furniture; ornamental bird baths; and maybe a fountain or two. Croquet anyone? This is a garden devoted to the exercise of connoisseurship, a garden where the merits of each flower must be clearly observable and easily compared with the others.

This is a garden whose individual parts are much more important than the whole. Its over-all design is usually reduced to the making of straight paths lined with rose bushes on each side, covered here and there by an arbor for the climbing varieties. Fine for a Sunday afternoon in a public park but falling far short of providing a full offering of a garden's potential.

Heaths and heathers threaten my resolve much less. As to variety and availability they are eminently collectible. They, too, are available in a variety of sizes from an inch or two to several feet and in a variety of decorator leaf colors—near white, green, brown-orange, yellow-red, and gray. Flowering times are so varied that such a garden can be in bloom twelve months of the year. The usual plan of a heath and heather garden is to incorporate many varieties of different colors into a scheme which eventually knits all into an innovative, patchwork quilt of soft texture and subtle color. They must be situated with some care since good drainage and full light are necessities, and they neither grow best nor look comfortable in the presence of sizable trees and shrubs. So in spite of their various attractions, I can easily stave off the temptation to collect them.

The dwarf conifers comprise an enormous group of plants with a wildly avid following. Nowhere in the plant kingdom do we find so much love and attention lavished on a bunch of genetic- or virus-induced freaks. With hundreds of cultivars to choose from, there is certainly a great variety: creepers, sprawlers, mounds, humps, spheres, weepers, ellipsoids, cones and the like. Some are thin and whispy, others dense and blocky, and as for color you can take your pick; there are reddish browns, silver blues, deep blues, platinum, pale yellows to burnished golds, and even some greens. The collector will turn up his nose at the ubiquitous and useful ground covers that arise from *Juniperus × media, J. sabina, J. horizontalis, Taxus media,* and such. These are too commonplace to be collector's items. The fascination is in the collection of the unusual, the strange, and the weird. As a group these are cute plants, custom made for petting and cuddling although the prickly juvenile foliage of many will dissuade even the most ardent admirer. I confess to having a few favorites like *Tsuga canadensis* 'Minima', *Abies balsamea* 'Nana', and the ubiquitous Birds Nest Spruce (*Picea abies* 'Nidiformis'), but most seem out of place in all those places I prefer as gardens. Indeed, most are out of place in any natural setting that uses full-size trees and shrubs. They even seem out of place in an alpine rockery, although this is one of their most frequent haunts. So many seem artificial and contrived. I enjoy them most when they are grown in a garden of their own, in the company of some boulders and some ground covers. But in my own garden I find such a planting too unresponsive to the change of seasons, too static and ultimately boring. More of a miniature stage setting than an environment, more of a toyland than a retreat, I always feel like an outsider in such a garden, never a part of it. Such gardens never meld with urban architecture and seem curiously out of place. So I reserve the enjoyment of such pleasures these plants afford for occasional visits to parks that grow them.

[4.3] EDIBLES

When it's apple-blossom time
in Orange, New Jersey
we'll make a peach of a pear.

Anon.

For the most part, I leave the growing of foodstuffs to the real farmers. They do it with much greater efficiency than I can and at less expense. Moreover, many of these foodbearing plants have been overdesigned to nourish the belly and underdesigned to nourish the soul. A full-grown apple or peach tree is a joy in spring when mantled by pink buds and white blooms, but a couple of months later, 30 bushels pregnant and on the verge of a multi-limbed hernia, trussed up with poles and wires like a cats cradle gone awry, it's at best an amusing distraction. Moreover, the growing of fruit trees and many of the fruiting shrubs is a relatively labor-intensive form of gardening. Feeding the trees, protecting them from disease and insects, thinning and harvesting is likely to leave little time to enjoy the fruits of such labor.

The grafted dwarfs are easier to manage in the home garden; spraying, pruning, and harvesting are done with considerably more ease, and the trees bear at a much earlier age. But in the garden they still look freakish to me, and some dwarfing stocks make for weak joints, so that even these dwarfs have to be trussed up for support, when in fruit. Of fairly recent origin, the genetic dwarfs offer most of the advantages of the grafted plants while avoiding the structural weakness of a poorly engineered graft.

I worry a bit about the chemicals that are used by the commercial growers to preserve that unblemished rosy glow on the peaches and impart that Shinola shine on apples, but almost every home gardener in these parts has become habituated to the use of an arsenal of pesticides, herbicides and fungicides. Hopefully our innards will adapt.

There is another factor which keeps my enthusiasm for fruit growing in check. Our neighborhood abounds with fruit lovers of far greater agility and dexterity than this one. We are beset by fruit-eating birds, squirrels and raccoons.

The raccoons climb the cherry trees, set table on an overhang under a bedroom window, and have a cherry jubilee. After a hearty repast and a healthy elimination under the window, they leave. I am hoping that raccoon coats come back into fashion.

And the Robins annoy me no end. They have adopted my mother-in-law's habit of taking a single bite out of each candy in the box to their cherry eating habits. They gouge a hole out of the plumpest part of each cherry and leave the rest for me.

Of course birds and raccoons can be thwarted by draping the tree with netting, not an easy task on a 15 ft. tree, and it creates a hideous, unmaskable blot on the landscape. And unless the tree is first framed by a wooden scaffold, itself not a garden ornament to brag about, branches are often bent into sorry shapes that cannot be corrected. So I begrudgingly share the harvest of cherries with the damned marauders rather than deface the landscape for a month by bagging an entire tree. Besides, I usually find an uneaten cherry here and there, and get my share.

We have tried hanging thread, inflatable owls, rubber snakes and other assorted doohickeys and clangors from the trees, but these seem to have no effect other than to make our trees look silly and provide amusement for the children in the neighborhood.

But the true fruit lover will not be dissuaded from growing his own by such trivial inconvenience. For that gourmet who twitches a nostril in contempt at the mention of McIntosh or Delicious, there is a vast variety of exotic and little known treats available only to the home grower. One nursery offers over two-hundred varieties of apple. But, in truth, many of them were superseded for reasons of taste, hardiness, and disease resistance, so growing them hardly seems worth expulsion from Eden.

There are fruit trees that can be an ornamental asset to the garden, and among these pears rank highly. They have it all, lovely blossoms, superb fall color, interesting winter outline (often fastigate and not too tall) and, of course, one of the most delicious of all fruits. A Comice Pear, wedge of brie, glass of wine and thou. Take care to select a blight-resistant strain and you have a treat for eye and belly.

Near the top of any list of ornamental fruit trees for the garden, the sour cherry offers a full, four-act show. Superb in flower, the blossoms large, slightly pendulous, with yellow-green centers, followed by decorative fruit as delicious and more flavorful than many sweet cherries, albeit more tart. Add to this its interesting shape and stunning bark, and you have a tree that won't embarrass you in any season.

Cherry plums are a hardy alternative to the larger commercial varieties, with excellent but small fruit, both sweet and tangy, attractively borne on small trees and bushes, easily pruned and sprayed. Typical plum blossoms, white blushed light pink, are borne in profusion and scent the garden with a pungent but sweet smell that I love as much as any lilac or viburnum. But it is not a scent that everyone finds pleasing.

Raspberries are a must and their leaves are bold and attractive even if the shrubs are somewhat ungainly and spread faster and further than bindweed. The berries are highly perishable, lose flavor quickly under storage and cost their worth as a gourmet treat when available at the local supermarket. Moreover, the commercial availability does not reflect the extended season of harvest that can be enjoyed by the home grower. The same can be said of blackcap, yellow, white and purple raspberries, blackberries and boysenberries even though the bushes are sloppier, thornier and harder to manage, and less of an asset in the landscape.

Currants and gooseberries make attractive ornamentals in almost any setting, especially the currant with its bold and interesting leaf and pendulous open clusters of red berries. Fresh gooseberries are not easy to come by in the local markets and when available can double the food bill. Moreover those brought to market are not picked at uniform ripeness and are usually of the American kind, well suited for tart pies a la mode, but not to be eaten out-of-hand, unless you want a persimmon pucker that Dizzy Gillespie would envy. The choice European and Canadian varieties that are so easily grown over a great deal of the country are almost unavailable at market. These should only be eaten out of hand, one at a time, accompanied by a nontrivial brandy.

Crabapples hold their own against any flowering tree, and many bear fruit that perks up the garden from August to November. The fruit is a treat for all sorts of birds; Cedar Waxwings in particular hang around for days in late October until the last crabapple is eaten. But if one is hard-hearted enough, the birds can be denied and the fruit harvested for jelly. In some varieties the crabapples are large enough to eat out of hand and are more than palatable.

Amelanchier is another dual purpose tree or shrub that is ornamental in every season. Currently it is receiving considerable attention in an effort to improve the quality of its fruit. In wild ones, the fruit resembles a small blueberry in appearance and even a bit in taste, but the texture is mealy and the flavor is insipid. The new varieties yield fruit which is larger, juicier, and much more palatable. It's possible that amelanchier berries will some day be grown as a substitute for blueberries in those places where blueberries are difficult to grow.

The flowers, fruit, and foliage of elders justify their use as ornamentals. Although some see them as coarse and weedy, I see them as bold, even tropical looking, just right for the side of a stream or the shore of a pond. Even the golden cultivars seem natural in such a site; neither garish or overly assertive, they blend beautifully with other water-side plants brightening the spot without detracting from its neighbors. But for quality and abundance of fruit one has to choose a green clone bred especially for the purpose, like John's or Adam's. The birds have a strong liking for the fruit—certainly much stronger than I have. I find it sickeningly insipid, and suggest that the legendary elderberry wine is better enjoyed in legend than at the table.

Chokecherry is yet another shrub with ornamental value and edible fruit; attractive both in flower and leaf, striking in its vibrant red, fall color, but inconspicuous when in fruit except to the birds. The fruit is used for making jelly according to the time honored one-to-one recipe: one chokecherry to one cup of sugar.

Where adapted one should consider persimmons, including the American, for its superb autumn color, shape, and leaves. Almonds, small-fruited apricots, and various bush cherries can be delightful and delicious additions. Is there anyone with a nose so dead that he would not grow a citrus plant for the scent alone if the climate permitted? And figs are such a delicacy that one might consider enduring the greatest hardship, like living in Los Angeles, in order to grow them. But again, let's take care that our stomachs do not override all the other amenities that a garden can offer us.

I would grow blueberries too for they are beautiful in flower and in fruit and spectacular in fall color. But winter protection from sun and wind and the need for fast-draining, acidic soil make it less worthwhile, and when in season blueberries are easily obtainable and inexpensive. Work is being done at several horticultural research stations to increase winter hardiness, but as yet none are reliable without snow cover or heroic measures and devotion.

The rheums include several spectacular, purely ornamental perennials, suited by nature and appearance to grace the banks of a lake or stream. But if the drainage is adequate and there is room for only one rheum, rhubarb might be the one to choose. Extraordinarily bold in leaf for such a hardy plant, and almost as bold in flower, it suffers in comparison to the others when judged by gracefulness. But this rheum can be eaten, which I love to do, especially when it is cooked up with sour cherries and topped with a dollop of sour cream or yogurt.

There are many other 'dual purpose' plants, some of dubious ornamemtal value, and others of dubious gustatory appeal. Quince, grapes, and kiwis are landscape possibilities, as are asparagus and sumac. One can raise daylilies in order to eat the unopened blossoms, and ferns for the taste of their young croziers, but this is like raising children for indentured service.

[4.4] HERBACEOUS PLANTS FOR COLLECTORS

Sooner or later we each take to collecting some sorts of perennials. A moderate collection seldom burdens the budget, doesn't require much time or effort, and is easily altered. I greatly prefer those plants that offer several seasons of beauty, and are not out of place in a natural garden, plants whose structure and leaf pattern are an asset even when they are not in flower. And where possible, I opt for those which are evergreen, or offer some interest to the winter garden as in the form of dried leaves or flower stalks.

Over much of the country, even in Zones 3 through 6, winter releases its icy grip for a couple of days here and there, the snow melts and the sun invites one into the garden. But the perennial beds are mostly bare and dreary, and do nothing to enhance the garden during these months. Now they hold no interest whatever, and inspire only a longing for spring and plans to give over these areas to something that will provide pleasure throughout the year.

Everyman's Perennials

I favor Siberian Iris, various species iris, single dwarf shastas, dwarf coreopsis and gallardias, the smaller campanulas and platycodons, some of the smaller hems and hostas, helliborous, true geraniums, ferns, ferns, and ferns, to name a few that have some interest besides flowers.

But I violently dislike the incorporation of those giant overbred and overblown caricatures of flowers. Those acromegalic, garish freaks that look better when decapitated and stuck in a vase than when standing top-heavy and slouched over in the garden. Included in this menagerie are the football mums, the giant dahlias, the super double pom-pom peonies, frilled and fimbriated giant German Bearded Iris, and a myriad of other grotesqueries developed on the assumption that bigger is better. These should be relegated to a cutting garden, as much out of sight as possible. We usurped the back side of our neighbor's fence for our cutting garden. It's not that we dislike our neighbors, but it was an unused and unsightly area anyway, and the cutting bed does little to detract from its appearance.

Alpines

Alpines are plants of the high country. Tidy and small, embracing an enormous diversity of shapes, and textures, and often flowering prodigiously, they comprise one of the most collectible of all groups of plants. Some are so small that two dozen can be grown in a 2 × 3 ft. trough and the troughs are usually designed to look like a part of a wild rockery, complete with stones. Indeed, "trough gardening" is itself a popular garden undertaking.

Overleaf. The alpine rock garden at the height of its glory in late spring. Denver Botanic Gardens, Denver, Colorado.

139

These plants have adapted to a rocky terrain and fast-draining soils, so in the garden they do best and look best in a rockery.

Designing a convincing rock garden and integrating it with the rest of the plan is not an easy task. A rock garden has such a distinctive character that it is often difficult to set it off properly in a planting featuring the usual shrubs and shade trees, a setting that is more suggestive of a woodland than of an alpine environment.

In particular, a design which aspires to suggest an entire mountain range will appear incongruous at best in such a setting. An enclosed courtyard might be a more successful location for such a project, but such gardens are more likely to come off as precious toys with no more ability to evoke the look and feel of the natural scene than a paperweight modeled after Halfdome.

This is not to say a boulder arrangement in a garden can't effectively suggest a rocky outcrop. But here the intent is not to capture the sweep and grandeur of an entire mountain range, but to excerpt some suitably scaled fragment.

Of course, the ardent collector will dispense with trees and large shrubs altogether, and give the entire plot over to the alpines. But there aren't many places where I would be content to give over my entire plot to an alpine rock garden. One finds a natural alpine garden in a surround as awesome and beautiful as this planet offers in the heart of a great mountain range. Isolate this garden and the sense of an environment is gone. Not surrounded by it, one doesn't feel a part of it. One stands above it, looks down on it, kneels to see some detail more closely. A beautiful hobby, and endless interest, but not an environment.

Cactus and Other Succulents

This is another group of eminently collectible plants; some beautiful, some curious, some grotesque and some a combination of these. A great many are collectibly small, and many of the larger ones are slender enough to pack into standing-room-only formation. So even a smallish garden can display an extraordinarily large collection.

I have even stronger reservations for gardens given over exclusively to cactus and succulents than I do for alpine gardens. As interesting as these gardens are, I find them woefully lacking in year-round interest and many of the amenities that other plantings offer. These gardens are without shade, without evaporative cooling, without privacy, without fall color, and without much winter interest. They integrate poorly with most suburban architecture and most other kinds of landscapes. Birds shun them, and only animals that crawl and slither deem them worthy of a visit.

Paradoxically, such gardens are common in the Southwest where the climate suits them perfectly, but where the attributes they lack are most sorely needed.

Apparently, most of the citizenry of the Southwest is in agreement. They turned their backs on the delights of Tumbleweed and Horsehobble, and set about greening the desert, carpeting the sands with blue grass and lining the streets with maples, oaks, and elms. And the cost of installing this New England landscape in Arizona? Astronomical and rising. The chronic

A small fragment the Eric Walter Suc lent Garden in Gold Gate Park, San Fra cisco, Califor

and worsening water shortage, brought on in large part by this water-insatiable landscape, may yet allow the desert to reclaim these gardens for the Prickly Pears and Locatillas.

I do not think that this greening of the desert is entirely due to an effort on the part of immigrants from our coasts to assuage their homesickness. Nor was it caused by a limited commercial availability of indigenous species. After all, nothing prevented them from transplanting the abundant and readily obtainable local plants to their gardens, as was done with spruce, fir, and pine in the more northern states. Strange and beautiful as a cactus and succulent garden is, it does not satisfy our need for some respite from sun and wind or our desire of a bit of congenial privacy. Most find such a garden interesting rather than hospitable, curious rather than comfortable, and most would prefer a garden with soft grass and shade trees rather than sand and Saguaro especially if surrounded by a desert.

On the other hand, there are highly drought-tolerant trees, shrubs, perennials, and grasses, and designing with these materials is a project of growing promise and importance. Plantings that use these materials and require only a modicum of supplementary water are called 'xeriscapes'. Most that I have seen appear eminently suited to their purpose, incorporating a preponderance of sages, sedums, euphorbias, and dry-land grasses that give a deserty look to the landscape that is hardly more inviting than an ordinary cactus and succulent garden. But there is such a wide diversity of plant material suitable for a xeriscape that it can have an almost lush and tropical appearance. For example, the Catalpa, Kentucky Coffee Tree, Russian Mulberry, Golden Rain tree, various sumacs and mahonias have the bold, large leaves that we associate with plants of wetter regions but are quite drought-tolerant. A garden designed around plants like these will not constantly remind the gardener of the dry heat and the scarcity of water, and yet will be responsibly water frugal.

And Many Others

There are many other specialty gardens that can be incorporated as part of a general landscape plan. Some fit in nicely, while others contribute to a whole that is less than the parts. Many of the herbs like tansy, lavender, rue, thyme, sage, chives, sweet woodruff, mint, and so on, can often be blended into the garden as interesting and attractive assets, but the old fashioned knot garden is best used as an adjunct to the state capitol grounds next to the rose garden.

The term "bog garden" has a dreadful sound, but a bog garden is the ideal environment for some of the most strikingly beautiful plants: rheums and rodgersias, primulas and iris, ferns of many sorts, superb grasses, elders and alders, birch of many sorts, red twig dogwoods, Tupelo, various magnolias, and many more. As in other cases, the desirability of such a garden depends on its location, the climate, and the surrounding landscape. This is not the garden for a Mississippi July. And what Floridian needs a bog garden with the Okifinokee swamp just down the street, in which one can slosh around whenever the fancy dictates.

Some grow plants whose primary purpose is to provide stems, seed pods, and flowers for drying and winter decoration. The weaver who is a purist might grow plants that yield dyes. Others might grow plants for their medicinal properties, their Biblical associations, or their use in occult practices. Those wanting an extra kick from gardening might consider growing cannubis, peyote, coca or poppies.

Unfortunately, I know too little about these garden interests and pastimes or I'm too chicken and embarrassed to comment on them. To learn something about them the reader is advised to consult the many specialty books that are available.

[4.5] CREATURE COMFORTS AND DISCOMFORTS

One of the most popular garden undertakings is the creation and maintenance of a wildlife sanctuary. Our family was in full agreement from the very beginning that this was an important goal, so we set out to make an environment which would encourage all sorts of creatures to visit and even take up residence.

When we moved in, the lot was bare except for a thin mat of bluegrass sod that had been tossed onto the dirt. Dirt is actually a euphemism for a stuff which was more like an alkaline concrete, pale, impervious to water, and of a pH higher than the range of our test kit. Save for bindweed, thistle, and grass, not a perennial dared rear its head. What few birds we saw—Grackles, Starlings, and Blackbirds—flew by with not even a curious glance. So we set to work planting trees and shrubs to provide protection and food for what we hoped would be a wide assortment of wild creatures.

AN OPEN INVITATION

I still remember the afternoon we found a live earthworm crawling through our soil. That night we uncorked a bottle and had a little welcoming celebration. As it turned out this was a scout who spearheaded a major invasion of creatures, large and small, cute and horrendous, some welcome and some very much unwelcome. The earthworms were followed by mice, rabbits, muskrats, squirrels, skunks, raccoons, and hoards of gnawing, biting, sucking insects. We corked the bottle, put away the glasses and rolled up the welcome mat. But it was too late. The creatures continued to come in swarms, droves, flocks and herds.

Creatures of all kinds have always been considered important garden accouterments. The Chinese had their deer, pheasant, and occasional elephant, the Japanese their ornamental roosters and koi. And everywhere, birds are welcome for their beauty and congenial vivacity. But before deciding to open the ark to all, a bit of caution is advised.

The problem is one can't be selective. Welcome one type of critter aboard, and a menagerie of undesirables will follow. Invite the birds, and you will surely have cats and then dogs. Rabbits, gophers, squirrels, and deer will be certain that the plants provided for the feeding and protection of any creature were meant especially for them. Provide some water and muskrats will search it out, and mosquitoes will gleefully multiply in it. The club can not be made exclusive, and in some places the riffraff that crash can drive the host from the party altogether.

Of course, there are alternatives like the dry landscape, the sculpture court, the tennis court, all of which have struck me as viable possibilities at one time or another. So far I've dismissed these options as unacceptable, and continue our open-door policy while trying to outwit, or at least outlast the uninvited creatures.

For some of the pests there is little to be done by way of personal protection for the gardener or the garden; stoicism and a locker-room tongue are about all that can be mustered in defense. For others, however, there are design modifications that can provide some measure of protection, if not thwart them altogether.

Bloodsuckers

I most dislike the mosquitoes, horseflies, deer flies, no-seeums, and all the other damn bloodsuckers that rob me of so much garden pleasure over such a long period of time. During a summer evening the most robust stroller retreats indoors anemic but swollen. And if you or yours are cursed by particular allergies to these demons, the itching and welts will remain for weeks. The deer flies and horseflies are particularly crippling, a bite on the back from one of these monsters will raise a hump that Quasimoto might envy.

Then there are the ceratopogonid flies, the infamous no-seeums, winged vampires, the size of a pin head, all tooth and venom and spleen. Too tiny to spot, too fast to swat, they can attack human anatomy at any point, but the ankles seem to be a favored target. In a moment they have you hopping about on one leg, madly scratching at the other, and shouting obscenities at the invisible. A scene much more appropriate to gardening in darkest Africa than in suburban U.S.A.

Sadism is not the creature's only perversion. As with Black Widows, wasps, and mosquitoes, it's the females who cause the trouble. The guys are just gonads on the wing. Once a male locates the pheremone fem of his desire he latches on and permanently attaches his genetalia to hers. One upmanship on a theme of Van Gogh. She responds to his love gift by plunging her proboscis through his head and sucking him dry. The ultimate hickey.

The mosquitoes are, by dint of stealth and numbers, the worst of the worst. The arrogance with which they fly about your face and up your cuffs, the persistence with which they continue the attack after you strike an errant and almost self-maiming blow, the crooked little side-stepping flight, all of these threaten to drive me to a condominium. How can a creature a couple of millimeters long leave a welt the size of a chicken egg? How can it extract that much blood and still fly?

Unfortunately, some of the features that most attract people to gardens also attract the bloodsuckers. Unless the garden is a Ryoan-ji West, plants play an important role in its design and often there is some water. But any body of water, no matter how small, has to be considered a possible pool of pestilence where mosquitoes can reproduce with sadistic abandon. The plants serve them also since the males are nectar feeders, and both sexes spend their leisure time resting on them.

Butterflies

This tirade should not be taken as a general condemnation of all insects, for there are many that are harmless, many that are beautiful, and many that are beneficial. Some of the beneficial ones are commercially available. For example Lady Bugs, Tyco Flies, and Preying Mantises, are marketed for the control of aphids, moths and butterflies and anything smaller.

Some people are so captivated by the beauty of butterflies that they design a special garden filled with lepidoptera turn-ons like Butterfly Weed, Purple Loosestrife, and Goosenecked Lysimachia. But those beautiful butterflies flitting about the Asclepias will soon lay delicate clusters of eggs, like tiny pearls in geometric close-pack, from which will hatch the larvae that will begin their growth into horrendous, voracious herbivors by feeding on plants, and always on the choicest plants. I have no doubt that a full-grown specimen of the Tomato Hornworm can fell a full-grown oak, either by gnawing through it or by the weight of its body.

Knowing this I still can't control my fascination with them, and although I haven't gone out of my way to attract them, they often favor my garden by a visit in just the right numbers to be an uncommon treat but not a common nuisance.

"You'll like this place, the salad bar is extraordinary"

The Unwelcome Zoo

For three seasons mice and rabbits are only moderately pesky. During spring and summer there are often enough greens to go around so that a little snack here and there may go unnoticed. Come fall and they take part in a general cleanup, nothing much to complain about here. But by winter the salad is gone, and the snow brings out the beast in them. The mice munch their way through the walls of the house and into the garage, basement or living room. Or they join the bunnies for a nash, pruning the shrubs to a crew cut, flat-topped at the snow line. That's the appetizer. For the serious course they turn to the trees, stripping away the bark so as to munch on the cambium, sometimes ringing the tree and killing it. I am seeking a good recipe for hasenpfeffer, but I don't know what to do with mice.

Muskrats have their own ideas on how to properly landscape the bank of a stream. When their tunneling has sufficiently undermined the bank, it collapses and the stream is diverted, often radically. But I've learned to cope with them by putting the industrious bastards to work for me. Our little stream separates our lot from our neighbor's, so when the stream is diverted in such a way as to give me a new cape or peninsula of land, I plant the family flag on it claiming it for my own. In this way I've increased my land holdings by some 10%.

Of course when they undermine my side of the stream my mind turns to thoughts of presenting my wife with a proper fur coat, but I wouldn't know what to do with the tails.

Teenage boys will often agree to come and trap the muskrats for their coats and musk oil, but only in the winter. The coats trash out with the first warmth of spring. They tell me that muskrats are a delicacy in the Southeast, but I don't think they're kosher, and I wouldn't know what to do with their tails.

One wonders what protects these seemingly frail and defenseless creatures like rabbits and muskrats. Certainly their gigantic libidos and unbridled promiscuity help, but it is probably their overwhelming, God-given cuteness that deters perfectly rational people from taking effective action against them.

The raccoons are the cutest and scariest of the lot. We made the mistake of feeding one, a very pregnant female. Later we were stuck with both her and her four brats. We didn't mind them coming to the back door for a nightly handout, but we did mind when they removed the window screen to steal a loaf of bread (whole wheat with honey) from the counter. They finished the entire loaf in one evening and left us the wrapper. I expected to find a note requesting some peanut butter, but even a raccoon doesn't have that much chutzpah. Charming and mischievous as they are, they are not to be messed with. Apparently they have no natural predators. Coyotes and cougars are too wise to risk a confrontation with them. A full-grown raccoon can easily dispatch a good-sized dog, usually by jumping on its back and clawing at its face. And don't believe that they won't attack a man. A well-known Boulderite stepped out of his house one evening to investigate some strange noises and was attacked by a raccoon. The creature thoroughly tore up his leg sending the poor man to the hospital for the better part of a week.

Another Boulderite unknowingly hosted a clan of coons in his attic for what must have been several seasons. One day he came home and slammed the door shut with enough of a bang to literally bring down the ceiling. It came crashing to his living-room floor, replete with mama coon, several good-sized kits, and enough scat to supply the mulch bin for years. The insulation was shot, the wiring was shot and the entire ceiling had to be redone at a considerable cost.

Even *Audubon Magazine*, champion of all creatures that have more hair than the editor, expressed certain reservations about the burgeoning raccoon population in suburban areas. What brought on the unexpected criticism was a raccoon raid on a bird sanctuary that left a rare crane without her young or eggs. The bird is on the endangered species list and is close to extinction. This clutch and brood belonged to the only female breeding in captivity.

And don't forget that these cuties are the potential bearers of a wide assortment of plagues including the black plague, tularemia, and rabbit and feline distemper. They post a distinct threat to family and pets besides being a nuisance in the garden.

Stinkers

As I write this, winter has taken up the battle again after a two-week cessation during which a skunk, maybe a herd of them judging by the odor, has again set up residence under the house, apparently near the flue of the heating system. It wants to keep warm after all. But the air intake ducts are nearby and when the rush of air through the flue startles the creature it lets one fly into the air-intake duct and the house becomes a miasma. So here we sit with the heat turned off and the house at 50° F in the middle of February.

Have you ever wondered how they do it. How do they procreate? Finding each other should be no problem whatsoever, but how do they get close enough? One would think that the fear of rejection would be enough to dampen the ardor of any potential suitor. But do it they must, because at this time of the year the roads are cluttered with their smelly remains. Maybe they have evolved in such a way that they don't smell themselves at all. One should be able to draw some deep philosophic insight from all this, but not when the odor is so potent it fogs the mind.

The Cure May Be Worse

Lion dung has been suggested as a bunny and deer repellent by our local animal control agent. These are such practical people. Actually, the scat of any large predator is thought to work, but lion dung is supposedly superior and free for the gathering at the zoo. Recalling the potent stench of the lion house I would imagine that it would be almighty effective at least in keeping humans far enough away from the garden that bunny damage would go unnoticed. I confess to not having tried it, but I'm dubious. Our garden is already widely decorated by the scat of lesser cats and a variety of dogs to boot but this seems to repel only the people. However, as a fly attractant it works quite well.

So we opted for less organic methods of control. Chemical repellents can be sprayed or painted on the trunks of trees and deciduous shrubs, and this has been fairly effective for us. The application is something of a bother and the white color of the stuff disfigures all it touches for a couple of months except for Aspen, birch, and other white-barked trees. Some say that certain commercially available tree wrapping works, but this is not convenient to apply and should be removed by spring since it provides shelter and protection for several insect borers. A 3 ft. high cylinder of wire mesh placed around the tree trunk and dug 6 in. into the ground will thwart the rabbits and mice. I have been forced to do this throughout the garden although it certainly does not improve its appearance.

Recently to my horror the highway department officially declared the road nearby to be a deer crossing. A couple of hungry deer can lay waste to an entire landscape in one day. Electric fences are illegal here and I did not and would not plant only deer-proof material. It rules out too many possibilities, and besides I did not have the foresight. So now I wonder and worry as to what the next winter will bring.

Semi-domesticated Creatures

In this lengthy diatribe on the creatures that plague and beset gardeners I must not forget to devote some space and rancor to those that some people harbor intentionally—the domesticated cat and dog, and the semi-domesticated, early teenager.

There will always be those neighbors who let their dogs roam freely. They are usually beady-eyed and mean-tempered with slack, dribbling jowls and narrow, flat cranial cases allowing for only a modicom of gray matter. Frequently, their pets share some of these same characteristics. The animals are usually well trained not to mess up the master's property, so they come to the neighbor's gardens. Often this is done in the middle of a walk, but the better-mannered mutts will excavate a temporary loo, usually where you just planted your choicest bulbs.

The breed fanciers over the years have shown remarkable skill in perverting heredity to suit their own tastes for the bizarre. They squash noses flat, perk up ears or flop them, dock tails, and genetically fix a whole sideshow of grotesque malformities. But never have they stopped to breed for brains or manners. A dog of any breed will treat your most exotic tree like a fire hydrant.

For years we suffered a daily visit by a Great Dane, Saber by name, Saber Dale. He would come over to piss on our Beauty Bush until he finally pissed it away. This damn dog was so big he could have pissed away a Sequoia. Saber was a harlequin dane, black patched over white. He gave us a lawn of the same design, brown patched over green in the summer, green patched over brown in the fall. The asynchronicity vexed me the most.

Dave, a lawyer friend, had a big, black, gouty mongrel called Shadow. His neighbor bred champion Afghan Hounds, and to protect his bitches in heat he built a six-foot high, chain-link enclosure. Shadow was too lazy, lame, and fat to climb a one-foot fence, but he could dig like hell. And one day, when the best of the neighbor's champion bitches was in heat, dig he did, until he was on the inside of the fence where he tied with the flaxen-haired beauty. Soon after, the outraged neighbor called Dave and told him that Shadow had violated his bitch, which necessitated not only an abortion, but the cancellation and default fine for the stud, and a cancellation of flight arrangements to and from the stud. All of this amounted to $210 in expenses and he wanted to know what Dave was going to do about it. Dave told him he would have to consult with his client, Shadow, and hung up. Later Dave called back and said that Shadow had thought it over and decided that it was only worth ten bucks.

Cats decorate your paths and lawns too, but with such discretion and grace that it almost excuses the necessity. There is no denying the elegance, grace, and beauty a cat brings to the setting. Whether alert on its haunches intently watching a butterfly, or ecstatically sniffing some herb, or in the serious business of tracking a grasshopper, their contribution to the setting is undeniable. A cat's leisurely pace seems to reflect a deep appreciation for your talents and efforts. They don't lope through the garden pausing only at the occasional vertical feature or a newly dug bed. Every sight and scent seems to fascinate them and hold their attention.

Unfortunately, they have an insatiable craving for the hunt, and the prey are usually the harmless and beneficial snakes and birds, although sometimes mice, rats, muskrats and rabbits are taken. I have asked the local cat owners to place warning bells on the collars of their tigers which seems to help. Even the most glutinous blackbird is able to hear the bell in time to dodge the pounce.

A truly big cat resides at the Hayes's funny farm about a quarter of a mile across the road. Dr. Hayes is a vet who keeps various wild creatures that were found injured or orphaned. They earn their keep through commercials and guest appearances on T V. His charges include a Black Bear, a pair of Timber Wolves, an Arctic Fox, a Badger, and a magnificent Cougar. Most of these are kept in cages but the Black Bear has romped unfettered in the fields with the family dog, Llamas, and children. The Cougar is a noted celebrity who appeared on the Johnny Carson show. She's kept indoors as a house pet and probably serves nicely as a watch cat. I asked Mrs. Hayes what it's like living with such a creature, and she assured me it's like living with any other cat—it even enjoys sleeping on the fridge. Now there's a way to enforce your diet. One New Year's morning I stumbled downstairs to make a pot of coffee with the hope of leeching some of the alcohol out of my liver. I opened the blinds and gazed out at a flock of eight Guinea Fowl being herded from my neighbor's yard back to the funny farm by six of Boulder's finest, billy clubs in hand. That opened the eyes more effectively then mainlining the coffee.

All the annoyances caused by these kept creatures are minor when compared to the depredations caused by a teenager on the rampage. Baring a grove of birch on your front lawn is an irresistible, lily-white invite for Sid to proclaim his undying love for Nancy by carving a heart with his and her initials into the bark. Too much immortality for what he deserves, it's disfigured forever. A grove of Aspen or beech is just as seductive and defenseless. Jack the Ripper on a skateboard.

I find it outrageous to be forced to compromise a design in order to discourage vandalism, but what else can be done? Maybe a planting of gooseberries or wild roses around the base would provide a natural and attractive compliment for the grove while staving off an attack.

But most of the kids present only a minor annoyance as in the street game of football, soccer, or baseball. The kid with the mighty but errant toe never lets an afternoon pass without sending a punt into the hemerocalis. A perfect hit. Not one flower stem left standing. Or Chub the "klutz" tries for a roundabout endrun through the gooseberries. May they grab him by the ass and flay off some of the excess. Unless you are a professional playing first base for the Red Sox, how can you be so clumsy as to let the ball roll through your legs and into the dwarf conifers every single time.

Strangely enough, Japan set the standard for barbarous affronts by man against garden in the 16th Century. Conquering warlords would plunder the garden of the vanquished and take off with its contents: trees, boulders, lanterns, everything.

This kind of barbarism had a resurgence here in the U.S. as late as 1968 when in Southern California small bands of later-day rustlers astride the bed of pickup trucks lassoed highly valued cycads on the front lawns of private homes, yanked them into the trucks and sped off. These hot cycads were later peddled for thousands. No one thought of putting photographs and descriptions of the missing cycads on the backs of fertilizer cartoons, so very few were recovered.

It's For The Birds

Even the birds are a mixed blessing, but here the mix is strongly weighted in favor of the creatures. Not only do they bring color and sprightly animation to the garden but many serve double duty in keeping the insects in check. A little stream borders our back garden providing a home for a colony of Mallards. In the spring and summer we set out trays of cracked corn on the back porch, and the ducks make the arduous trip from stream to porch, family by family, several times a day. Each family will eat its fill of corn, stroll around the porch a bit, and then plop down for an hour-long siesta. After the nap, they stretch up in unison, shake out their feathers, simultaneously poop on the patio, and make for the water in a single-file beeline. With half a dozen chicks in tow, fist-sized fuzz balls in baby down, the trek is a burlesque stumble-bumble that raises serious doubts about Darwinism but leaves no doubt about the benevolence and humor of the Creator.

We have half a dozen feeders set out, some with thistle some with sunflower seed, some with a mix of cracked corn, sunflower and white millet, and some with suet and seed or peanut butter. This tiny investment brings embarrassingly rich dividends through each season.

In the spring we watch the Goldfinches molt out of their somber grays to the perky gold and black that puts them in step with the burst of color all about them. Bluejays, brash by nature, dress and bearing, usually come by to clash color with the finches. We are also blessed with warblers, occasional Western Tanangers, Western Bluebirds, Ruby-Crowned Kinglets, Western Orioles and a treasure chest of other jewels. In the summer we see an occasional Ring-Necked Pheasant, a solitary Kingfisher, Snowy Egrets (more common here than the Common Egret), and an occasional daylight-dazed Great Horned Owl, looking befuddled and confused as though locked out after an all night binge.

With mixed feelings we also play host to several fierce raptors—Sparrow Hawks, Sharp-shinned Hawks and Ferruginous Hawks. You know when they're about, since all the other birds dart for cover, and nothing stirs. They'll take perch on a locust tree and coldly and methodically scan the entire garden. At times their taut patience pays off and some silly sparrow tries a fifty-yard dash from one juniper to another. The hawk gives chase and the unnerved sparrow is flushed out to try another dash for another juniper. It seldom succeeds the second time, and in a silent flurry of feathers the sparrow is throttled in mid-air. A small woodland drama, on stage in the back garden.

By autumn, many of these birds leave, but House Finches and a half-dozen species of sparrows remain. More somber in dress, they are wonderfully complimented by the colors of fall. Only the Evening Grossbeaks sport a bit of color to match the Aspen.

Come winter we play host to some of the most whimsical creatures birdom has to offer. Chickadees, brazen and bold, stand their ground and scold you for your interest. Downy Woodpeckers bring to life a child's cuddly caricature of a bird. Plump but suave Juncos, dapper in brown and black velvet with silver beaks, disport themselves with frenetic abandon. And Nuthatches, their tails probing the sky for gravity, somehow creep head downward along the suet log looking for food.

In fact hosting the birds may bring its greatest pleasures during winter. On the coldest day in January, with a foot of fresh snow on the ground, one can sit at the window, in the warmth and comfort of home, watching a mob of boisterous House Finches, oblivious to the cold and snow, bickering over who is the toughest or handsomest red head in the lot. But on the coldest days they mostly just hang around, puffed out and still, perched in the branches. Now even the downiest woodpecker looks chilled and miserable, and by contrast you are made even more aware of the warmth and comfort of your roost.

But it's not all pleasure. We also endure the feeding and pooping frenzy of regiments of Red-winged Blackbirds, Grackles, and Starlings. And the male Yellow-headed Blackbirds, as beautiful as they are, have a raucous monosyllabic call that must offend all but the most hormone-driven female of the species. These birds don't sing, they harangue. They hurl expletives. Even Louis Armstrong would have cringed at the gronk of these golden heads.

It seems that many species feel particularly comfortable at the edge of a wood where they can reconnoiter a large open area with the security of a dense stand of trees at their back. This makes the quarter-acre plot an ideal sanctuary for birds, attracting many more than one would imagine judging by local density.

An adequate shelter of trees not only offers the birds a place of protection, food, and nesting sites, but also provides a blind for the avid back-yard naturalist and voyeur. With binoculars in hand, partly hidden in a grove of pines, one can spy on the Hairy-chested Nutscratcher tending his compost pile next door, or the beauteous belle of the cut offs and tank top as she manicures her petunia patch.

The birds offer us so much pleasure throughout the year that I think of them as a necessary part of the garden and consider any effort to encourage their presence well spent. But, in fact, very little effort is needed, and almost every garden scheme can be easily modified to accommodate them. After all, besides food and water, their need for a bit of privacy and seclusion is quite compatible with our needs, and supplying them in the garden will be automatic. We might want to supplement the design with a few more berrying trees and shrubs and some thicket-forming plants for cover, but this is a small tax to pay for the companionship of such a joyous crew.

Stream-side gardens for the collector
of ferns and other moisture-loving
plants.
Above. This small step fall in the
author's garden is a modified runoff
sluice for street water.
Right. A stream bank garden in the
Quinault Rain Forest, Olympic
Penninsula, Washington.

154

The alpine rock garden designed by
Herb Schaal of EDAW Inc., in the
Denver Botanic Garden, Denver,
Colorado.

Photo by Seth Malitz

157

157

More views of the alpine rock garden
at the Denver Botanic Garden.
To the left is *Campanula garganica.*

The rock gardens of nature are often considerably more spare than our cultivated ones, with far fewer species in an area of given size. These examples are from Rocky Mountain National Park, on the shore of Dream Lake (left) and off the Fern Lake Trail (below).

159

Above. A pool and massive boulders provide a microclimate for alpines.
Below. Semperviviums fill a seam.
Both scenes from the alpine garden in the Botanic Garden, Denver, Colorado.

Analogues from nature. Both
scenes from Rocky Mountain
National Park, Colorado.

Oceanside rock gard
at Point Lobos State
Carmel, California.
Above. Monterrey
Cypress form a biza
but beautiful backdr
Left. Crassulas pick
way along the seams
massive rock outcro

Two views within the Eric Walter
Succulent Garden, Golden Gate Park,
San Francisco, California.
Left. An Australian Grass Tree, *Xantho-
rrhoea arborea*.
Below. A wall garden featuring
crassulas and other succulents.

163

CHAPTER 5 *Customizing Plant Forms*

[5.1] INTRODUCTION

Most woody ornamentals have a highly impressionable nature. Their form and character can be altered dramatically with a modicum of persuasion. Trees can be converted to shrubs and shrubs into trees. The high and the mighty can be dwarfed and bent. The crooked and not-so-noble can be straightened and enobled. Control can be effected mechanically, horticulturally, or genetically. There are lessons to be learned from arborists, fruit growers, and those masters of plant sculpture, the growers of bonsai.

The pliant tolerance and adaptability of plants is astounding. Trees can be tied into knots that befuddle topologists, and yet continue growing for centuries. Willows planted upside down will convert their former crowns to roots and their former roots to crowns. To protect their giant tree ferns from our Allied bombing raids, the curators of Humbolt Arboretum in West Berlin stripped the ferns of all their fronds and roots and stored them stacked like hairy cordwood in deep tunnels. Eighteen months later, when the war was over, they were brought up, potted, and placed in a glasshouse. Within a year they sprouted new roots and fronds to continue life without a hint of their hibernation as shaggy poles.

In view of these and many other examples, it is not surprising that many of our woody garden plants are tolerant of a wide variety of seemingly cruel and unusual measures that alter their shape and control their growth. Nature suggests several methods of control and is an inexhaustible source of templates for the modeling of tree forms. Here is where I look for the first examples.

[5.2] WIND SCULPTURE

The effect of the elements on plant form is most dramatically seen in the high alpine reaches. Here at timberline is the bastion of the Bristlecone Pine. Some have held fort in this inhospitable place for more than 4,000 years, the short summer and harsh nine-month winter forcing them to meter out their lives cautiously and very slowly. These are the world's oldest living trees, older even than the giant sequoias of the high Sierras. They begin as seedlings huddled in the shelter of boulders, mere scruffy bottlebrushes a foot high after decades. After millennia, sufficiently toughened and

bonsai masterpiece ;oshin" created by hn Naka. Eleven oemina Juniper", " tall. This specimen now in the U.S. ational Bonsai •llection of the ational Arboretum Washington, D.C. oto by Peter oomer

165

thickened by wind and snow, they dare to raise themselves inch by yearly inch into the full force of the weather. Then they continue their development into giant hulking forms with twisted limbs pointing the direction of the prevailing winds, and broad backs, flayed free of bark, hunched counter to the force of the gales.

Now they wrestle with the elements for thousands of years until the gales get the upper hand over brittle old age and the new growth can no longer keep pace with what is lost in the storms. They begin to die. But having reached maturity so slowly and under such adversity, they do not relinquish life easily or quickly. They persist for several more centuries, three quarters of their bark flayed off, a strip of cambium on the lee side the only artery left to the few remaining branches, until these too are ripped from the tree. Then as jutting snags they still stand in defiance of the elements for yet another hundred years. Even when finally uprooted and thrown to the ground they yield slowly and reluctantly, the bare hulks alternately sun baked and frozen to bone white brittleness, until they break up much like the boulders around them, masking the rot and decay which so rapidly and prosaicly sends their lowland cousins back to the earth.

Yet this same pine adapts fairly easily to garden culture. And then what a change there is. The gladiator grows fat in his retirement. The tree acquires a plump lushness from its dense branching that begins at ground level to its luxuriantly green, foot-long, yearly growth of candles. This domesticated stoutness is superficial since the bone and muscle of the tree, its bole and limb structure, is much thinner than that of its alpine counterparts. Still a beautiful tree, but largely without the noble mien of its mountain kin, it is now unable to evoke the wild inhospitable spirit of the high ramparts that are its traditional home.

Other pines too, like the Limber and Jeffrey, stand their ground at timberline. Their form is more sinuous, more resilient and yielding to the winds and storms. More graceful but less powerful and defiant, they show the centuries' long fight by bending into the contour of the land for protection. But bring them down into the garden, and they become symmetric, elegant, upright trees with little hint of their steely fiber.

The same is true of the Alpine Fir, as symmetrically cone-shaped as a Blue Spruce in the garden, growing to a height of 90 ft. But at timberline it cautiously creeps and crawls a foot or two above the ground, extending the length of its branches barely an inch a year. A tree three centuries old may reach a height of only 2 ft. and a width of 8 ft.

Other climates and other sites also sculpt the trees into dramatic shapes. Monterey Cypress, perched on cliffs above the Pacific, are sheared flat by the off-shore winds, their boles and limbs flattened to wide planks, reducing wind resistance without sacrificing strength. Their wide-spreading, flat-topped form at oceanside is a far cry from their garden shape, indeed a reversal leading to a symmetrical, graceful cone-shape under inland cultivation.

The desert too is a sculptor of trees. Here Pinyon Pines, and various upright junipers are moulded into adaptive shapes to cope with the extremes of temperatures, the intense sun, and the persistent draught. They stand erect, but their growth shows the frugal spareness dictated by limited water, shelter, and nutrients available. Under the caring ministrations of the gardener, they become pleasingly plump—attractive but not inspiring.

erratic angularity
Monterey Cypress
testifies to the
of the coastal
s. Seventeen Mile
e, Monterey,
fornia.

167

Above. The Veteran Tree, an ancient Monterey
Cypress, overlooking Monterey Bay before the
winds that forged it finally tore it free and tossed
it into the sea.
Above right. Monterey Cypress is always pic-
turesque but unfortunately of limited
adaptability inland.
Below right. A Laocoon grouping of Monterey
Cypress. All three views are from Point Lobos
State Park, California.

It's trees like these, trees that won their character through the centuries' long fight for survival in the harshest climates and sites, that inspire so much bonsai. Indeed, some of the most renown examples of bonsai were plucked from the mountains when already hundreds of years old. Other bonsai, grown from seed or cuttings in the nurseries, have been sculpted to emulate these mountain dwellers. Wrappings of copper wire train limbs to mimic the wrenching twists caused by mountain winds; candles are pruned to ½ in. stubs to illustrate what growth is possible in a three-month, off-winter season; and roots are partly exposed to emulate the effects of erosion.

Sometimes ancient trees too large for bonsai are brought out of the mountains to grace a garden with their hoary nobility. This requires considerable care, and often the transfer is effected over several years. First the tree is root pruned in its mountain site and tied in to prevent the winds from taking advantage of its weakened hold and sweeping it away. There it is left in place for at least a year. It may be top pruned as well to relieve some of the burden on the lessened root mass. When the tree is brought down into the garden it is carefully staked, wrapped for protection against the winter, and cautiously watered and fed. Now care and skill have to be exercised in order to maintain its form. Once the tree is settled in and growing there is always the danger that the easy life will encourage a luxuriance of growth that will mask its stoic past producing some weird amalgam of disparate shapes lacking the ability to evoke either the grandeur of the mountains or the hospitality of its new home. The tree becomes a grotesque hodgepodge. The gardener guards against this by diligently adhering to a pruning schedule, and watering and feeding the plant sparingly and with caution.

A dozen or so of these wind-sculpted pines were dug from the nearby Rockies to grace the Japanese Garden in the Denver Botanic Gardens. They do a great deal to give the garden its interest and character, although the mountain images that the garden evokes are of the most gentle and benign sort, even though the trees are carefully managed to retain their indominable character.

Many gardeners versed in a variety of specialties care for these trees. One very small, very expert Japanese is in charge of pruning these pines. He is just the right size and shape to move up and down the branches like a nuthatch, removing all but a bit of each candle. In the fall he actually reduces the length of the needles clump by clump. The effect is superb, but the patience and time required limit the technique's applicability to the very few who are sufficiently well heeled to farm out the grooming chores to a caring and knowledgeable professional.

[5.3] CONTROLLING SIZE

Nature is pushy. Plant a group of trees and shrubs together and each will push and shove to get its fair share of light and soil. Seldom can the shape of a garden's woody plants be left unattended year after year, and in older gardens the shaping chores may constitute the bulk of the upkeep time.

Maintaining a tree or shrub at a given height is usually a practical as well as aesthetic concern that arises all too often when impatience dictates the choice of fast-growing and ultimately overly large plants instead of genetically controlled slow growers of more modest height. But sometimes the right plant for the design is a large grower that has no suitable substitutes of smaller size. In such cases one must acquire the plant, realizing that the choice necessitates some additional labor.

There are all sorts of influences that control the height of a woody plant. In the garden control can be exercised by obvious measures, like "off with its head" to more subtle ones like root pruning. Here we want to mention some of the less obvious practices that control height.

Exposure

Exposure to the elements can have profound effects on the form of a tree and its ultimate height, as is so strikingly exemplified by the contrasting growth patterns of Alpine Fir and Bristlecone Pine near timberline and in the garden. Another good example is the Vine Maple. Multistemmed, shrubby, and short in the open, it conforms to its name under the forest canopy, becoming all strung-out and viney. Studies have been done in the wild on stature and trunk thickness as a function of the distance of a tree from the perimeter of the grove. For some species the influence of location is dramatic. Trees on the perimeter show a marked thickening of the bole and a reduction in height. So in the garden, one can expect that trees grown on the exposed perimeter will grow less quickly becoming more dense and compact, and maybe more picturesque.

Shrubs too can be quite responsive, becoming denser, less leggy, and shorter with more exposure. Careful placement can do much to maintain the shape of a shrub without the need for frequent pruning.

Restricting Root Growth

The growers of bonsai no doubt know as much about controlling the height of trees and shrubs as anyone, and some of their tricks can well serve the gardener who wants to limit the size of some specimen. Control by the bonsai specialist is exercised in several different ways: restricting root growth, limiting the amount of nutrients, and judiciously pruning the top growth.

The root growth of bonsai is partly controlled by growing the plants in very shallow containers. Every year or couple of years, depending on the species, the tree is removed from its container and root pruned.

In the garden a tree or shrub can be grown in a container buried in the ground to its rim. One has to take care, as with bonsai, that adequate drainage has been provided. Every few years, the plant is yanked from its container, some soil is removed from the root ball, the roots are pruned back, new soil is added, and the tree is replaced in the container. Of course some pruning of the top to balance the loss of roots is a requisite part of this procedure.

Sometimes a site can be chosen which forms a natural barrier to the roots, such as a concavity in a rocky outcrop, or a ledge, or the side of a building. In such cases instead of unearthing the tree every year or so in order to prune the roots, something of a chore with a 15 or 20 ft. tree, a long-bladed shovel is used to cut a circular pattern around the base of the plant. This method of root pruning is even effective in open ground in the absence of a root barrier, provided that the species being trained is shallowly rooted. For example, Aspen, birch, and many maples do not seem to suffer from such treatment, yet their growth, including the size of the individual leaves, is strongly restricted. This sort of treatment often causes a circle of saplings to arise around the parent tree, but these are easily removed.

Some constraint on root growth results if a plant is placed in close proximity to other plants, but each species reacts in its own way. With many, such as *Acer rubrum, Fagus sylvatica*, walnuts, Lodgepole Pine, and Douglas Fir, it's not at all clear that root competition affects the ultimate height of the tree, although it certainly affects the growth pattern in the way that competition for light usually does. Indeed, as in the case of the Vine Maple (*Acer circinatum*), this effect may be spectacular—the tree growing in height much more vigorously under competition then when growing alone.

Trees and shrubs grown for their flowers or fruit, are often encouraged to bud out at a much earlier age and with greater profusion when root pruned. For example, wisteria that have never bloomed are often prodded into spectacular display by this technique. Perhaps the plants interpret this pruning as a threat to their existence and are programmed to procreate before closing shop. Strangely, this kind of management does not seem to shorten the life or the productivity of the plant at all. Indeed, trees grown as bonsai often live far longer than when grown without restrictions.

The amount of fertilizer and water that a plant receives is almost invariably a strong determinant of its rate of growth and final size. For bonsai only the gentlest fertilizers, like those made of fish meal, or soy cake are used, and then only sparingly. The pot the bonsai resides in is shallow with ample drain holes and the soil used is highly porous, all of which minimizes the danger of overwatering. In the garden one might forego fertilizing a plant altogether except in the most impoverished soil, and give a minimum of supplementary watering. This will not be very effective for the draught lovers and nitrogen fixers, but may have an almighty effect on water hogs and gluttons like buckeyes, poplars, and various fruit trees.

Bonsai Techniques for Dwarfing

There are other techniques used by Bonsai specialists to control the growth rate and size of their trees. For example, they may diligently pluck off every new leaf of a maple tree. The tree responds by sending out a new crop of leaves, but this time they are considerably reduced in size and so more in harmony with the size of the tree itself. Japanese Black Pine is another tree favored for use in bonsai. It's a plant of strong character with many interesting variations—some showing twisted needles, some a blue or yellow tint, and others an extremely rough and corky bark. But in most the needles are 3–4½ in. long, and even though bonsai culture dwarfs them somewhat, it is not enough to bring them into scale with the rest of the plant. So the gardener prunes the needles to a third of their length. It's reasonable to conjecture that these practices reduce the over-all vigor of the plant and help to control its height. On the other hand, these are not techniques that are easily adapted to a garden of full-scale plants—too much time and labor would be required. But one might consider such practices on a small scale in order to manage a few choice plants.

However, it is usually better to search out species and cultivars that will fit the bill over the long run. There are forms of Japanese Black Pine that will grow to a height of only 6–8 ft. with needles one-third the size typical of the

172

species, and Japanese maples with fingernail-sized leaves that grow to a height of only 2–3 ft. Some of the dwarfs will try your patience as they slowly reach their mature height, and full-sized trees and shrubs chosen for characteristics like horizontal branching or fastigate shape may not show these traits until full grown. Nevertheless, the end result is invariably better, more certain, and attained and maintained with less labor when the plant's heredity is on your side.

Grafting

The fruit growers have shown us the efficacy of grafting as a means of controlling height. Grafting can make a 6 ft. dwarf out of a 40 ft. pear, a 30 ft. cherry, or a 20 ft. plum. Depending on the stock and on the kind of interstem graft, the height of the mature creation can be custom designed to within 2 ft. of any size between the dwarf and the untampered height. However, the graft union is often an obvious and unsightly lump for a number of years, and when not well done is a point of structural weakness.

Grafting of fruit trees is commonly used to impart hardiness, tolerance to certain soils, and disease resistance. But ornamentals are seldom grafted for purposes other than increasing the supply of specific clones that do not come true from seed or can not be rooted easily. Moreover, the use of hormones and new rooting techniques have decreased the need for grafting considerably. But it is conceivable that certain ornamentals can be given a boost in hardiness, a boost in soil tolerance, or a change in mature height by judicious grafting. The benefits to ornamental horticulture would be considerable. For example, the Eastern Dogwood is particular about the soil it grows in—preferring slightly acid soil and demanding good drainage. These requirements strongly limit the use of the tree over much of the Midwest. On the other hand, there are dogwoods that are extremely hardy and tolerant of all sorts of soils. Could the former play scion to the latter's stock? It might be worth a try.

As an extreme example of the grafter's art and enthusiasm, we should mention that they have created flowering crab apples on which three varieties, a red, a white, and a pink, are grafted onto a single stock. However, the popularity of these contrivances seems to be on the wane even in the absence of international agreements to prohibit the practice. But where space is severely limited, both in the garden and between the ears, these creations might be of some use.

Where fruit production and not appearance is the primary concern, the practice makes more sense, allowing several varieties to be grown in a small space—a definite advantage in the restricted area of a private garden particularly if the grafted varieties require cross-pollination.

174

WIND SCULPTURE

Left. An ancient Bristlecone, alive in the year 1 A.D. now stands beneath a contrail streaked sky. Crater Lake National Park, Oregon.
Above. Another Bristlecone, this one entrenched on the shore of Lake Hiyaha at 13,000 ft. in Rocky Mountain National Park, Colorado.
Right. A bonsai created from a juniper allegedly 1,000 years old.

BONSAI

The last word in shaping trees and controlling growth.

Above. An azalea clinging to a rock calls up images of offshore islands.

Left. A Japanese Maple bonsai provides a model for the shaping of a garden tree. Photo by Susan Malitz

Maple (*Acer buerqeranum*) 30 years old, 1' tall.
Bonsai provides excellent models for arranging
trees in a grove, and many of the species used in
this style are equally suited for a garden grove:
Japanese, Fullmoon, and Trident Maples, various
birch; Aspen; and many varieties of pines. Photo
courtesy Shufunotomo Co., Ltd., Tokyo.

[5.4] CONTROLLING OVER-ALL FORM

Plant forms can also be manipulated over a wide range, and some species are more amenable to manipulation than others. Some are pliant and can be easily twisted and bent into shape. Others alter their growth pattern dramatically when severely pruned. The gardener can take advantage of these amenable plants and create shapes custom-made for the design of the garden.

Trees vs Shrubs

Often the distinction between a tree and a shrub is a reflection of the way the plant has been managed. The Carolina Silverbell, Virginia Fringe Tree, Canadian Redbud, Kousa Dogwood, various viburnums and hawthorns, Red Buckeye, certain magnolias and many, many more can be grown in either form and are beautiful and natural as trees or shrubs. Most of these species seem unable to make up their minds anyway, and the smallest inducement can set them off in one direction or the other. To obtain a tree form prune out all but one or a few stems and eventually remove the lower branches. To obtain a shrub form with multiple stems prune heavily or cut a vigorous young plant to the ground. Sometimes nicking or severing some of the roots will give the same result.

Plants that are more set in their ways require more persuasion to change. For example, much beheading can change a Silver or Norway Maple, White or Green Ash, Ailanthus, or Box Elder into a large, coarse, and multi-stemmed shrub. On the other hand, *Cotoneaster lacteus*, Peegee Hydrangea, and Black Haw Viburnum, to mention a few, can be grown as small trees if given enough attention and bullying.

Even some vines, like wisteria, can be induced to straighten up and fly right, masquerading as trees with aid of strong braces, heavy ties, judicious pruning and inexhaustible patience. Conversely, some trees can be humbled into a vine-like form as is done with Weeping Fig, twining three stems together in a braid. This kind of degradation can be carried still further through the wonders of grafting. Absolute shrubs like Cranberry Cotoneaster, lantana, and roses can be grown on top of a 4–5 ft standard as a sort of mock minitree, but looking less like a tree and more like a shaggy lollipop thrust face high so that the disfigurement can be examined more closely.

Trees in Clump Form

Some trees look their best and do their best when grown in clump form with several stems. Birch and Aspen certainly are of this character, and I think that the Eastern Dogwood, Katsura Tree, many of the hawthorns, pear, ash, Honey Locust, Beech, Horsechestnut, and many others look particularly impressive when grown as clumps. Katsura trees, hawthorns, and Honey Locusts lose none of their grace and elegance, while trees like Beech and Horse Chestnut, massive and powerful as they are when grown on a single bole, are even more impressive when grown with multiple trunks. Many trees mature at a considerably lower height when grown with multiple stems, and yet have the same initial growth rate. Ash and Honey Locust are examples. This is a considerable advantage if such large-growing species are to be accommodated on a small lot. In addition, many horticulturists believe that trees which are marginally hardy in a given region have a better chance for survival if grown in clump form. Some suggest that this is due in part to the tree shielding itself against wind and too much sunlight, but I suspect that if this phenomenon is indeed genuine, as experience seems to indicate, there is a deeper reason.

Many of the trees mentioned above have a tendency to form multiple trunks without any encouragement from the gardener. Others need to be prodded. Sometimes placing several nicks in the trunk close to ground level will do the job, as is the case with White and Green Ash, Honey Locust, crab apples, hawthorns, poplars of most sorts, and many more. A more radical approach that is often successful with the same trees is to lop them off at ground level, and then just wait and pray. The best chance of success is to be had with young trees only a couple of feet tall and in vigorous growth.

One might even consider grafting some branches or buds onto the base of the tree, but most trees that can be encouraged to grow multiple stems will not need this kind of inducement, and very little time is gained by it, Again, it seems much less of a hassle to work with a tree that has a preference for growing multistemmed than to coerce an inveterate single by hacking and sawing.

[5.5] SHAPING TO SUIT

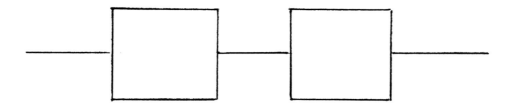

Brassiere worn by a Picasso model

Pruning is the most common method of controlling the shape and character of woody plants. Beside determining its height and width, selective pruning can emphasize a plant's special features. For example, the framework of Japanese maples is often thinned to accentuate their airy grace. Stewartias, Snake-Bark and Paperbark Maples, Korean Mountain Ash, and various birches may be thinned to display their colorful and wonderfully patterned bark. Azaleas, boxwoods, alpine currants, hollies, and privet are often sheared not only to shape them but to make them denser. Ailanthus, some sumac, and Devil's Walking Stick are often pruned to the ground annually—a practice which induces a strong growth of suckers with huge tropical foliage, much larger than on old wood.

Kerria japonica, shrubby dogwoods like *Cornus alba, C. seriaca*, and some willows have superb winter stem color—clear red or yellow or green. These colors often show best on young stems, so these shrubs are usually pruned heavily each year, cutting the oldest stems to the ground.

Most junipers, tams, and yews have extraordinarily beautiful and distinctive growth patterns, so the gardener is usually cautioned not to use an electric hedge trimmer to give such shrubs a crew-cut as this mutes the texture and shape and kills the individuality of the shrub. While it is true that it does, it is no more permanently disfiguring on young stock than a like cut on an army inductee, yet garners several advantages. The shrubs grow with greater vigor, and the pruning encourages a denser branch structure. After a few years of growth, should the shrub require pruning for shape, health, or to restrict its size, the added branches will stand the gardener in good stead. Now entire branches can be removed if need be, and the remaining growth will soon mask the correction. Moreover, you will have several choices of which branch to cut. This is much better than pruning a thick stem at its midpoint to reduce height, a practice which usually results in an ugly, clearly visible wound and side branches that grow from the region of the cut at an unnatural angle that is likely to be incongruous with the over-all shape of the shrub.

Even when junipers are pruned to a mounding, billowing shape, I do not find the look objectionable. The effect is much like the clipped boxwoods and azaleas in the famed Japanese gardens Daichi-ji and Shoden-ji, but the texture of clipped junipers is even more dense and fine. Moreover, this may be the only alternative to clipped boxwood or azaleas in climates that are inhospitable to these plants.

Most trees and shrubs do not object to heavy pruning, some even seem to enjoy it and cooperate, growing with increased vigor, sending out new branches, suckering, or sending out new stems from the trunk. Sometimes this cooperation can be more like an aggressive counterattack, joining a chronic, year-to-year battle between the gardener's attempt to control the errant plant and the plant's attempt to avoid being pruned out of existence. Poplars, willows, shrubby dogwoods, and most fruit trees are among the many that respond in this way.

Others of a more wimpy constitution are so affronted by the touch of the loppers that they may abort the offended limb or even abort themselves altogether. Some of the daphnes and some of the mulberries are of this unforgiving bent.

Then there are those that suffer the loppers stoically but refuse to cooperate. Woody plants usually become more intractable as they age, a trait not uncommon among life forms. Cut back a limb and the stump will remain an ugly, scarred-over reminder that this job should have been done years earlier, or the plant may make some pitiable attempt to mask the scar with some uncharacteristic, misshapen jumble of twigs. Many rhodos, Burning Bush (*Euonymus alata*), Smoke Bush (*Cotinus coggygria*), some viburnums and many trees are compliant when young but uncooperative when mature.

Often the desired form can only be reached by a sequence of successive approximations carried out over a decade or so, and the gardener must patiently suffer through the ungainly or downright ugly intermediate stages. For example, a pine planted near a path to someday form a shady canopy over the stroller's head must simply be tolerated until enough height is obtained so that the lower branches can be removed. Meanwhile the gardener must contend with branches which jut into the path and which have to be shortened or bent out of the way in some stop-gap fashion which is unlikely to be an asset to the garden. There is no alternative when the tree is 6 ft. tall and you need 8 ft. of clearance.

A magnificen
Lebenon Cedar wit
multiple trunk

Pruning is an art when done for the sake of art. Pruning a tree to increase its structural integrity, or its fruiting proclivity is fairly straightforward. There are well-established rules and guidelines, and it is hard to make a mistake that can't be corrected by another year or two of growth. On the other hand, there are few rules and canons to guide one when pruning for aesthetic reasons. Removing a major tree limb results in either a major improvement or a major disfigurement. Since it is usually much easier to dismember than to remember, it is best to proceed slowly and with caution. With no time records to be set, mark the limb slated for removal with paint or a cloth tie, and remove it only in the imagination first. Live with the thought of its absence for a year or so before deciding whether to cut or not.

The world's speed record for limb removal, according to the *Guinness Book of World Records*, is held by Dominique Larrey, Napoleon's chief surgeon, who amputated a leg in 15 seconds. Unfortunately the patient died. Haste makes waste.

It's unlikely that even the most careless and impulsive gardener will cause such a tragedy although mistakes are made that threaten both life and limb in both pruner and prunee. Such mistakes are usually announced by some terse exclamation that chills the marrow and ices the heart even on the sunniest day. Words like:

Won't it grow back?

I thought it was dead.

What do you mean it wasn't this branch?

More ominous still:

Where's the first-aid kit?

or

I thought you were holding the ladder.

Trees in Bondage

The custom of tree binding has long been practiced in Japan where it is openly condoned. It has been a standard device for training garden trees and bonsai for centuries. While trees in bondage may not be a pretty sight, and some possessed of particularly delicate sensibilities may object on humane grounds, long-term effects can be obtained in this way that are otherwise impossible.

I'm not suggesting that the tree be bent into total submission to a faith not of its heritage with the risk of breaking limbs to boot. The intention is not to encourage the growth of sequoias in the Kengai (cascading) style or like foolishness. Rather, taking the lead from the bonsai devotee, we want to encourage the tree to grow in some natural way, natural to its species, or at least possible under some natural circumstances. We want to build character into the tree, perhaps to evoke a sense of resilience, permanence, or stark stoicism. Mutilation only evokes pity and disgust.

In bonsai the most common way to alter the shape of limbs and trunk is to coil copper wire around them and then bend them to the desired position. The wire holds the desired curve until after several years the bend is permanent. However, trees possessing a delicate bark, like cherries and other prunus species, are injured by this technique, and so are configured by different means. Limbs are reshaped by tying them to various parts of the pot in which the bonsai is growing, or to heavy braces of metal or wood, or even to different parts of the plant itself.

In the case of a garden tree wiring is obviously unworkable, but the alternate methods are easily adapted to the task. Rather than tying branches to a pot, the branches are tied to boulders, ground stakes, the trunk of the tree itself, other branches, or even other trees. Care must be taken to avoid injuring the tree as by girdling a branch with a tie left in place for too many years.

There are all sorts of variations on this method. To affect the look of an old pine whose branches no longer have that upward sweep of youthful exuberance, but are held parallel to the ground or even bent downwards at their midpoint, bamboo poles are secured horizontally across the trunk, and the limbs are tied to these.

As a further embellishment of this device, a lattice is constructed of bamboo poles and suspended on stakes parallel to the ground. Several branches are then spread onto the lattice and secured. The end result is a dense plane of pine boughs. This is sometimes done at a height that will provide a canopy for the stroller, and at other times, as is the case with a superb specimen in the Japanese Garden at Golden Gate Park in San Francisco, at a height of only a foot or so making a thick-pile, floating carpet. Although I find this effect quite beautiful, it strikes me as contrived and unnatural, something I enjoy seeing occasionally, but nothing I want to stare at in my garden day after day. Nevertheless, it's a fine example of the malleability of trees and the techniques that can be used to take advantage of it.

Some trees, such as pears, have a tendency towards weak, narrow crotches. To correct this proclivity, fruit growers use a sort of primitive gynecologist's device consisting of a short narrow board notched at both ends. The board is wedged between two branches that need spreading, with each notch engaging a branch. This is also a useful ploy for the reshaping of ornamental trees for strength and for aesthetic reasons.

Sometimes dogs and other pets are tied to trees, but this method of shaping is unreliable since the animals tend to move around a lot and have to be brought in for the winter.

For those with kinkier tastes, there are trees that can be debased by knotting the trunk or limbs, coiling the trunk like a gigantic spring, or braiding several trunks together. I don't know why people do this sort of thing except that they can, and maybe it keeps them from doing it to other people.

With any of these bending techniques the desired position must be forcibly maintained from one to several seasons depending on the bend and the species. If the restraints are removed prematurely the tree will counter the effort to reshape it by exaggerating its previous form—the branch returning to its initial position and then some. But eventually, with enough increase in the girth of the limb, the desired position will be held.

TOPIARY

Two superb examples of the dotty art in Longwood Gardens, Kennett Square, Pennsylvania. Left. A green dog threatens a leafy fire hydrant.

184

Espalier, Topiary, Mazes

Some pruning practices, such as pollarding, topiary, and espalier, pay no heed at all to the plant's natural growth patterns. A tree is pollarded by chopping off its branches to within a couple of feet of the trunk, and then pruning the current year's shoots all the way back to the stump every autumn. Over the years this encourages the stumps themselves to grow into massive lumps, so the trees take on all the charm and grace of a heavily corned and bunioned foot resting on its heel.

An espalier is a tree grown splat against the wall of a building or trellis. In order that the full extent of the gardener's domination over the plant be made apparent the branches are usually pruned to absolute bilateral symmetry. While this device has some justification in the management of fruit orchards where it saves space, facilitates picking and spraying, and encourages heavier fruiting and at an earlier age, it is not likely to make a positive contribution to the appearance of the garden. However, an espalier is a space saver and when viewed from the side is almost invisible.

Topiary makes poodle dogs and giraffes out of perfectly respectable boxwoods, yews and junipers while at the same time converting the garden into some kind of green Disneyland. This could make for a child's favorite spot, and it's a wonderful pastime for the frustrated and uninspired sculptor. For the rest of us it's a curiosity that demonstrates the infinite tolerance of some plants and the infinite patience of some men. One would think that in the age of the electric hedge trimmer there would be some opportunity to expand the scale and create new forms in this medium. Perhaps some Christo or Heizer will take it into his head to clip some erotic image out of the great coastal forests of the Northwest. But until that time, topiary will continue to rely on a rather stodgy lexicon of forms and continue to amuse us with its quaint charm.

For the large English estate, well supplied with hedging-shears and a galley's worth of grounds keepers, the garden labyrinth with walls consisting of meticulously trimmed shrubbery was a must. Some were enormous. No one knows how many intrepid British explorers lost their way in these great, green labyrinths, never to be seen again. The danger has been lessened with the decrease in size of suburban lots, but a labyrinth is still a wonderful place to send a mischievous child or in-laws who have overstayed their welcome.

[5.6] GENES DO IT MORE EASILY

Managing the shape of woody plants is a continuing task in most gardens, but unlike lawn care, there is some opportunity for a bit of creative expression. However, a garden full of trees and shrubs can soon outgrow one's enthusiasm, and counter creativity with endless demands of tedious, mind-numbing drudgery.

The obvious way to avoid this situation is to plant trees and shrubs that are genetically programmed to approximate the height and shape called for by the garden design. This may seem to be a pie-in-the-sky solution, but it is frequently realizable. For example, if something like a Norway Maple is needed, but that tree is too big, then maybe *Acer truncatum* will do. If a

Japanese Black Pine is wanted that does not grow taller than 8 ft, one can choose from a dozen or so selected clones that fit the bill. Spruce, junipers, thujas, hemlocks, crabapples, flowering cherries, Japanese maples, magnolias, and many others are available in such a diversity of forms and sizes that there is no need to plant varieties destined to dictate the weekend's activities.

Locating the right cultivar may take some additional money, time, and effort, but in the long run, much more is saved than spent. Moreover, when height or shape are controlled by considerable pruning, the result is never as convincing or natural as when the genes do it for you. One need not worry that this approach will eliminate the opportunity for a little creative expression since heredity can not be expected to determine more than an approximation of the desired form. The fine tuning, the choice of permanent branches, of a trunk that is upright or leaning, of single stem or multiple stem, are all choices the sculptor-gardener is free to exercise. But roughing-out is best left to the genes.

CHAPTER 6 *Design*

[6.1] GOALS

What excites and intrigues me most about designing a personal landscape is the possibility of transforming a quarter-acre chunk of dirt into an environment, a private sanctuary. One can capture the look and feel of a forest, or an alpine meadow, or suggest a windswept coast in one's own garden even on a nondescript plot of the most modest size. And the wonder of it is that it can be done in a handful of years with abundant pleasure being the reward from the very beginning.

I hope that what has been said so far has not convinced the reader that planning a landscape is such a monumental task, requiring such a wealth of knowledge and inspiration, that the only solution is to seek the services of a professional landscape architect, take a second mortgage to retain him, and set him to work designing the garden.

Even if you were lucky enough to hire some genius at his moment of greatest inspiration he could not be expected to attend to your special interests as you would. Nor could the end result possibly be as close a reflection of your personality and aesthetic sensibilities as if you had designed it yourself. Moreover a genuinely creative architect could not stand to mimic himself over and over again. He would be tempted to create something new, something different with each commission. The result could be a unique masterpiece or a failure. Even Beethoven had his *Wellington's Victory*. So you take a chance upon a chance—finding a talented landscape architect whose sensibilities are closely attuned to yours, and hiring him when his muse is at his side.

On the other hand, creating a landscape is one of the most rewarding ego trips possible, and sharing the results with family and friends one of the greatest gardening pleasures. But first you have to have some idea of your personal Eden and what its principal functions are to be. Will serving the stomach be its primary purpose—heaping the table with fruits and vegetables? Maybe the goal is a rose collection, or beds of iris. Or maybe the seclusion of a small wooded retreat is what is wanted. Usually, it's not that simple. The garden may have to serve several masters and perform several functions, some of which may be horticulturally or aesthetically incompatible.

This is where the marriage made in heaven will have its mettle tested here on earth. He wants a vegetable patch, she wants an annual bed. The kids need a badminton court; the dog, of course, has to have a run. Politics, marriage and gardening are the great teachers of compromise.

Assuming that some amicable agreement has been reached and a separation hasn't left one without a plot to landscape, the next step is to take stock of the lot's assets and shortcomings. The availability of water and light are major concerns. One needs to know the location of public easements, underground pipes and cables, and septic fields. What is the nature of the soil? Is it heavy clay or is it sandy; is it sweet or sour? What is the hardiness zone of the site? What is the length of the growing season—the average date of first and last hard frost? All of these considerations will in some measure determine the species of plants that can reliably grow, and so will determine, to some extent, the appearance of the garden.

Use What You Have

Don't despair that rose bushes have thorns
Rejoice that thorn bushes have roses.

Anon.

Almost any habitable place outside the Sahara and the Arctic Circle will provide the correct conditions for so many desirable species that the vast majority will have to be ignored. Of course, those that one wants to grow most of all are invariably unsuited to the site. Rhodos are taken for granted until one moves from Connecticut to Kansas. The Oregonian who never noticed the stewartias, Japanese Maples, and flowering cherries, now longs for them in Nebraska. The high plains drifter who settles in Georgia might go to any ends to grow those glorious alpines that blanketed the foothills of his former home. And the Floridian wonders how he can survive the rigors of a Minnesota winter without the palm trees and strelizias.

But the first consideration in choosing trees and shrubs has to be adaptability. Can they be expected to do well in your region? Survival is not enough. An exotic novelty, marginally adapted to the climate, will be no more than a shabby, curious misfit in the garden, whereas a more commonplace specimen, thriving and grown to perfection, might be a considerable asset on the same site. The traditional Japanese view is to rely on plants indigenous to the region in which the garden is located and to then grow them to perfection.

If one can achieve variety in the design without compromising unity or ease of maintenance, not only will the garden offer more interest, but it will be protected against complete obliteration by some disease or insect pest that is species-specific. What a heartbreaking, backbreaking, walletbreaking chore to uproot a stand of dead trees and start again with a batch of new seedlings. Consider the decimation of the American Elm under the onslaught of the Dutch elm disease. Whole avenues have been stripped bare of their noble honor guards, summarily vanquished by a tiny beetle and a fungus it carries. Plantings of crabapples, pears, and hawthorns wither and die or are grossly disfigured by an attack of fireblight. Pines are killed in one season by the pine beetle or blister rust. Spruce tip moths and galls disfigure and can be lethal if seasons pass without control—and control is difficult. Deciding to make any highly vulnerable species a primary and extensive element in your design is a risk to be carefully considered.

Often susceptibility to a given disease or insect depends on the climate and cultural conditions. But one should not underestimate the adaptability of pests and diseases or their ability to migrate from state to state, from coast to coast, indeed from country to country. The slow march westward of the tent caterpillar, the pine beetle encroachment on stands further to the South, the Mediterranean fruit fly invasion of California, all bear witness to the adaptability of plant pests and diseases.

It is usually much more rewarding and less frustrating physically and financially to work with what you have. This is not to say that special challenges and interests can not be met and catered to within smaller areas of the garden, but converting an extensive rocky slope to a vegetable patch might be more work than its worth and less rewarding than making a rock garden out of it.

Every house has a north or northeast side that can shade a fern garden. There is always some warm spot near the foundation that will up your zone a notch or two. No lot is so narrow that it can't support a clump of fastigate trees and a few shrubs. If the drainage is poor, consider a bog garden; if it's high, dry, and rocky, forget the bog dwellers, and opt for alpines. And what an opportunity the edge of a woodland presents.

Of course for some the game is in flaunting the odds. They want the joy of growing something ungrowable—growing it for the novelty, for the challenge to their horticultural skill, for the science of it, or just for the hell of it. A well-grown planting of rhodos is commonplace in the Northwest but is a delightful novelty in the semi-arid plains about Denver. Alpine gardening in Georgia is hampered by the humidity and winter wet, but the challenge piques the interest of the rock garden enthusiast.

However a sack race is still a sack race, and most of us should choose the bulk of our landscape material from that which is well adapted to our region. In the case of the larger trees and shrubs, this approach is not a reflection of timidity or lack of curiosity. Rather it is simply good sense. A cold snap that breaks a fifteen-year old record and kills a fifteen-year-old planting of trees is enough to drive the most enthusiastic gardener into a condominium.

Of course, there are those sites that are so perfect, so complete, that nothing can be added without subtracting from the whole. For those very few who have such an ideal, ready-made garden, exchange this book for one on fishing or golf. Our only advice is control yourself; "leave it be". This book is for the less fortunate, for those who find themselves outside of Eden on some quarter-acre piece of dirt stripped bare of topsoil by the developers, or for those living with some hodgepodge landscape creation that brings only boredom and perhaps a few practical amenities.

Now, hopefully, with sanity and marriage intact, all compromises, concessions, and agreements struck, the designer is ready to begin. One sits down with muse, spouse, children and dog by one's side, hundreds of ideas percolating in the mind, cracks Part II and whips off a couple of designs. In fact it's a good idea to whip off more than a couple. Think about the alternatives and discuss them over a period of some time. Be as critical as possible and locate the strengths and weaknesses of each. Evaluate them from the point of view of aesthetics, horticulture, maintenance, and use. Consideration should be given to scale, the growth rate of the plants and their upkeep requirements, the look of the garden in every season, rockwork, grading, and all sorts of other things that are best thought about before construction of the garden is begun.

Scale

Commonly, plants are scaled in keeping with the available planting area—the smaller the area the smaller the plants used. One advantage to this approach is that as wide a variety of material as a larger garden has to offer can be incorporated into a smaller space. For the collector of alpines or dwarf conifers this is the only solution—even a small plot can house an almighty collection. If the plot is delimited by physical constraints, like buildings or fences, the effect is somewhat paradoxical. The viewer who can focus attention on the planting and become totally absorbed in it, sees it as convincing and considerably larger than it actually is, and the physical barriers blot out the visual elements that are incongruous with the design. On the other hand, if note is taken of the over-all scene, these barriers appear to constrict the garden. By their size alone they define the environment, the mood of the garden, and give it a claustrophobic feel. But there are certainly other choices for the design of a small planting.

For example, a strip of land 10 × 30 ft. can be converted into a forest path, using clusters of fastigate trees like Canoe Birch, Aspen, certain cherries, crabs, pears and many others, on each side of the path. Add a few boulders, some foresty ground cover, say *Mahonia repens*, or *Pachysandra terminalis*, perhaps some ferns and a clump or two of perennials and you have an alternative that is likely to be much more pleasing—an environment within which one can experience some of the amenities of nature directly, and not like a visitor to a natural history museum viewing a diarama.

The Japanese have mastered the art of small-scale landscaping, and through the centuries defined and refined an idiom for courtyard gardens that is now emulated everywhere. Simplicity is invariably a dominant theme. A few plants chosen for their structural interest rather than their flowering proclivity are skillfully arranged around some boulders, stepping stones, stone basins and lanterns and then pruned and maintained to perfection. Botanic variety is intentionally sacrificed for quiet harmony; yet these are gardens that provide long-term enjoyment by the perfection of their design. The lesson is again "more is less", and for those whose goal is not collecting, it can be a lesson worth learning.

Four-season Design

Designing a garden that is interesting in every season is a challenge, but designing one that is interesting and dramatically different in every season is an even greater challenge and proffers even greater rewards. This is not easily done with evergreens alone since most show little color change, and most of those that do, modulate to dreary and sullen hues that emphasize the negative aspects of winter, while their textures and compositional role in the garden remain largely unchanged. Many of the rhododendrons and evergreen euonymus curl and droop their leaves to express their displeasure of cold, and this presents such a sorry sight that one wishes they would deciduate altogether and start fresh in the spring. Of course, if they have to be bagged, or require a tent around them for wind and snow protection, their winter appearance will be radically different, but not one to brag about. So for the most part, the challenge of creating a design which changes dramatically in response to the seasons is met by using deciduous and perennial elements. These are the elements that create the dramatic changes. However, evergreens set the stage and provide a contrasting backdrop that emphasizes the changes.

Winter

Commonly a design will ignore the delights of winter, even though a garden in winter can offer special pleasures. Winter is not just a time for callouses to soften and backs to straighten; it's not just a holding pattern waiting for spring. After the first snow quenches the last embers of autumn, the design of the garden is laid bare and offers its most dramatic contrasts. Naked, seemingly frail Aspen are counterpointed against the massive darkness of spruce. A Redtwig Dogwood's scarlet tracery is highlighted against the snow, and an oak flexes its massive limbs against the chill blue of a November sky.

The mowing is done, the fall cleanup is finished. No bugs to worry about, no spraying. The garden is at rest. No pushy perennials clamor for attention. Now the garden's major features have center stage, and one can enjoy the design as a whole.

In Zones 5 and below, six months may pass before the last leaves of autumn are replaced by the first leaves of spring. What a shame it is to ignore the potential of a full half year of garden pleasure. Yet many do. They give in too easily to the seductions of spring and fall, to the more easily obtained pleasures of the gentler seasons. They overplant tulips, daffodils, mums, and asters. It's easy, and results are obtained quickly. But then come the dull and dreary months. At least they seem so when you go out into a dull and dreary garden. Nothing is left except the shriveled stubble of the now dormant perennials and the memories of warmer weather. What a waste! With a bit more thought and a bit more effort this time can be bridged by a garden tuned to respond to the snow and ice with a show of beauty unsurpassed in any other season, and with enough variety to match that of the rest of the year.

Winter is also the best time for evaluating an existing design and planning modifications. Now the composition is seen most clearly—all the fine ideas and all the silly blunders stand out in bare relief. The flaws aren't masked by clouds of blossoms or the blaze of autumn. Attention isn't diverted by dozens of mindless chores. One can focus on the design without being hurried or harried, and work out a strategy to improve it. It's all sport and pleasure since one doesn't have to act on the decisions for months, at which time some of the more grandiose plans can be moderated to something less ambitious. But never mind, this dreaming and planning is one of the most enjoyable winter sports.

Winter is also a good time to move new rocks into an existing garden. With the ground frozen and the perennials dormant, a considerable amount of weight can be moved over them without doing any harm. Rocks being hauled on a hand truck are far more easily moved across frozen ground than over a surface which yields under the weight. An alternative method for moving rocks in the winter is to lay down boards and then pack them with an inch of snow, providing a low friction slide over which the boulders can be pushed.

This is also a good time to refine the pruning and a good time to decide if the design can be improved by removing some plants. After all, the deciduous trees and shrubs are nine-tenths gone at this time anyway, so it is

Overleaf. Window view of the author's garden after a December snow.

191

easy to imagine their complete absence. Most of the perennials have simply disappeared from view altogether, requiring no imagination whatsoever to clear them from the mind's eye. So one can act on a decision to simplify as soon as the ground thaws. Moreover, it is psychologically less painful to chuck a dormant and seemingly lifeless plant in the middle of winter than one in full leaf, or worse still, in full bud.

I look forward to winter as enthusiastically as I look forward to any other season. Come November and I'm ready to put away the mower and shovel for a few months. I want to see the frost silver the junipers, to see the mahonias burnished to copper, then purple and red, and I want to see the trees weave cords of snow into huge macrame. I want to see the landscape simplified, and in a quieter mood. Of course by March, like everyone else, I've had enough, and grow more and more impatient with winter's dallying retreats and repeated counterattacks. I can't wait for spring to drive it off altogether, brandishing the flimsiest of weapons, a handful of daffs, a few crocus here and there, and a myriad of swelling buds. But six months later I'm again ready to say goodbye to the mosquitoes and the tired, tattered foliage, and look forward to the first snows of winter.

Keep It Coherent But Interesting

Interest and coherence are two design goals that are somewhat at odds since the first suggests variety and the second simplicity. What is desired is some balance between the two. If coherence is achieved through an over-simplified design the result will ultimately be boring. If interest is obtained by emphasizing variety the design may come off as a jumbled hodge-podge, which will also be boring in the long run, although isolated features might continue to have interest.

Coherence is difficult to characterize. We know it when we see it, but necessary and sufficient guidelines for creating it are illusive. Coherence is a property of the design's composition and there are numerous books on color composition and spatial composition, both of which concern the garden designer. But unless one has two left eyes, a coherent design is recognized as such when seen. So instead of postponing the garden until a masters degree in fine arts is acquired, take inspiration from some wild or cultivated garden that is seen as coherent, and quite likely a design will follow that will be coherent.

The elements that make a design interesting are even more illusive and more personal. Variety is often a contributing factor, but not always. The dry landscape at Ryoan-ji strikes everyone as interesting, but few say that it has a great deal of variety. A design that strikes the eye as being different is likely to be considered interesting. The design might be different because of some curious or even grotesque features, or it might be different in a more subtle way that suggests the work of a creative designer. The first is more akin to a cheap trick than art, and the interest is likely to disappear after a short time. The latter will likely sustain interest over a much longer period.

For a collector, say of alpines or dwarf conifers or cactus and succulents, the principle of coherence conflicts directly with collecting interests. A collection is usually as broad and diverse as possible and new items are continually added, and nothing stifles the joy of collecting more than the realization that the collection is finished—that there isn't the space to cram in

another plant. Although this kind of garden can be very interesting, it is not the kind of garden that interests us here.

One way of achieving both coherence and variety is to hang the variation on some simple main theme. Establish the theme with the largest features of the garden and then relegate the task of bringing variety into the scheme to the lesser features. For example, the central theme might be that of a pine and Aspen grove, the composition of these trees defining the garden's primary structure and establishing its mood. A selection of perennials to add variety can be incorporated into the scheme later. In fact there is little reason to consider minor elements at all when drawing up the design plan since virtually any design provides an abundance of corners here and there in which small shrubs and perennials are a welcome asset. This approach not only simplifies the design process but almost assures coherence.

[6.2] FAST GROWING VERSUS SLOW GROWING

Had we but world enough and time—
Andrew Marvel

One of the more vexing decisions the designer is faced with is that of using fast-growing trees or slow-growing trees. Only the most selfless and altruistic soul would choose to plant a garden whose pleasures are largely reserved for future generations. So the choice comes down to fast-growing trees that will reach up to provide you with shade at the rate of 8 ft. a year, or a few slow-growing trees purchased as large specimens.

The first choice doesn't strain either patience or wallet—at least not initially. In this category are trees like the Silver Maple, Box Elder, Plane Tree, willows, and all sorts of poplars. True, they grow at a rate of about 8 ft. a year and will quickly give shade—but at a price. Such trees are usually brittle and crack easily in wind or under ice or snow. This drastic self-pruning is unlikely to accord with one's ideas of the picturesque and often produces something that is grotesque and out of place. So those not wanting to gamble on nature's pruning have to do it themselves in order to keep the trees structurally sound and attractive, and to prevent them from growing out of scale. Often such trees are disease- and insect-prone, so proper measures have to be taken to protect them from all sorts of creatures and plagues. All this takes a yearly commitment of time and energy. Moreover, these trees are often genetically programmed to self destruct at an early age, and an untimely demise of a sizable tree may necessitate the unceremonious use of heavy machinery to unearth the cadaver and cart it off to some funeral pyre. The tree might now be sorely missed, not for the way it contributed to the garden when alive, but more from the hole left by its passing. Its replacement is likely to be much smaller and completely out of scale with the rest of the planting.

On the other hand, there are places like the bottom of a gully, the bank of a stream or lake, where nothing fits as well as a willow or clump of White Poplar, and there's no substitute for an Aspen grove. Moreover, in such situations weather-worn and beaten trees can look picturesque and not at all out of place. With the Aspen and other poplars grown in a grove, the natural cycle of reproduction from seed and runners will constantly renew the planting, so the occasional unhealthy tree can be removed without disturbing the design at all. Here you have all the advantages of rapid growth and avoid many of the disadvantages.

It is sometimes expedient to plant a fast-growing tree close by a slow-growing one that is to be the permanent feature of the landscape, permanent at least in the scale of human lifetimes. When the slow grower reaches respectable size, its stand-in is removed. But in this case the total expense and time involved may be more than the cost of purchasing and planting a larger sized permanent tree, and it might require some very artful planning to come up with a design that will be tolerable during this transition phase. Moreover, competition between the two trees is likely to leave the slow grower at a disadvantage. This is not the same as overplanting a stand of the same species and later removing trees here and there to thin the grove, a strategy that is unlikely to cause either horticultural or design problems.

Fast-growing and ultimately expendable trees are often used in a fresh planting as nurse trees, to act as a buffer against the elements, as with a shelter belt planting. Here a temporary line of weed trees, like Lombardy poplars, will offer wind protection and some shade to a new planting until it can become well enough established to hold its own. Many trees and shrubs are initially tender but quite hardy after two or three years of coddling. When the permanent planting has established itself the nurse trees are removed, although suckers of the more vigorous species may crop up to haunt the garden for years.

For the most part, the design should be based on trees of moderate growth rates, and initial sizes chosen commensurate with purse and patience. Even at a rate of a foot or two a year, a few twelve footers will soon give the shade and feel of a young forest. The ultimate size of the trees and their structural integrity should be of concern, not only for aesthetic and horticultural reasons, but from the point of safety and legal liability. Slower growing trees that are easily managed by pruning can at least forestall these considerations for decades, if not indefinitely. But the faster growing kinds can present a problem within a dozen years.

Another consideration is the amount of maintenance a tree or shrub will require. Will it require elaborate winter protection, say crutches to support its limbs, or a wrapping to prevent sunscald. Maybe the tree requires massive yearly pruning to stay in health and shape. Perhaps it has to be sprayed on a regular basis in order to ward off insects and disease. Or maybe you have to clean up its clutter of leaves, pods, or fruit. These are problems that grow as the tree grows, and are very easy to overlook when thinking about its aesthetic and design potential.

Problems arise with the fast-growing shrubs and perennials also, problems which may or may not be commensurate with the size of the plant.

Once settled in, plants like the larger shrubby junipers, 'Pfitzer', 'Sea Green', 'Hetzii', and so on, can grow unexpectedly large in an unexpectedly short time and may then require a yearly trim. If these junipers are used extensively, a yearly trim grows into a considerable chore.

Flowering quince, barberries, shrub roses and many other shrubs look their best with an occasional thinning, but their thorny belligerence is usually enough to dissuade even the most conscientious gardener from taking the clippers to them.

Removing the faded blossoms from an expansive rhodo collection, blossoms that otherwise would turn brown and hang on forever, might entail nearly as much time as the flowering display itself, and leave you wondering about the fairness of the tradeoff. The same shortcoming applies to extensive beds of daylilies, iris, and many other perennials. And the enthusiastic growth of others, like Physostegia, Lychnis, Rudebekias, and so on, can do much to broaden your definition of weed in just one season. Containing the growth of some of the better ground covers, like the thymes, sedums, creeping veronicas, vinca, Snow-in-Summer, Creeping Jenny, and others, can become a horrendous, time consuming chore. In fact it's their rambunctious, weed-choking growth that makes them so useful as ground covers. But if they invade a perennial planting, the next choice of ground cover might be concrete.

In each of these situations it's usually possible to choose an alternative plant with approximately the same look, but with a more tractable growth habit. For example, the juniper 'Arcadia' can serve as a small 'Pfitzer', 'Buffalo', looks like a restrained 'Tam', 'Miss Jykle' is a restrained *Vinca minor*, *Sedum minor* 'Green Acre Minor' is a dwarfer and more controllable 'Green Acre', and *Arctostaphalos uva-ursi* is available in many clones, some of which are particularly slow growing, low and tight.

As the trees grow from their purchased height of 8–12 ft. to their mature height of 20–60 ft. and as the shrubs grow from their 2 ft. purchased height to some 4–12 ft. and fill out, the appearance of the garden undergoes a profound change. Creating a garden that can be enjoyed from the time it is established to the time it matures is one of the more challenging design problems. Of course there are elements of the design that have a fixed size, like the rockwork, paths, and fences, and those which have a very limited range of size like the ground covers and smaller perennials. But it's this juxtaposition of a 4 ft. perennial with a 6 ft. tree that throws the design out of whack.

In some cases overplanting helps bridge the gap between the young garden and its mature form at least with respect to the density of plant material. For example, junipers used as a ground cover that require some 4 ft. of space between mature plants can be planted initially at 2 ft. intervals. Later, as mature size is reached, every other one can be removed. Trees, also, can be overplanted and later thinned, but it requires a tremendous amount of cold-blooded resolve to remove a young and thriving tree.

Often a design is greatly enhanced by using different sizes of the same species. The effect is not that of a static, climax forest, but rather of a young and vibrant stand in full growth, and such a planting can bring a great deal of pleasure from the moment it is set in place. Another way of achieving the same effect and maintaining it with much less labor is to plant different clones of the same species or even different species that have a somewhat similar appearance but mature at different heights. For example, Austrian Pine and large clones of Mugho Pine go well together even though the Mugho is multiple stemmed. Japanese Black Pines are available in many different clones of varying sizes. The same is true of Japanese Maples, various spruce, flowering crabs, and to a lesser extent Norway Maples, Red Maples, and flowering cherries.

Except for those with a maximum supply of patience and a minimum supply of bucks, a new design will usually call for the installation of several large trees at the onset, although young stock has several advantages. In general, younger plants are much more amenable to being moved—they recover quickly from the experience and quickly get about the business of growing. Shrubs such as daphne, and trees like the taprooted hickories, and some oaks, so resent transplanting that they may curl up and die out of spite. Others, like many of the larger pines, spruce and fir, show their displeasure of being moved by refusing to show significant growth for several years, enough time for a plant purchased at a smaller size to catch up. Still others, like yews, kalmias, and dwarf conifers, are extremely slow growing and so are often prohibitively expensive or unavailable in larger sizes. Of course, planting smaller stock not only saves the buck but also the back.

Yet where patience cannot be stretched over a period of years, the planting of a few large trees gives an instant effect, and provides a microclimate that fosters growth of other plants in the garden, and this may well justify the initial expense and labor.

[6.3] EVERGREEN VERSUS DECIDUOUS

What percentage of the planting should be evergreen? Some have tried reducing this to a formula—not more than 30% says one. But I don't believe that any such formula makes sense.

Some of the most impressive winter landscapes I remember consisted solely of leafless trees: a forest of beech trees in Zeist, Holland, the massive boles of the trees straight, fluted and muscular, setting a mesh of gray twigs and branches against a gray sky; the lean austere elegance of a birch stand along the Connecticut River, or an Aspen grove in Colorado; almond trees in California contrasting their jagged angularity with the precise geometry of the orchard; the serpentine tangle of branches in an oak forest in Pennsylvania. All of these without an evergreen in sight.

On the other hand there is the ethereal beauty of a stand of Colorado Blue Spruce in a light snow flurry—the chill of winter emphasized by their color and the way their limbs serve up platters of snow; or Ponderosa Pines, green laced with white overhead, trunks a rusty orange, fissured and checkered, straddling a trail.

If there is a general principle that can be drawn regarding the balance between the evergreen and deciduous elements in the landscape, perhaps it is this: the longer the winter, the greater the number of evergreens.

[6.4] CLIMATE CONTROL AND OTHER PRACTICAL CONSIDERATIONS

In addition to horticultural and aesthetic considerations there are some mundane but important practical problems that the plan should address.

For example, shade is a most desired garden amenity in many climates. In addition to its garden benefits a leafy shield from the southwest sun can do much to keep the home cool during the summer. The drier the climate the more efficient evaporative cooling is, and a slight breeze blowing through a tree's canopy can reduce the temperature beneath by 12° F. Although conifers cast very dense shade they have less effective surface area for evaporation and are thought to be far less efficient than decidious trees as evaporative coolers.

In the garden it's not just the people who enjoy the climate moderating influence of trees and large shrubs. Many plants appreciate it too, while others are downright dependent on it for survival. Many ferns, woodland flowers, rhododendrons, kalmia, and pieries have a hard time surviving over much of the U.S. unless they are grown under the protection of trees. The deciduous shade lovers don't mind a deciduous host, but most of the evergreens appreciate the year-long protection of an evergreen tree. Conifers confer additional perks. The needles they drop form a mulch that suppresses weeds, conserves moisture, and upon decomposition nourishes and acidifies the soil. In climates with particularly cold and snowy winters, evergreen trees act as a snow catch—a consistent snow blanket is a blessing to shrubs that would be freeze-dried by the winter sun and wind. A snow blanket moderates soil temperature, retarding rapid freezing and thawing which causes roots to split or be heaved from the soil altogether. Moreover, dormancy is enforced preventing premature spring growth that is so susceptible to late frosts.

The use of trees as a windbreak for a planting has already been mentioned, but the house itself might need protection from the wind. Here the conifers have all the advantage and also provide the most efficient visual screen and sound screen.

In addition to these considerations one might have to attend to a sliding hill or a low, wet area, and again the proper planting can do much to alleviate the problem or at least ameliorate it. The challenge is to address all of these practical considerations without sacrificing the integrity of the design.

[6.5] DESIGN PRINCIPLES BORROWED FROM THE ORIENT

Several principles inherent in much of the landscape architecture of China and Japan are eminently applicable to Western gardens. These are simple principles which can be exploited to increase the beauty and interest of a design within virtually every landscape style, without destroying its character.

Principles include:
  i) Framing,
  ii) Borrowed Landscape,
  iii) No All-Encompassing Views,
and iv) Unifying Interior and Exterior.

Framing

"Framing" is a device used to isolate a fragment of a scene and focus attention on it. The fragment of the garden that is framed is presented as something special and usually is designed to be something special. For example, the frame may be an opening in a grove of trees through which the viewer sees a particularly striking rock arrangement. Or the frame might be an open fence gate, or a hedge broken by a path. Commonly the frame is architectural—a door, window, or overhanging eave.

Overleaf. Another view of the author's garden, from another window on another day.

199

Choice window views do a great deal to assure the year-long enjoyment of the garden. The effect is profoundly private and personal—after all, such views are available only from within the home. What better way to experience the rush of spring than to open drapes and be met by a crabapple in full bloom.

But no doubt, framing confers its greatest satisfaction during the harshest seasons when the comfort of the home is in sharp counterpoint to the inhospitable scene viewed through the window: when the damp, chilling mists of March invite no one out, but the crocus, tulips, daffodils and flocks of impatient birds; or when a December snowstorm brocades the trees and the thermometer settles at 0° F and even the birds move more slowly and deliberately, often just sitting on the branches all puffed up and fat against the chill. Maybe it's the window view after an ice storm in February that is most vividly remembered, when the garden seemed forever inert, encased in a sheathing of ice which sparkled with a brilliance that mocked the chill.

Considering all the pleasures afforded by framing and the ease of realizing this principle, it should be a feature in every personal landscape.

Borrowed Landscape

This is the device of incorporating a scene outside of the garden into the design of the garden. The principle has been translated as "borrowing a landscape" or "capturing a landscape". This technique is often used in conjunction with "framing" the view being captured by the frame.

A scene close by with elements common to the garden is seen as a continuation making the garden appear more spacious. On the other hand, if the view from the garden is radically different than the garden, the effect is quite opposite. Then boundaries between properties are emphasized, and the plot appears to be smaller than it actually is.

The second effect is seldom desirable, and in this case it is better to restrict the view by some visual screen. But unless the landscape being considered for capture is totally out of sync, it is usually possible to incorporate a few complimentary elements into the scheme. Just a hint of continuity is all that is needed to suggest that the garden and borrowed landscape are linked. For example, if the captured view is of spruce, one or two spruce trees in your garden can secure the capture. Even trees of a different species that occur naturally in association with those in the borrowed landscape might work. For example pines and Aspen are commonly found with spruce, and look natural with them. An opening in a grove of Aspen provides a perfect frame for a distant stand of spruce, even more perfect when the frame is gilded by crisp autumn nights.

My preference is for landscapes that seem larger than they are, landscapes that offer some expansive view. Gardens surrounded on all sides by 6 ft. fences or high hedges give me a claustrophobic feeling, one more akin to being in a small room than being outdoors. On the other hand, there may be a distinct need to block off some objectionable view, or insulate the garden from extraneous sights and sounds, or simply to have some privacy. These are demands that are in direct conflict with the "Borrowed Landscape" principle. But where no such conflict arises, borrow, capture or steal a landscape whenever you can.

No Point of View Encompasses All

There is a strong temptation to plaster the interesting features of the design against its perimeter and leave the interior free and unobstructed for walking and viewing. This approach allows the entire garden to be seen from any point within its interior—but then strolling yields no surprises. With this kind of design, a small garden shows its size all too clearly, and may even appear smaller than its dimensions.

A seldomly stated principle which is frequently used in the Japanese stroll garden runs counter to this sort of scheme: *No view should encompass the entire garden.* When this principle is followed, the garden seems larger than it actually is, and one must walk through it in order to enjoy its entirety. This device fosters variety without disunity through the use of visual screens to separate disparate features, while paths can be designed so as to gradually and naturally modulate the changes. For example, a rocky outcrop might have a sunny, open, southwest face that houses a planting of scree-loving alpines, whereas its shady northeast side might suggest a rocky woodland. Seen side by side, the two would strike a discordant note, but if no single vantage point encompasses both, they can coexist in harmony.

Another advantage in using this principle is that corners of secluded privacy are created—something which most suburban gardeners regard as a highly desirable feature in a garden.

A barrier can be opaque such as a rocky outcrop, a thicket of tall evergreens, or part of a structure. Alternatively a grove of sparsely branched trees like birch or Aspen can be used to form an open, lattice-like screen which changes character dramatically from season to season. An opaque screen tends to visually cramp the area making the garden seem smaller, while a more open type of screen makes the garden seem larger than it is, and a glimpse at what lies behind serves as a cordial invitation to walk around the screen.

The challenge of creating a garden that honors the principle that no view encompasses the whole is like designing a huge piece of walk-into sculpture. But when the challenge is met a garden of long-term interest is created, and that more than justifies the effort.

Melding Exterior to Interior

So strong is the Japanese love of nature that much of their architecture is designed to minimize any sense of a barrier between the interior and the landscape. Their traditional buildings are not the brick or concrete fortresses of the West which so effectively seal out our surroundings, but are much more delicate in construction and open in design. Unfortunately, in many cases, our buildings are sited on locations which are best hidden away from the senses. But the idea of melding interior to exterior is not new to the West. Frank Lloyd Wright was a great exponent of this approach and widely espoused it in word and deed. His masterpiece "Falling Water" is perhaps his most compelling argument for the principle. The building is sited in a forest in Pennsylvania beside a waterfall. The terraced design mirrors the terraced boulders over which the water tumbles. Local stone was used in the construction to bolster the harmony, and the considerable use of glass dissolves the distinction between dwelling and surroundings. There are extensive bal-

Above. Boulders in the author's garden.
Below. A velvety green moss and an enormous flat boulder combine to make a ground cover of extraordinary beauty at Dream Lake, Rocky Mountain National Park. Even gardens that feature large boulders and stepping stone paths seldom use flat stone slabs as ground cover.

conies open to the sky, sort of half structures that further blend the house with nature.

Japanese design often goes a step further, shunning heavy walls of stone for walls of wood or "shoji" (movable screens of wooden lattice and translucent rice paper). The idea being that the more delicate the building materials the less the sense of a partition between dwelling and nature.

This design philosophy has many adherents in California and other places where a mild climate permits the luxury of such an aesthetic. But for those of us living in climates where there is real weather, some compromise has to be struck between aesthetics on the one hand and habitability and comfort on the other. Besides, very few have the luxury of designing both their dwelling and garden simultaneously, and so those sympathetic to the principle of unifying dwelling and landscape must be content with some approximate version.

Using windows to frame various views of the garden honors this principle to some degree. Houseplants situated by windows and in planters on the patio help a bit. But for most of us, the melding of architectural design and garden design is a goal that can only be approximated.

[6.6] ROCKWORK

There are several distinct styles of rock arranging that are current and popular, some of which are described below.

1) *Let-your-rocks-fall-where-they-may style.* This style is also commonly called the dump-a-load or heap-of-rubble style. It is quite natural, like a rockslide or a building leveled by an earthquake. To realize it, have the trucker back up to the site, and simply dump. The heap is then lightly covered with dirt and planted with some rampant ground cover that will hide it completely. At least it never has to be mowed, and may someday be the site of an archeological dig.

2) *Seed-a-rockgarden style.* This is a style that makes ingenious and parsimonious use of materials. A number of smallish rocks are placed at a considerable distance from each other with the hope that they'll grow and fill in. Although such an arrangement is not likely to disturb the landscape unduly, its low profile makes it invisible to the nearsighted and so it should be roped off for safety.

3) *Mineralogist's style.* This is a style dear to the heart of all rock hounds. Here, a collection of stones, as disparate in character as possible, is assembled and displayed for their individual novelty and interest, usually on a bed of sparkling quartz or spanking white, marble chips. The integrity of the design is sometimes marred by placing plants nearby, say within a hundred feet or so. Again, this is an arrangement that can be recommended for its ease of maintenance, and although it will accumulate dirt after awhile, nobody will give a damn.

4) *Chain-gang style.* This is something like the "let-your-rocks-fall-where-they-may" style, except freshly quarried stones are stacked to show as many cut edges as possible. The character of the rock is important. Each should be cut with some precision in a facsimile of a tombstone so that they can be easily stacked. This style is ideal for games of king-of-the-mountain, and it, too, should not be cluttered up by plants.

5) *The iceberg style.* This is a time-honored oriental style which dictates that 8/9 of the rock be buried under ground. The very act of burying the rock is fraught with meaning, and the underground part is thought to be the most significant.

I do not bury 90% of the boulder as some have done in Kyoto, or even 40% or 50% as is common practice there. My pocketbook won't permit such extravagance and my sense of thrift would be offended. I don't see the limit to this dictum. Why not bury 99% of the boulder and leave only a pimple. Conspicuous consumption. Potlatch gardening. Pretentious earth works art in the style of the day. Some even say that this approach gives the composition the feel of power and permanence and provides the viewer with a sense of the real weight of the stone. But knowing half of the rock was buried would only weigh heavily on my wallet. The bottom of my feet are too calloused to detect those powerful below-ground vibes. My Zen imagination can't override my frugality. Deep setting is only warranted if the shape is such that leaving more exposed would expose some ugly portion or create a form that's ugly or unsuitable. If the stone is set in a stable position, appears stable, and contributes to the composition, I consider it well set.

In fact, I'm so frugal that I use scavenged concrete slabs as underlayment for any rock arrangement consisting of several levels rather than building up layers by burying perfectly good rock so that others can sit on top. Although freshly set concrete will leach a considerable amount of alkalai to the surrounding soil, concrete weathered for a year or so is virtually inert. By tailor making the soils that fill the seams, one can grow acid lovers or alkaline lovers with equal ease.

I even use slabs of concrete as a footing for large boulders that are to sit at ground level, but I don't know why. If the boulder has a relatively flat bottom, it should settle and sink at a rate no greater than the heavier combination of boulder and concrete slab. Certainly the stability is not increased by using the slab. But I have the concrete, so I do it out of stubborn habit and superstition. According to the same sources that advocate burying 1/3 to 9/10 of the volume of the rock, the Japanese seat their boulders on sand or gravel. This might facilitate making minor adjustments in the position of the rock once placed, but otherwise I see no reason for this practice either.

For those seeking a source of inspiration outside of the above styles we suggest a hike in the mountains, or along a rocky coast or river bed. Look at the rockwork to be found in the wild—the boulder outcrops, the canyon walls, the rocky stream beds, and moraines. Here one finds more than enough ideas and inspiration to rock over the entire planet.

What size rocks should one use? Some say the bigger the better. When boulders are being used as decorative elements per se, this is not a bad dictum as long as the space around the rock is not so confined as to seem to imprison it or set it off like some monstrous gemstone or freak. The guideline is simple enough. The rockwork should be in harmony with the rest of the garden. But there's the rub. The rest of the garden will feature trees and shrubs many of which will be set in place well before they reach their mature size, and therefore the scale may be wrong at all stages of growth except one. The 6 ft. boulder that trivializes a 5 ft. pine will later be trivialized by a 30 ft. pine. Here is a real design challenge. Create a design that will be satisfactory from start to finish.

Contouring the land into hills and valleys often adds considerable sculptural interest to the garden. This does not necessitate the construction of a Mount Fuji or the excavation of a Grand Canyon, but something larger than a molehill is called for. Hills on the order of 2–6 ft. in height are usually quite adequate in the scale of a personal landscape. From a design standpoint the contours establish a rhythm for the eye to follow, guiding it from one corner of the garden to another, while at the same time blocking the view of certain portions of the garden.

Furthermore, there are several horticultural advantages to be gained by contouring a site into hills and valleys. On a lot like ours where the dirt is atrocious—impermeable clay laced with bentonite in which no self-respecting thistle would condescend to grow - mounding improves drainage immeasurably. Moreover, by ad-mixing amendments to the stuff, special soils can be custom made to the tastes of the most finicky plants. A hill of scree can be constructed for the pleasure of alpine plants, or one of peat for the ericaceous ones. The resulting perfect drainage prevents the buildup of salts that usually becomes a problem after a few years when a peat bed is installed at ground level. Of course, the low points are useful too, they cater to the water hogs—those bog dwellers that don't mind standing in standing water.

Even a 30 degree slope will give you the edge on exposure, enabling you to grow plants that would fail on the flat. A south or southwest facing slope is the spot for those drought-loving steppe dwellers or Mediterraneans that need to basque in the sun. This exposure is the first to clear of snow and so undergoes the most wrenching changes in air and ground temperature. A northeast slope, on the other hand, particularly one planted with some shrubs, is far more moderate. There is less exposure to the sun in summer and far less in winter. The snow on the slope lingers, providing smaller plants with an insulating cover—a blanket that protects them from the wind, insulates them against more severe cold, prevents the alternate freezing and thawing of the soil, and prevents the flow of sap in the winter that occurs when the sun warms a woody plant sufficiently and often causes the wood to split at night when the temperature plummets.

A dramatic example of the effect of snow cover is seen near timberline. Alpine fir creep along the ground, sheared to a height of 3 ft. or so with a precision that a topiarist could brag about. This shearing is the work of the wind and sun hacking away at the new growth which is exposed above the snow cover.

However, there is a drawback to hill plantings. They usually require more effort to maintain, particularly if weeding or mowing is a concern, and one or the other will be unless the hill is concrete.

Other reasons for moving dirt from here to there on a large scale include the preparation for a pond, a stream, or God forbid, a swimming pool. But for whatever reason, if extensive regrading is called for, or a considerable amount of soil preparation is needed, one either has to bring in some heavy machinery or rewrite the marriage contract. Assuming that the first option is chosen, the machinery has to be brought in early in the construction, before the installation of a sprinkler system, paths, and plants.

This is also the time when the major rockwork should be set in place, another project for heavy machinery unless all the boulders are wimpy or one has the resources of Pharaoh. It is possible to move sizable boulders by people power, and I have the scars to prove it. For me there was no other choice since our current home came complete with a lawn and sprinkler system, but nothing else. Stones of ½ ton were moved with the help of a hand dolly, two strong sons, and a wife harnessed to the handles. Much larger stones can be moved across relatively flat ground by sandwiching rollers in the form of wooden rods or metal pipes between a plank of wood resting on the ground and another plank on top. Once the boulder is shoved, rolled, or coaxed onto the top plank, it can be pushed along by a three-year-old child. However, even if you have a three-year-old child, this kind of work is most efficiently and safely done by the dumb machinery that blesses this century and is almost always worth the expense.

Unlike many other components of the garden, the land contours and the position of massive boulders will be unalterable fixtures and so deserve more care in their design and placement.

With the grading and rockwork completed, a sprinkler system can be installed. Those who live in a region with hot, dry summers and have a passion for mosses, ferns, rhodos or other plants that benefit from a cooling fog on a hot summer's day should consider installing automatic misters. The misters themselves are inexpensive and use a modicum of water. The resulting evaporative cooling can be significant, creating a little oasis, a microclimate where both man and plants feel more comfortable on hot summer days.

The sprinkler system, too, is usually placed where it will remain, and since the well-being of the plants will be dependent on it to a large extent, it deserves to be planned with special care. However, neither the contours, rockwork, sprinkler system, nor planting can be designed independently of each other in spite of the fact that their time of installation will be different. Each has to compliment the other horticulturally, and with the exception of the sprinklers, visually.

[6.8] HONOR THY NEIGHBOR

Deference, courtesy, local covenants, or even the law might unavoidably cramp your style. The law seldom grants artistic license. Should one's desire for privacy conflict with a neighbor's desire for a view, the local covenant might give him the edge and force that unkindest of cuts, the beheading of a tree or a grove of trees, and the need to redesign and replant an entire section of the garden. This is unlikely to improve the over-all design of the garden or the relationship with the neighbor.

Another potential source of contention is the clutter a planting might shed into a neighbor's lot. Autumn winds that sweep your garden clean could cover his in leaves. All the unpicked fruit, unreachable and worm-eaten, might be blown off to rot in his yard. This summer's crop of samaras could give rise to an unwanted regiment of volunteers stationed throughout his plot.

A planting can cause more serious offense. That Norway maple or cottonwood seeking to secure its hegemony might spread its roots far into a neighbor's garden, perhaps even invade his sprinkler system or septic field.

Large spreading trees that are strong of spirit but weak of limb present several non-trivial hazards. A major branch cracked off in an ice storm could flatten his Ferrari or open a skylight above his living room. Since these mishaps usually occur during winter, the skylight might be particularly unwelcome. In these cases one doesn't have a case, and it may be time to read the fine print in the liability section of the homeowner's insurance policy.

In addition to these major affronts the garden can offer various minor ones. These usually involve something one likes, but at a distance. The flowers, fruit and autumn color of *Viburnum trilobum* are superb, but the blossoms are malodorous so it's planted away from the house against a neighbor's fence. Siberian Maple is delicious in flower but attracts bees, so it too is planted away from the house against the neighbor's fence. The raspberries are a necessity for the fruit but aggressively thorny and run uncontrollably, so they are placed away from the house next to the property line.

Usually it pays to consider such possible annoyances before the design is finalized and the planting begins, or at least before the lawyers are contacted. Often it is possible to strike some compromises between art and the neighbor's concerns and come up with a design that can be lived with and enjoyed, one that changes in response to the owner's desires and not the county law.

[6.9] AND THEN

In view of all the previous considerations the project of designing a garden may now seem hopelessly complex. This is because there are so many possible goals and so many ways to attain them, and such a wondrous diversity of material to work with. However, this is what makes it possible to create a uniquely personal garden and makes the chore an exciting, creative challenge.

As soon as one decides what the main objectives are, the complexity of the task and the number of approaches is quickly reduced to manageable levels. A stock of examples, man-made or natural, further reduces the complexity and brings the goal into sharper focus. Then it's time to conceptualize a few of the possibilities and visualize some of the alternatives. Part II of this book is intended to facilitate this stage of the process.

Views of the author's
garden, this page and
opposite.

210

Right. Nannyberry
(*Viburnum lentago*) in
autumn.
Below. A variegated form
of *Miscanthus sinensis* is
set aglow by the western
sun.

In the author's garden. Even the commonest plants like Pfitzer Juniper, Redtwig Dogwood, and Austrian Pine have uncommon splendor after a snowstorm.
To the left, visual haiku—a terse but exquisite note to the end of autumn and the beginning of winter.
Opposite page. Ordinary cottonwoods and willows laced with snow.

Winter lingers in the author's garden. Opposite. A Corkscrew Willow by a stream that runs black in winter even under sunny skies. Right. Austrian Pines finally yield and sag under heavy snow. Below. Like an oriental carving in ivory—a Black Chokeberry in snow.

Scenes from Rocky Mountain National
Park that suggest garden designs.
Above. Stacked stones on the shores of
Dream Lake.

216

Right. Aspen abuting pine, Bierstadt Lake Trail. One is often cautioned to give each plant in the garden enough space so it can develop its species' characteristic shape. Nature often ignores this dictum, creating novel and striking compositions of disparate colors and forms. It's a device that works very well in a naturalistic setting. Below. Juniper forms a ground cover below Aspen along Bierstadt Lake Trail. They are common companions in the wild, although Aspen is usually thought of as a moisture lover, and juniper as a dryland plant.

217

A borrowed landscape above
and opposite. The stream
defines the property line and the
author borrows the spruce and
junipers from the neighboring
garden of Mike and Loretta
Tucker.
Left. A section of the author's
front garden is framed by the
patio.

219

The foothills of the Rockies as a
borrowed landscape—highly
recommended.
Above. From the author's patio,
framed by a Honeylocust.
Left. From the front garden of
Dick and Frieda Holley.

Right. It isn't the Golden Pavilion but the neighbor's redwood deck does add an oriental touch to the author's garden.

Below. A section of the author's garden is framed by a window.

221

A neighbor's fence is
borrowed to complete a
section of the author's
landscape. Compare with
pages 200–201.

Two views, one direct and one reflected, of a superbly framed courtyard garden in the Engineering Center of the University of Colorado at Boulder.

CHAPTER 7 *Meditations of a Mad Gardener*

[7.1] LASTWORDS

Gardening is my pleasure—from the planning stage right down to the dirt. Groveling around on all fours, begging for yet another kick from Mother Nature, I may bitch and complain from spring to autumn. But as soon as my October railings are done I begin to dream of another spring.

By December the plant catalogs start trickling in, I no longer walk with a Neanderthal stoop, and there is no detectable shoveling motion in my handshake. I begin to entertain the projects for the next spring. Come January and February I can't wait to get my hands on the shovel and work up a sweat, to be out on a sunny spring day breaking my back once again. Will the garden be finished this year? Fat chance!

I don't want this garden to be finished, not ever. A great measure of the joy and pleasure is derived from working it, maintaining it, planning it, and watching it slowly evolve and mature. When the growth of the trees and shrubs overtake my lagging inspiration and outstrip my muscle to move them around, when I no longer can play musical plants, I'll move and start again.

If my back gives out before my eye or my mind, I'll retire to to the foothills, lake, or streamside, give up the bulk of those tedious chores like weeding, maintaining a lawn, moving rocks, and planting trees, and take more time to enjoy the doings of the Great Gardener.

But in the meantime, I'll continue to tend to those mindless garden chores though there are other things I'd much rather do on a Sunday morning. One can probably argue that mowing is healthful exercise, more relaxing and mentally less taxing than watching the weekend lineup of TV ball games. You don't have to remember that Mooney Winsome bats 320 overall, but only 210 against Oily Boid because Oily is a lefty and Mooney is a Protestant. It's not as demanding as hockey where a slap-shot can easily be confused with a cheap-shot. Nor does it require the attention of basketball, where one has to be able to distinguish between a double dribble and simple incontinence, even while distracted by the bouncy cheerleader with the bouncy basketballs directing a thousand-voice hallelujah chorus of air-heads chanting a-i-r—b-a-l-l, a-i-r—b-a-l-l, a-i-r—b-a-l-l. All one has to do is push the damn mower.

[7.2] TO VISIT AGAIN

My main complaint is that there isn't enough time in the span of a human life to pursue the art of the garden to any great extent. How little opportunity one has to become familiar with those out-of-the way gardens, seen once or twice and then only briefly. There is even less opportunity to realize the imagined gardens—those that are planted in the mind and develop out of sight of all but one.

I would like to visit Kew again and enjoy the orchid houses, catch the Victoria Lily in bloom, enjoy the great palm house, the filmy-fern house, the Australia house, and most of all, the enormous variety of trees and shrubs planted on the grounds. I wish to visit the Humbolt Arboretum again and see the miniature underwater gardens displayed in dozens of superbly aquascaped aquaria—Cellophane Plants, Amazon Plants, Madagascar Laceleafs, dozens of cryptocaryne species, all grown to perfection as nowhere else, without a blemish to tell of accident or disease. I wish to see the Borghese Garden in Italy again, but this time without a mob of other tourists obliterating its tranquility and masking its geometry and sense of time and place.

However, the "gardens" I most want to return to are less well known and more inaccessible—those seen at enough length to make a startling impression, but fleetingly enough to allow the imagination free rein to enhance and embellish what is already extraordinary and exotic.

Venice, Italy

From my dreary room in the penzione, I could look out over the filthy rooftops and hear the ceaseless, grinding arguments of trains blowing off steam at each other, screeching to confront the next mob of tourists, snorting impatiently as the tourists boarded, and then clangorously banging out of the station. But below the drabness, in a small courtyard, surrounded on all sides by centuries-old, dingy, brick walls, was a monastery garden, laid out in precise squares, rectangles, and circles, and planted with flowers, small fruit trees, and vegetables. With great patience and skill the monks coaxed a plentiful bounty from this small plot in the heart of the city, despite the pollution and the stingy issue of sunlight admitted by the surrounding buildings. In its perfect blending of utility and beauty, in the peace and contentment communicated by the monks caringly tending it, this tiny formal garden moved me more than the grand geometry of the Borghese Gardens. Indeed, in its brave show of beauty and self-sufficiency in the grimy core of the city, it moved me far more than any other formal garden I have seen.

Between Campinas and São Paulo, Brazil

I remember my one and only glance at a climax forest of araucaria seen from the window of a speeding van on the way from Campinas to São Paulo to catch a plane.

All the trees had grown to the same enormous height, and all were perfect in their absolute radial symmetry. Each tree had its place; the branches of one barely touching those of its neighbors—little or no undergrowth—a garden as is. The foliage of a Brazilian Auraucaria is as black a green as that of any conifer, and the color and form of its parts made the stand seem more like the girder skeleton of some gigantic building complex rather than a living forest. How curiously contradictory for a tree of such ancient lineage to present such a contemporary image. How strange to find it in the tropics where helter-skelter is the usual rule of growth. Here was another definition of a formal garden—formal by inherent structure and not by imposed design—constructed by nature in the constructivist idiom on a scale she usually reserves for her free-form style.

Too excited and too disappointed in not having been given the opportunity to visit the place, I dispensed with the courtesy that my gracious hosts so well deserved, and asked why I had not been taken there. I was told there was the danger of poisonous snakes, that the land was privately owned, and was a wild and useless place anyway. This is a typical reply to such a question throughout most of South America where public lands and national parks are virtually unknown, a cause or a reflection of a general lack of interest and appreciation for the wondrously rich and varied natural beauty that graces that continent.

The Brazilian Araucaria is a popular landscape tree in much of South America. One sees it in public parks and private estates, almost always as an isolated specimen. Grown in this way its huge size, dark color, and uncompromising symmetry dominate the landscape, formalize it, and reduce all else to an inessential embellishment. I have never seen them planted in a grove so as to capture the appearance of a forest. Of course, this would require considerable space, but the effect would be extraordinary. What would it feel like to walk through such a grove? Could one maintain a sense of time and place. Would the sighting of a pterodactyl be surprising? Might such a garden transcribe to suburbia, or is it impossible to accommodate its size and unique form in such a setting. Maybe it's even out of place in the subtropical Brazilian landscape. Maybe it should be the sole plant on the Galapagos Islands. Maybe it's the only plant that can stand behind the stone heads of Easter Island. On the other hand, maybe it can transcribe to a personal landscape on a large site backing a low, stone dwelling. But then what else could be planted with it? What else would be needed?

Outside of Caracas, Venezuela

I remember a trip from cosmopolitan Caracas through miles of impoverished, tin shantytowns, to the Venezuelan coast and paradise. The beach we sought access to was privately owned by twenty or so individuals. My companions told the guards that I was a wealthy Gringo with pockets full of U.S. dollars (the dollar was a currency to contend with then) and was interested in purchasing a piece of beach property. That, and what was equivalent to a five-buck tip, gained us entrance into paradise.

A fair-sized river leisurely wound its way to the shore through a tamed but wildly luxuriant forest of palms, Jacaranda, Flame Trees, and an understory of philodendrons, gingers, Birds of Paradise, Monstera, Cyperus and bamboos. Epiphitic ferns and orchids lifted the flamboyance overhead so that the garden surrounded one on all sides as well as above. Clearly a planned garden, but like any planned garden in the tropics it showed the struggle in keeping with its design and a tendency to return to jungle. The garden succeeded in keeping the jungle at bay without making it heel, and this tension between control and flat-out, unbridled luxuriance made it as exciting and exhilarating as any garden I have seen. Sensual throughout, and offering the senses a full measure of pleasure at every turn—exotic fragrances of exotic blossoms seen and unseen, enormous leaves in manifold shapes and textures, leaves that know neither hail nor frost, some furry, some smooth as patent leather, some creped or puckered and many patterned and painted in colors that flowers or birds in temperate climates would be proud to wear—all in such abundance that it was difficult to perceive an over-all plan; just a richly textured, highly scented, and brilliantly colored exuberance cascading down to the beach.

This theme of abundance was carried to the white sands that collared the cove in a 50 ft. wide expanse where well-tanned women strolled the beach, not bare breasted as the site suggested, but barely strung with string bikinis—more string than bikini in accordance with the wonderfully sensible style of the tropics. Looking back from the sand, it seemed as likely a place as any for the site of Eden.

This was the embodiment of my dream of a tropical paradise, a dream that grows more vivid as each December marks its passing on yet another bony joint of my anatomy. Maybe, when more warmth is needed to route my hormones about, I'll move to Florida and give such a garden a try. But then I fear that some sympathetic resonance will set up between my mind and the climate causing me to langorously vegetate away the rest of my days in harmony with the garden.

Between Bogotá and Medellín, Columbia

In Bogotá, I asked about the weather. "There are four seasons, two wet and two dry, and the temperature remains in the seventies for most of the year", I was told. Within a couple of hours drive of Bogotá one can ski above the line of permanent snow, or stroll on the sands of a tropical beach, or trek through a tropical rain forest.

It was somewhere between Bogotá and Medellín that we found ourselves on a small coffee and sugar cane plantation, the plaything of an incredibly wealthy businessman who vacationed there one month out of each twelve. The location was subtropical, warmed by a near-equatorial sun and cooled by its elevation and the breezes which roled off the hills. Here the year-round temperature and humidity was as perfect as anywhere else on this planet, so perfect and reliably constant that the weather was not an interesting topic of conversation. The plantation realized barely enough profit to offset the upkeep of its small mansion and the retinue of servants and farm hands who cared for it even during the owner's eleven-month yearly absence. The spacious garden surrounding the house was neatly partitioned into verdant islands of various shapes and sizes by paths and drives that led to the house. Each island had its own interest—some featured a boulder arrangement and a grove of small palms or bamboo, others a bench or a fountain and a Jacaranda tree, or an Orchid Tree, or a Datura. On the patio and in the islands, orchids grew in pots, on cork, and on tree-fern slabs. Besides a sizable number of indigenous species: cattleyas, epidendrums, and laelias, there were all sorts of exotics like cymbidiums, dendrobiums, and paphiopedelums, many blooming prodigiously.

At the rear of the house the garden spread out to meet the hills where the high jungle alternated between regular plantings of coffee and sugar cane. A bracingly cool stream made its way out of these hills to cascade from a height of 15 ft. into a large, irregularly shaped swimming pool, tiled at the bottom, but edged with boulders so as to fit quite naturally into the garden scheme. Giant Monsteras made their way upward on each side of the falls, and a host of tropical and subtropical plants in the ground and in pots availed themselves of the moisture that the falls and pool fed into the air. Philodendrons and strelitzias, camellias, hibiscus, gardenias, azaleas and fuchsias, exotic ferns and callas and cannas and more orchids basked in the warm sun and cool, moist breezes.

Halfway between city and jungle, this garden fused urbane formality with rustic informality. Borders and paths were tiled and precisely laid out—not in totalitarian, toe-the-mark straightedge, but rather in flowing free-form, clearly delineating the half dozen, disparate, small gardens while tying them together into a harmonious whole. Exotics mixed with native species to create a planting sophisticated enough to reflect the owner's status, means, and taste, and casual enough to blend with the wild surrounding and take the edge off the unavoidable ostentation. It was a garden for casual and refined living where a well-heeled urbanite would escape from the frenetic realities of the world of big business and take his ease for a few weeks. Indeed, this place irresistably encouraged every visitor to relax and enjoy the incomparable climate and the tamed and untamed landscapes.

I was told that the region had many such estates and that Medellín was famous for its private gardens. I wish I had seen them then. That was nine years ago, before the coke barons had fully sunk their talons into the country. Many of them settled in Medellín so it is no longer safe for a gringo to visit. Maybe in a few years the world will have had its fix and Columbia will be able to heal itself—but I doubt it.

Near Santiago, Chile

I remember Roli's garden on the outskirts of Santiago—a gentleman farmer's garden maintained to provide a few treats and staples for the table as well as give pleasure to the eye. The climate is maritime like that of the San Francisco Bay Area. The political climate is far less temperate—alternately hot with anger and deep chilled by repression.

The garden occupied about 5 acres. A third of it was given over to a grove of old almond trees precisely planted in a latticular array. Although long past their prime as fruit producers, they continued to gain character. Their time of greatest distinction was in November, mid-spring in the Southern Hemisphere, when they set the most delicate pink blossoms in contrast against their leafless, black and knobby frame whose angularity chronicled the year-by-year struggle to reach for the sun in spite of the orchardist's sequiturs.

Another third was given over to a vegetable garden of no special distinction except for the excellence and abundance of the harvests, a reflection of the gardener's skill and a most benevolent climate. There were two small groves of eucalyptus, each with only a dozen or so trees. The eucalyptus has such power of regeneration and rapidity of growth that these two groves were the sole source of firewood for the farm. A pig sty was partly hidden by one of the groves; its odor was not.

There was an abbreviated soccer field and a small swimming pool surrounded by a hodgepodge of spectacular plants including a huge, variegated agave, crassulas of several sorts, and some camellias.

The rest of the garden, about 20% of it, was given over to ornamental plantings. There were magnolias, more camellias, a small rose garden, and a huge auraucaria towering over all.

This was a garden of relaxed informality. Certainly not one in the "natural style", but its hard-edged geometry of precisely laid-out beds and walks had been softened by years of benign neglect, and the garden approached natural canons more and more each year. Nowhere have I been more at ease or more comfortable than in this bucolic yet sophisticated garden. Rich in innuendo, rich in variety, rich in purpose, the history of its various owners is entangled with its design and the way in which the garden was maintained. Fascinating and intimate, it is as personal a statement of aspirations, priorities, and tastes, pruned by economic and political realities, as one can find in the art of the garden, and I loved going there both to relax and to work.

One hazy summer afternoon in December, seated on the farmhouse porch, immersed over my head in some mathematical problem I've long since forgotten, my concentration was broken by the squeal of a pig being butchered out by the sty. Half an hour later, there was this huge pig, clean shaven to its pink skin, lying on its back overfilling a wheelbarrow, being pushed with great difficulty along the path of the rose garden. A slaughtered, pink pig in front of a hedge of scarlet roses all set off by the blue grandeur of the coastal range. Cruel and gentle, absurd and sublime, a garden of contradictions, well suited to a country of contradictions.

Zeist, Holland

I remember a great beech forest in Zeist, a forest I came to know rather well over a period of several months. Three days a week our family ran the mile-long obstacle course laid out there, a sort of human steeplechase that no equine with horse sense would choose to run, but the winter was unusually mild, and we had the company of those grand beeches.

They stood like a battalion of giants in close formation. Unable to spread to their full width, they presented themselves at rigid attention against Holland's winter sky, gray against gray, their huge boles fluted and muscular under the skin-taut bark.

The forest floor was black and spongy with the decay of centuries of beech leaves—a black velvet setting for the glistening mosses and saliginellas which grew there, and the extraordinarily beautiful polypore fungus, looking like sheets of agate shingling the decaying hulks of the fallen trees. A cool, damp forest with a somber mood, not darkly so, but meditative.

I would like to see this park in full leaf under a summer sun, if the sun ever shines during Holland's summer. Entering it then must be like entering an enormous cave—a sudden drop in temperature, a sudden eclipse of light, and a deep solitude. Nothing claustrophobic about it though, it's too vast, too expansive, and its dome is too high. Maybe it's most like a Black Oak forest in the eastern United States. But the beech trunks are more massive, more columnar, taller and closer together, and they support a leafy canopy that is much denser. I don't think there is a close analogy between a beech forest and any other.

Even a single beech is too much tree for a small, private garden. But for a proper estate, or at least an estate-sized lot, what could be more impressive than a grove of beech—a living cathedral, mysterious, cool, musty, and opulent.

[7.3] GARDENS OF THE IMAGINATION

There are other gardens that I dream about, gardens that exist only in my imagination. Had I a cat's share of lifetimes and the necessary material wherewithal I would build them all. But in the meantime I continue to nurture them in my mind where the upkeep is minimal, help is cheap and willing, and there are no mosquitoes.

A Garden of Brushed Stainless Steel

I have in mind a garden of brushed stainless steel, icy blue and seemingly cool on the hottest day, detached, remote, and a bit mysterious, cast out of Blue Spruce, the most silvery blue with the longest needles, like 'Thomson's' variety. Ground covers would match, restricted to blues and grays only. 'Wiltoni' junipers, Pussytoes, and Snow-in-Summer would fit the bill nicely. I could tolerate a spot of yellow from the flowers of Lavendar Cotton or Chamomile in order to get their silvery grays. White and blue flowers would be so welcome that I might admit a modest patch of green to support them—Siberian Iris, Shastas, and Asters would do. I could even tolerate, indeed condone, some metal lawn furniture, painted white and not too Roccoco. Here, in the surreality of this garden, one could dream up many others, or write a poem, or prove a theorem.

A Cypress Garden

I have such a fondness for water and for those plants that have a deep affinity for it that I often imagine a garden of islands situated on a sizable lake.

Swamp Cypress would be the predominant tree, planted in clusters and small groves right at the water's edge, and on the rises. A decidous conifer, the Swamp Cypress offers a strikingly different appearance in each season. The feathery, dark green, summer foliage turns a bright golden brown in the fall. Its winter form is starkly dramatic, with a rapidly tapering trunk whose steep lines of convergence from its unusually wide base create the illusion that this tall tree is much taller than it actually is. In the spring, the spare, naked power of its winter aspect is muted by a cloak of delicate, feathery leaves in the brightest of lime greens.

All sorts of marvelous shrubs are candidates for the understory: Bottle-brush Buckeye, with its extraordinary mid-summer display of upright pannicles of white blossoms above the palmately compound leaves, would be a top choice, as would the Eastern Dogwood. False Spirea, chokeberries, and various viburnums would be favored. And of course on the higher ground, azaleas and Mountain Laurel would play a prominent role.

There is certainly no want for perennials that would enjoy such a situation. One could use primulas and macleaya, lythrum, and ligularia, ferns and hostas, rodgersias and iris, contrasting the delicate and the bold in an almost tropical manner. Sedges and grasses are a must at the water's edge, and the lake itself would feature water-lilies.

Of course, a bench would be needed at lakeside where one could sip Jack Daniels and read a bit of Tennessee Williams.

And Others

There are all sorts of other gardens that hang in the mind, like a garden based on Sassafras trees, or Sugar Maples, or Red Maples, or some large, green-leaved clone of Japanese maple. Any of these will contradict the prophecy of winter by setting autumn afire. Or consider a garden dominated by a grove of Sargent's Cherry. This is the largest of the cherries grown primarily for flowers, although this one has typically superb cherry bark and atypically brilliant fall color. A planting of these will prompt spring with an explosion of pink that is unrecognizable by any other season. Where shade is not a major consideration, imagine a design with a predominantly vertical motif, one based on fastigate clones of English Oak, or Ginkgo, the groups of trees skirted by flat-growing junipers like 'Broadmore'. This is a garden where some narrow upright conifers could be used in groups here and there with good effect to emphasize the verticality of the composition and contribute some textural contrast. Or imagine a large garden with broad lawns and several groups of Lebanon Cedars, each group like a vast temple, whose free-form columns (the boles of the trees) are spaced widely enough to allow generous paths to wind between them but close enough so that their crowns meld into one contiguous canopy.

This daydreaming is pleasant sport but I'd much rather be out in the garden puttering around, redesigning this and that, or just allowing my senses free reign. Not that daydreaming and down-to-earth gardening are in any way incompatible—indeed each fosters the other. But still, I would rather be out in the garden savoring the scents, sounds, and sights directly.

What a luxury it is to have a private landscape; what an endless source of challenge and interest. Every effort is fruitful and every concern is repaid—or at least frequently enough to keep enthusiasm at high pitch. Almost every error is correctible and few decisions need be final. No other environment is so forgiving, so encouraging, and so rewarding. Though there are many gardens that I want to visit and many that I would like to construct, my own holds a lifetime of pleasure, and I enjoy it more each season and look forward to the next season as though it were going to visit the garden for the very first time. Of all earthly delights, none surpass the private garden.

PART II:
THE PAPER GARDEN

CHAPTER 8 *Designing by the Book*

[8.1] THE PLAN

Can't place perspective in perspective? Wonder where vanishing points disappear to? Feel more confident rendering chicken fat than botanical subjects? Don't despair. The method described here requires no drawing skills whatsoever, and even those who are accomplished draftsmen will find it faster and more efficient than drawing. The technique can be used to create overhead views as well as ground level views, both of which are needed to effectively visualize the full, three-dimensional aspect of a design. The garden can be pictured in leaf and out of leaf, and even at various stages of growth.

Only the following items are needed to implement the technique.

1) A **plat map** giving the exact shape and dimensions of the lot, the size and location of the house, driveway, walks, and public easements, will prove to be a great convenience. A plat map is usually transferred to the new owner of the property at the time of purchase, but if it has been misplaced a copy can be obtained from the office of the county clerk. Of course a layout plan can be made by taking careful measurements; but this is a hassle if the shape of the lot is complicated.

2) **pen** and **ink** (both white and black) that can be used on plastic are useful but not necessary.

3) Access to a **copier** capable of making transparent copies on plastic from opaque originals and vice-versa is essential. Copiers that reduce and enlarge offer an additional advantage. Most copiers have these features, and most commercial copying firms can supply this service at a very nominal fee.

[8.2] GROUND LEVEL VIEWS

The design method suggested here makes use of plant forms printed on sheets of transparent plastic. Here is a step-by-step description of the process:

1) In the appendix there are several pages picturing various tree and shrub forms. These are generic forms in the sense that they are not intended to accurately represent specific species but rather any plant having the given shape. The designer selects those shapes that have a potential role in the plan and copies them onto transparent sheets.

2) The transparent sheets are cut into cards so that each card has a single plant form.

3) The sections of the drawings which represent light colored plant parts are made opaque by applying white ink. For example, forms that are to represent trunks and branches of Aspen or Paper Birch should be penned over in white ink. On the other hand, dark tree trunks should be made opaque by applying black ink. In either case, if trunks and limbs are left transparent, forms placed behind them will be read as being on the same plane, a confusing and misleading effect that is easily avoided using pen and ink.

4) The cards are then arranged on a sheet of white paper or cardboard until a satisfactory design is attained. Overlaying one card on another gives the appearance of one plant being in front of another. This facilitates a design that makes full use of three-dimensional space.

5) The cards are then secured to the paper or cardboard by transparent tape, and the design is copied onto white paper.

[8.3] OVERHEAD VIEWS

The bird's-eye view of the suburban garden is unlikely to be appreciated by any except the birds, but it's the view which most accurately indicates the position of the various design components. Here is where a plat map comes in handy. The map itself can be copied, piecewise if necessary, and enlarged or reduced as required. Cutouts of the various overhead views of plant forms are then moved about on the map until a suitable design is found. As with the lateral view, the cutouts are then fastened to the map with transparent tape and the assemblage is copied.

It is often easier and less confusing to use opaque overlays rather than transparent ones when designing the overhead aspect. An opaque overlay is obtained by copying the plant forms directly onto opaque paper and then cutting out the form. On the other hand, if the design has many layers with the upper ones shielding the lower ones from view, as is the case when the plan features broad-canopied trees above an understory of shrubs, both opaque and transparent overlays are useful—the opaque being used to represent the understory planting and the transparent overlays to represent the upperstory.

The drawings of the overhead views that are provided are more abstract and schematic than those of the lateral views since plant differences are often less apparent when viewed from above, and simplified forms facilitate "reading" the design. Moreover, the loss of realism is of little consequence in a view that will be unavailable.

The overhead and lateral aspects are usually developed simultaneously, modifications of one calling for modifications of the other. This is easily done with the techniques described above and hopefully most will find the task game-like and entertaining.

Besides its usefulness in organizing the woody components of the design, the method is easily adapted to all sorts of other applications, like the planning of rockwork and perennial beds. For example, in the latter application a clump of a certain perennial can be represented by an amoeboid blotch of the appropriate color on transparent plastic, or simply by a cutout of colored paper without the transparent backing.

[8.4] EXPANDING THE PAPER ARBORETUM

The supplement is easily augmented if one does not find the necessary variety or quantity of forms needed for the design.

For example, iterating enlargements on the copier will grow a sequoia from a thuja in a matter of minutes. Enlarging is also helpful in visualizing the garden after some years of growth. Reducing rather than enlarging allows big trees to beget little ones after their own image, creating a garden of miniatures in no time at all. And copying in the original scale will clone a forest with exponential speed.

Besides altering the size of the image, variety can be obtained by positioning the trees at varying angles, by scissoring off or whiting out unwanted parts, by inking in embellishments, or flipping a transparency over so as to reverse the image.

New additions to the paper arboretum can be gleaned from many sources. Drawings yield the most customized additions. Photographs of plants can be copied or traced. A black and white photo on high contrast film works nicely, but even an ordinary black and white photo can be reproduced and given more contrast by most copiers. If the process is repeated several times the grays are washed out and the result looks like a line drawing. Any of these images can be modified by applying black and white ink.

In addition to enlarging the arboretum, these techniques can be used to supply the design with all sorts of inanimate accouterments—boulders, birdbaths, lanterns, bridges, follies, and gazebos. The more whimsical can affix a photo of Mt. Fuji as a backdrop to the garden or replace the house by a photo of the Golden Pavilion. Add a touch of class by picturing Botticelli's Venus rising from the lily pond. For something more scandalous, try setting Manet's Picnic on the front lawn, or reclining his Olympia in some secluded corner; but check the covenants before actually installing such a design.

[8.5] OTHER VISUAL AIDS

Even with plans showing both overhead and ground-level views, it is sometimes difficult to work out the exact placement of components. This is when props—makeshift standins for the various designs can be a considerable help.

For example, wooden poles can be driven into the ground to establish the position of a tree or the spatial relationships between the members of a grove. Boxes and buckets of all sorts can represent shrubs and boulders. Hoses can delineate paths and boundaries.

Even people can be used as standins for trees or shrubs when wooden stakes seem too wooden or too fastigate. But people usually tire of standing still after a few hours—everyone wants to vegetate in his own way and in his own time. So for the most part, it is best to rely on inanimate standins.

Although the technique of designing with opaque and transparent overlays is fast and easy, the process should not be rushed. The design will never be as readily modified as it is in this stage. Cards are moved much more easily than trees, and reducing an image on the copier is far more expedient than pruning a stand of shrubs or heading a tree. In fact the method is so efficient that one might as well compose several alternative designs, imagine what each will offer in the various seasons and over the years, consider their relative installation and maintenance costs, and then decide which will best realize that private paradise.

CHAPTER 9 *Figures*

The preceding chapter describes a procedure for designing a landscape through the use of transparent overlays. This chapter provides drawings which can be copied onto sheets of plastic to make the transparencies.

In order to use the images as prescribed they have to be separated by cutting the plastic copies, making it necessary to arrange the forms so that they do not overlap. This was done in figures A-1 through A-26 which should not be construed as landscape designs. On the other hand, figures A-27 and A-28 are intended to illustrate the method of building up a design using the technique described in chapter 6.

For the most part the forms were drawn in black and white only since some copiers do not reliably reproduce grays. The stippling seen in the overhead view of a spruce tree in figure A-6 was originally drawn in gray and black, and then copied by a Thunder Scanner (software product of Thunderware Inc.) which interpreted the grays by a stipple pattern.

In several figures copies of the same form appear in various sizes—the reductions having been made on a copier.

The shapes illustrated are intentionally ambiguous, and are intended to represent any of several plants having approximately the same form. More or less plausible interpretations are suggested below.

Figures A-1 through A-4 feature pines like Austrian, Japanese Black, and Ponderosa, but in desperation they can be taken to represent Scot's, Japanese Red, Eastern White and others. A-4 is a bird's eye view. Scrawny, deciduated tree forms are included in A-3. These can be taken as birch, Aspen, and many others. The deciduous shrubs in A-2 and A-3 can represent hollies, dwarf viburnums, rhodos, euonymous, and so on. The shrub form in A-1 can be taken as a Red Twigged Dogwood, Bayberry, Winterberry, Chokeberry, and many more if one is not too picky.

A-5 and A-6 focus on spruce, fir, and less convincingly, hemlock. Overhead views are included in A-6, while A-5 shows some deciduous shrubs (see above) and another in leaf, perhaps a barberry, privet, pyracantha, or who knows what.

A-7 through A-10 feature shrub forms in both lateral and overhead views. Those with an unfettered imagination might see junipers, chams, thujas, yews, dwarf spruce, fir, and hemlock. Among the broad-leaved forms search for barberries, cotoneasters, nandina, privets, quince, rhodos, euonymous, mahonias, lilacs, viburnums, etc. A-10 also pictures some narrow deciduous tree—maybe a poplar, alder, oak, maple, Ginkgo, or linden to name a few that are available in fastigate varieties.

A-11 represents some poplars and willows; stretching the imagination, some cherries and crabs might be suggested.

A-12 and A-13 feature elm, Honey Locust, or maybe Hackberry along with a few shrub forms representing some of the species mentioned above.

A-14 gives us two more shrub forms and the outline of an oak, beech, linden, maple, or any one of several other megatrees.

A-15 pictures overhead views of shrub forms along with a lateral view of some yew or juniper, and a decidiated tree—say Metasequoia, Swamp Cypress, or linden. Of course some of the overhead views of shrubs can be taken to be groves of trees, and the tree form can be read as a dead spruce if one is a brown-thumb pessimist.

A-16 is a bird's eye view of four deciduous trees in an arrangement that is as uninspired as possible.

A-17 pictures a trio of decidiated birch, Aspen, Japanese Maple, some hawthorns, or other tree of like elegance. The same three trees are pictured as a three-stemmed clump in A-18, while A-19 is an overlay of A-18 by A-17 with A-18 rendered in gray to clarify the relationship.

A-20 and A-21 show the same three-stemmed Japanese Maple (or hawthorn, or some other light and airy species) decidiated and in leaf. A Mugho Pine and some other shrub share A-20 while two rhodos or the like share A-21. The smaller shrub in A-21 was reduced from the larger by the copier.

A-22 shows birch or Aspen in leaf, the clump of three made up of the three singles; and the shrub might be Fatsia, viburnum, or just wishful thinking.

The left side of A-23 gives us a plum, apricot, cratagus, crab, or other; the right side might be a fastigate clone of linden, drab, cherry, young oak, or young maple. The shrub might be barberry, spirea, some shrub rose, or cotoneaster—but your guess is as good as mine.

More megatrees are illustrated in A-24, this time in full leaf. Lets say the one on the left is a maple, oak, beech, or ash, while the one on the right might pass for an elm, Honey Locust, or Hackberry to the indiscriminate. The shrub is another your-guess-is-as-good-as-mine.

A-25 gives us another maple, oak, or ash. On the right are two shrubs, one a reduction of the other, that can play the role of Kerria, or barberry, or chokeberry or whatever. The one on the left is a different sort of whatever.

Fig. A-26 is dominated by another elm, locust, or Honey Locust. Maybe it's a young Norway Maple, Pagoda Tree, or Silk Tree. Conceivable it's a Washington Thorn. It might even be some sorbus species. The shrubs are what you make them. Grape Holly or true holly on the left: Creeping Grape Holly, dwarf quince, lilac or mockorange below right; chokeberry, Winterberry, thinned barberry, quince, etc. on the far right.

Fig. A-27 illustrates the use of transparent and opaque overlays to build up a ground level plan.

Fig. A-28 is an overhead view of a part of the author's garden. Compare with the photograph on pages 200–201. The three deciduous trees near the patio are Honey Locusts; the deciduous tree at the bottom is a crab apple. Except for the Mugho Pine at the lower right, the others are Austrian Black Pines. The penninsula in the center features Aspen—spectacular in all seasons against the dark backdrop of pines. Creeping Grape Holly skirts the Aspen and complements their gold by scarlet in the autumn and then turns purple for the winter. The shrub at the upper right is Nannyberry and that in the upper center is Boulder Raspberry—free flowering and growing strongly in spite of heavy shade. In front of the Boulder Raspberry are *Daphne retusa* and *D. tangutica*. The evergreen shrub to the right is a Pfitzer Juniper. Not indicated is an understory of "Sea Green" junipers beneath the Honey Locusts, and "Wiltoni" junipers around the crab apple and Mugho Pine. Sheltered beneath the leftmost pine and also not indicated is a small woodland rockery (see top photo, page 204). Bluegrass is the ground cover in the Y-shaped region, and gravel covers the area outside of this region.

Fig. A-29. It's been a long winter.

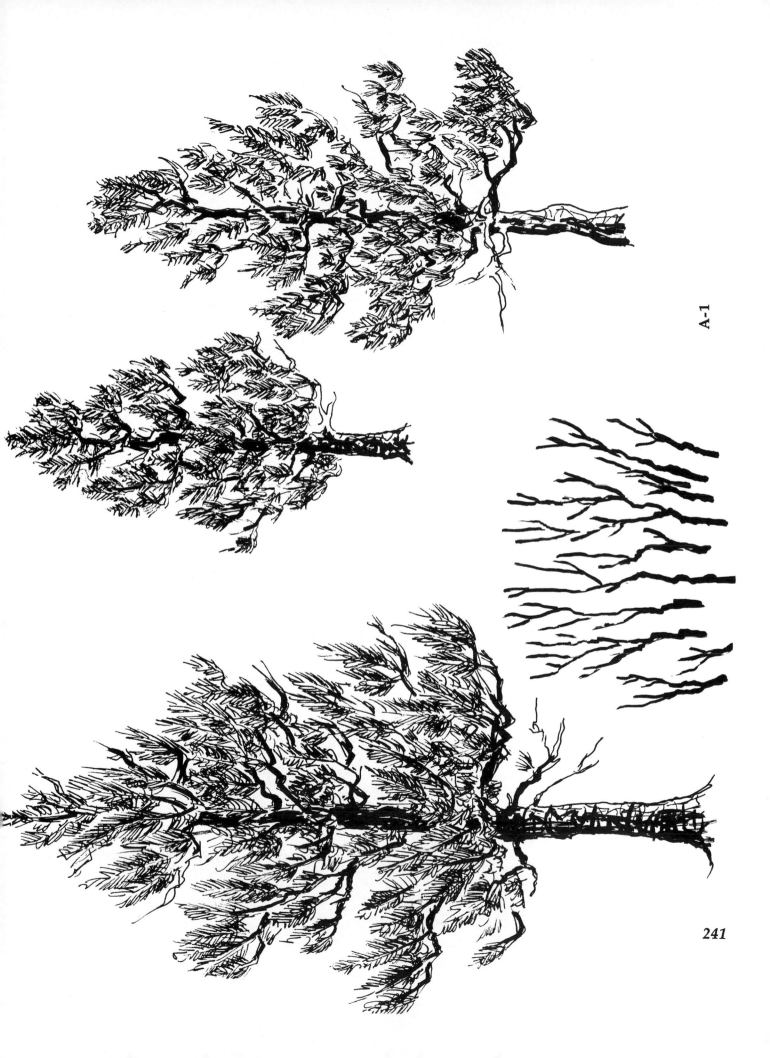

A-1

241

242

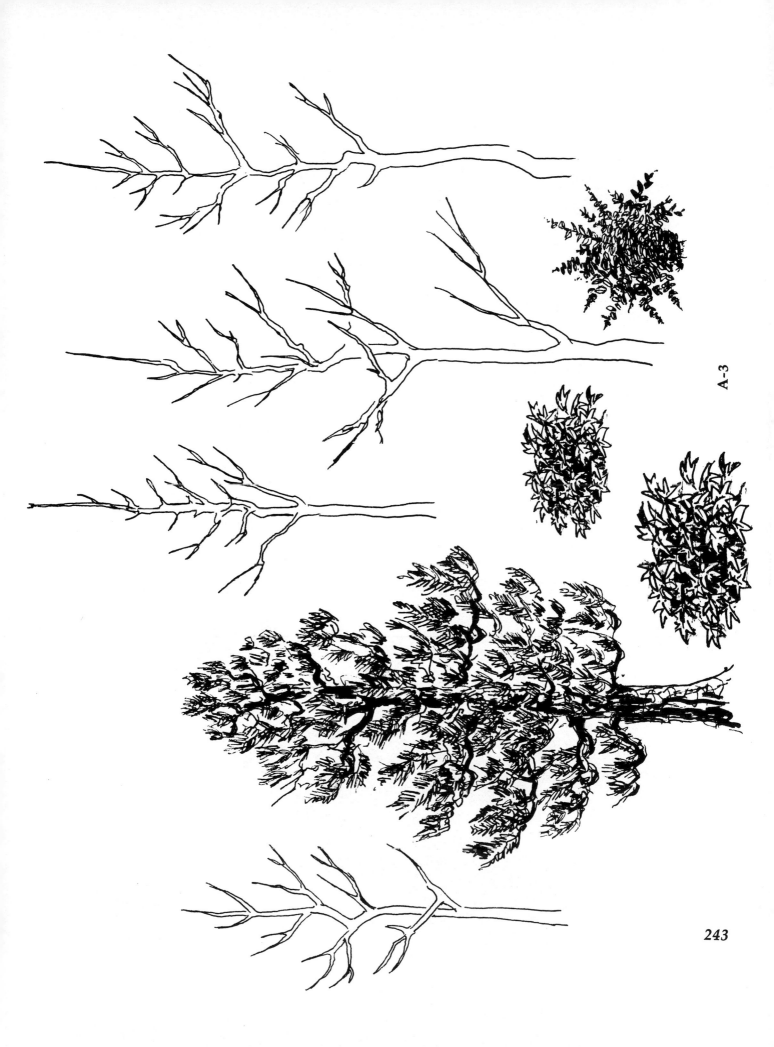

A-3

243

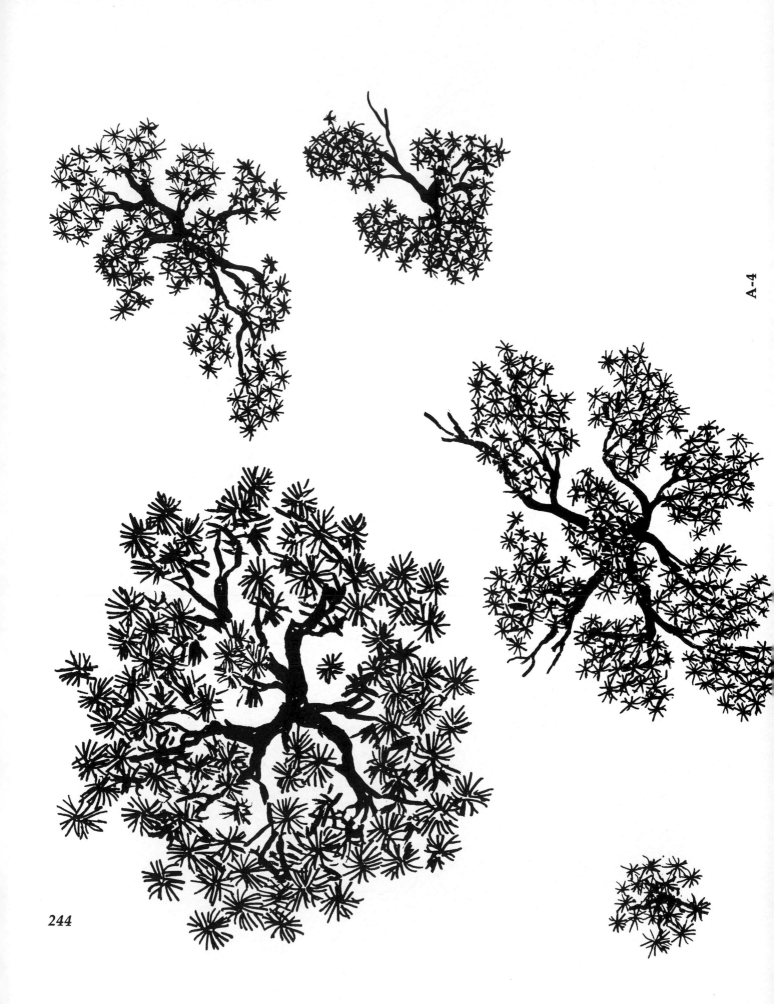

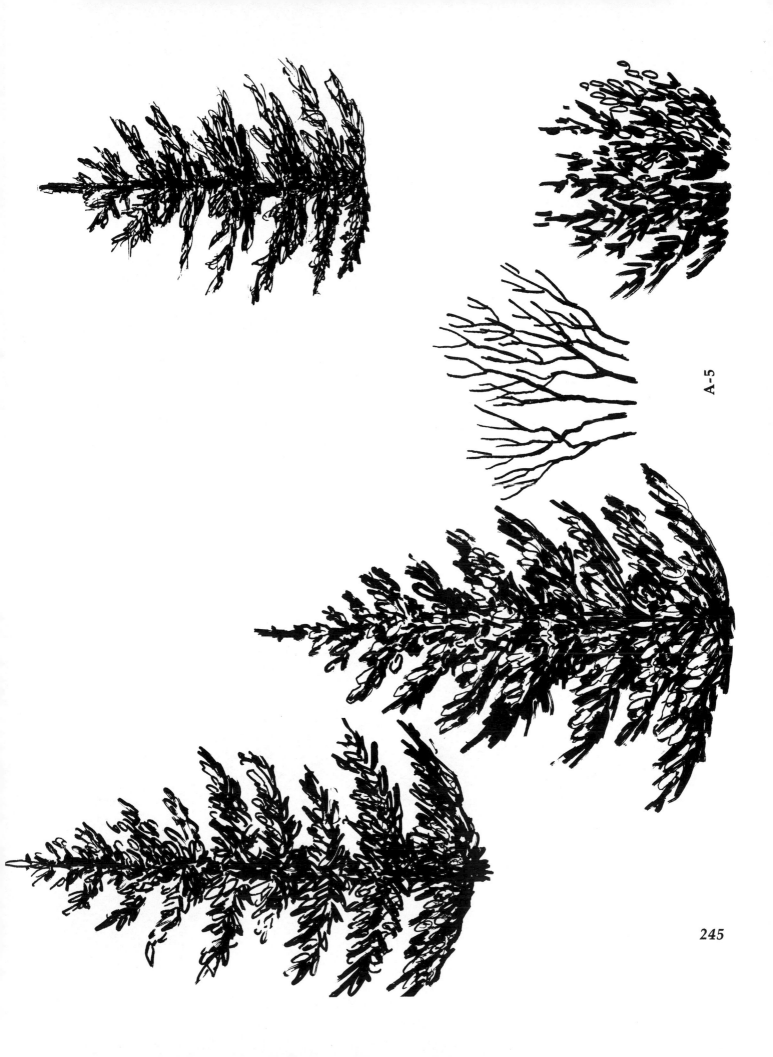

245

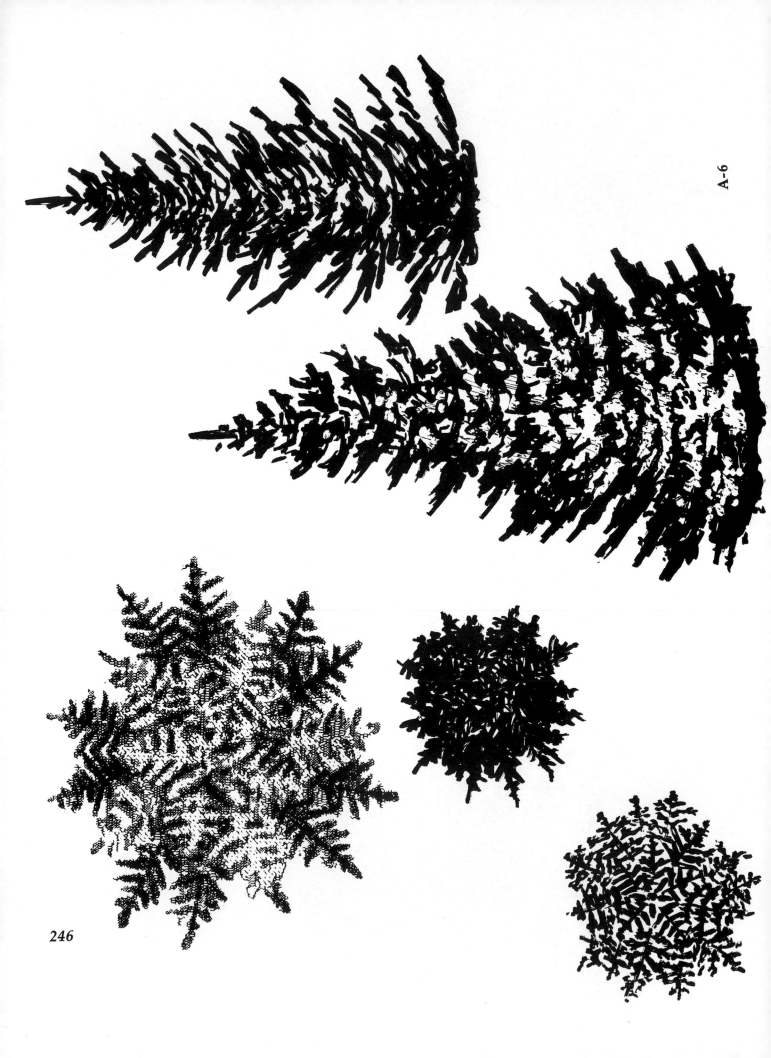

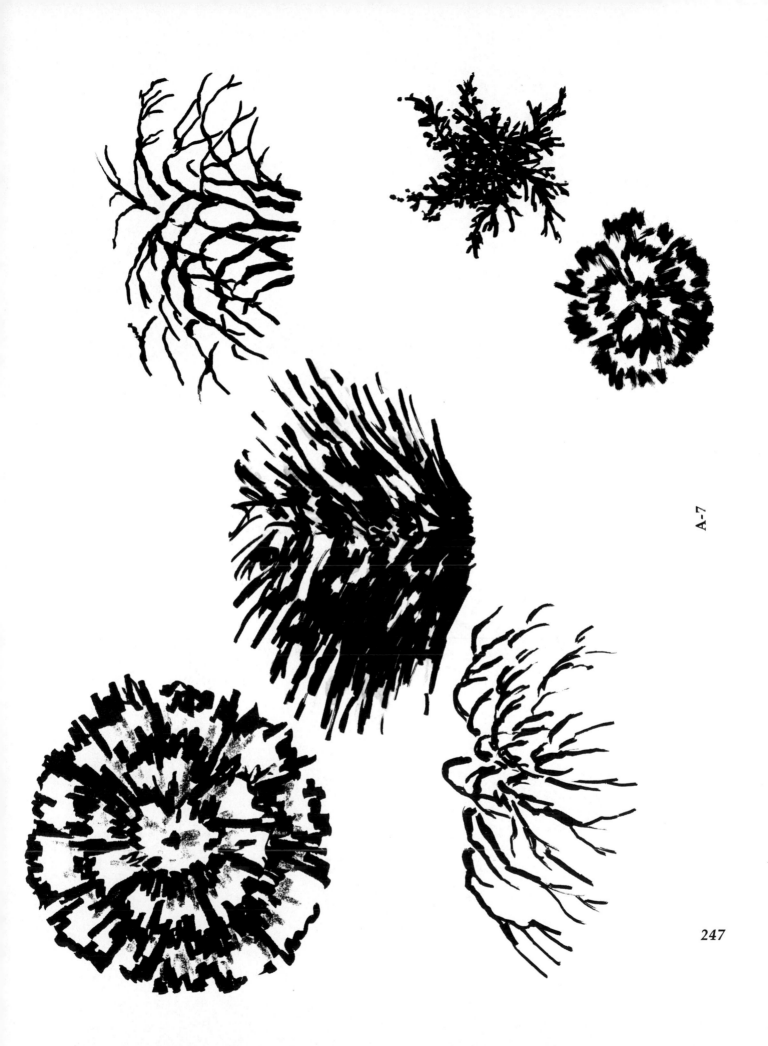

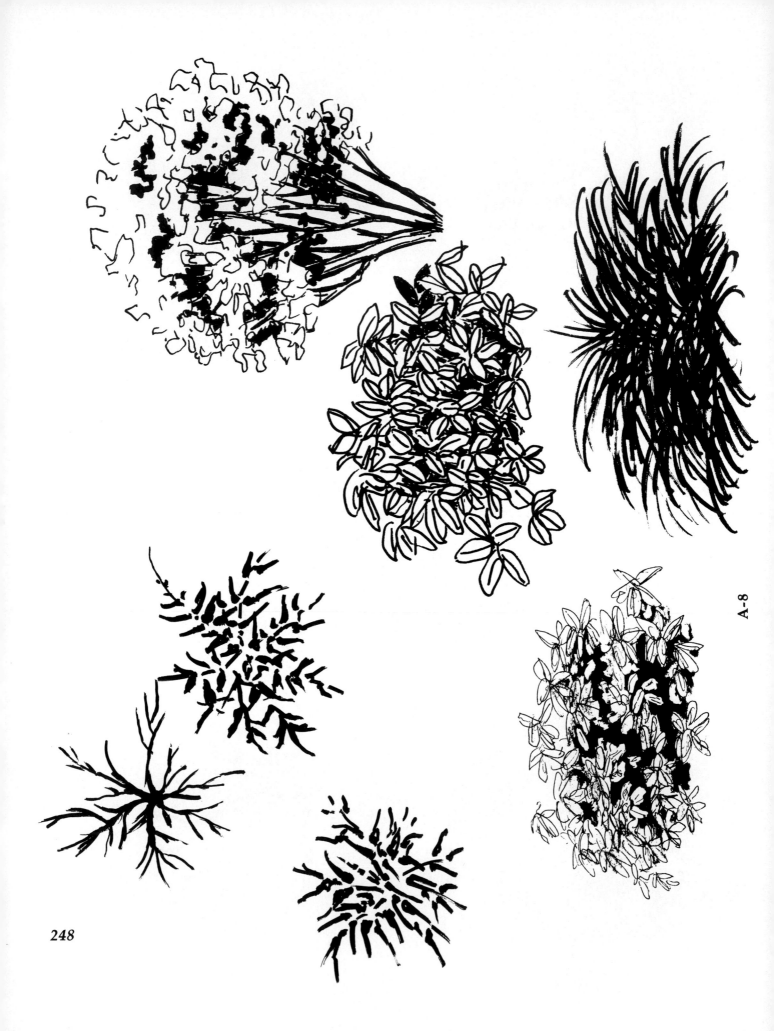

248

A-8

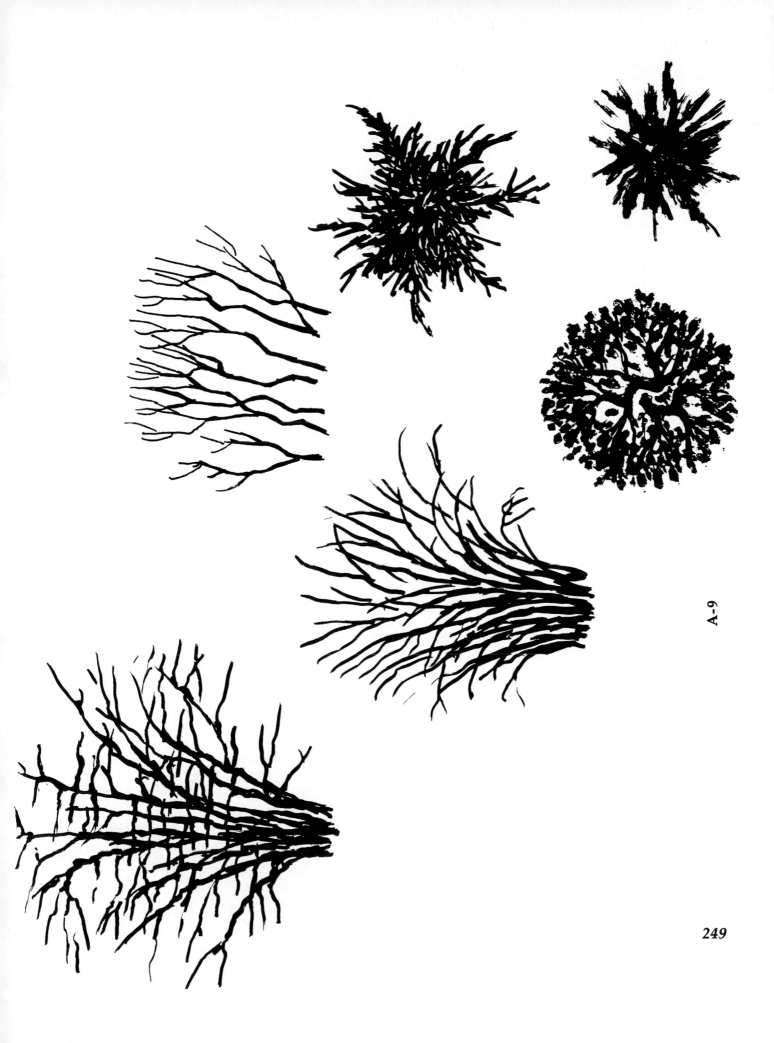

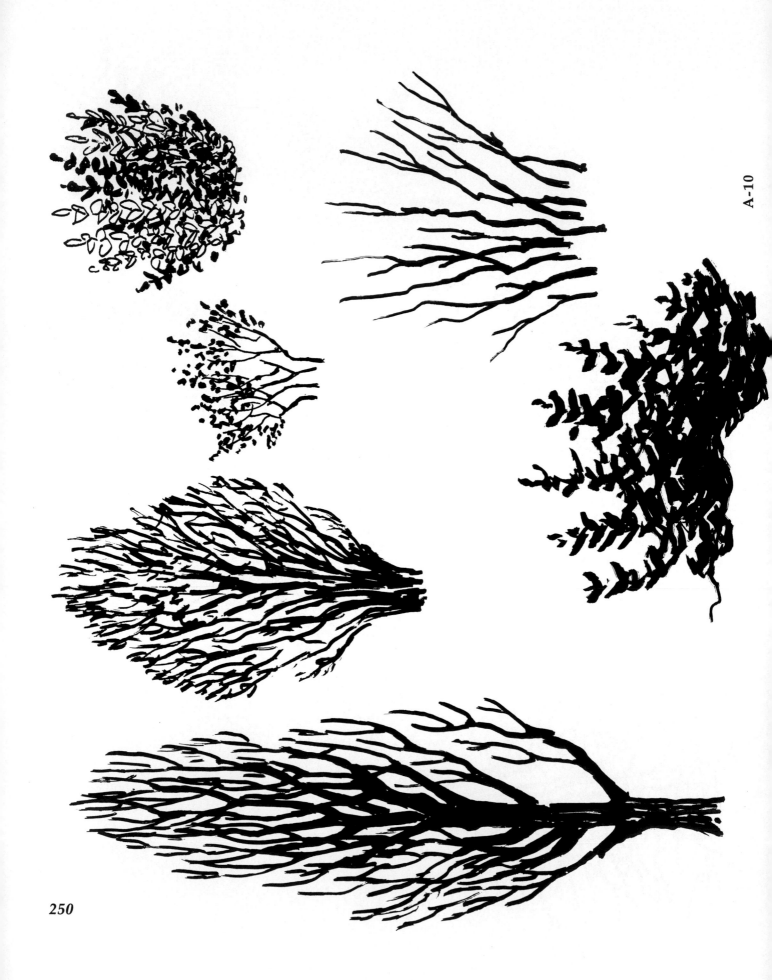

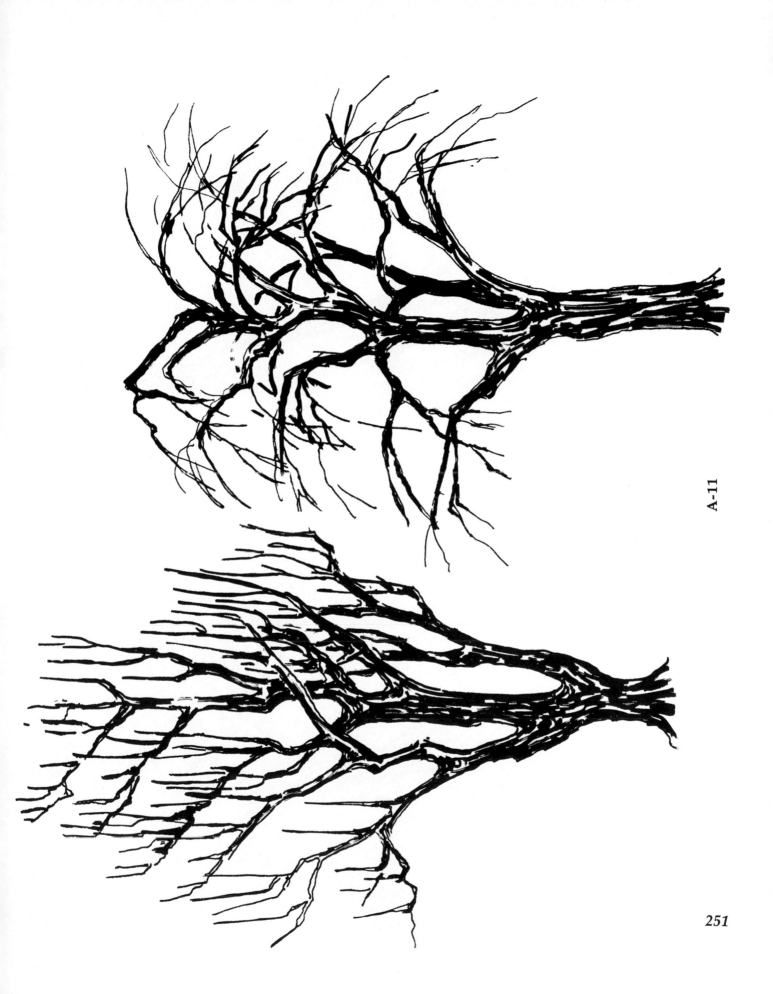

252

A-12

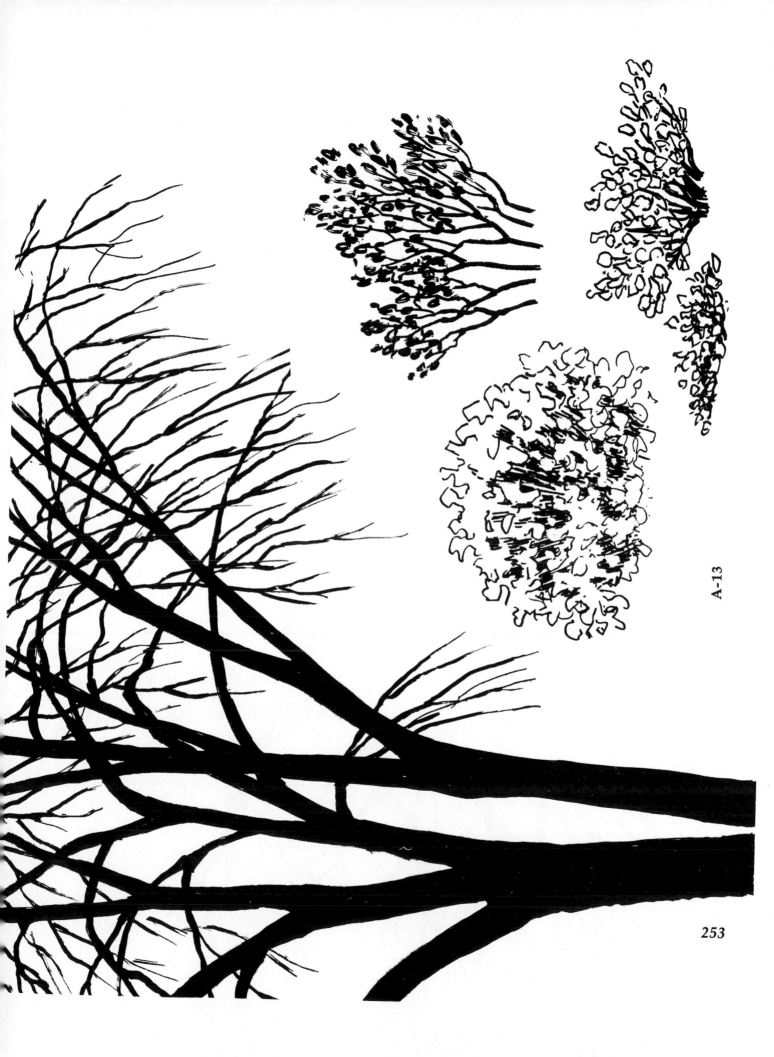

A-13

253

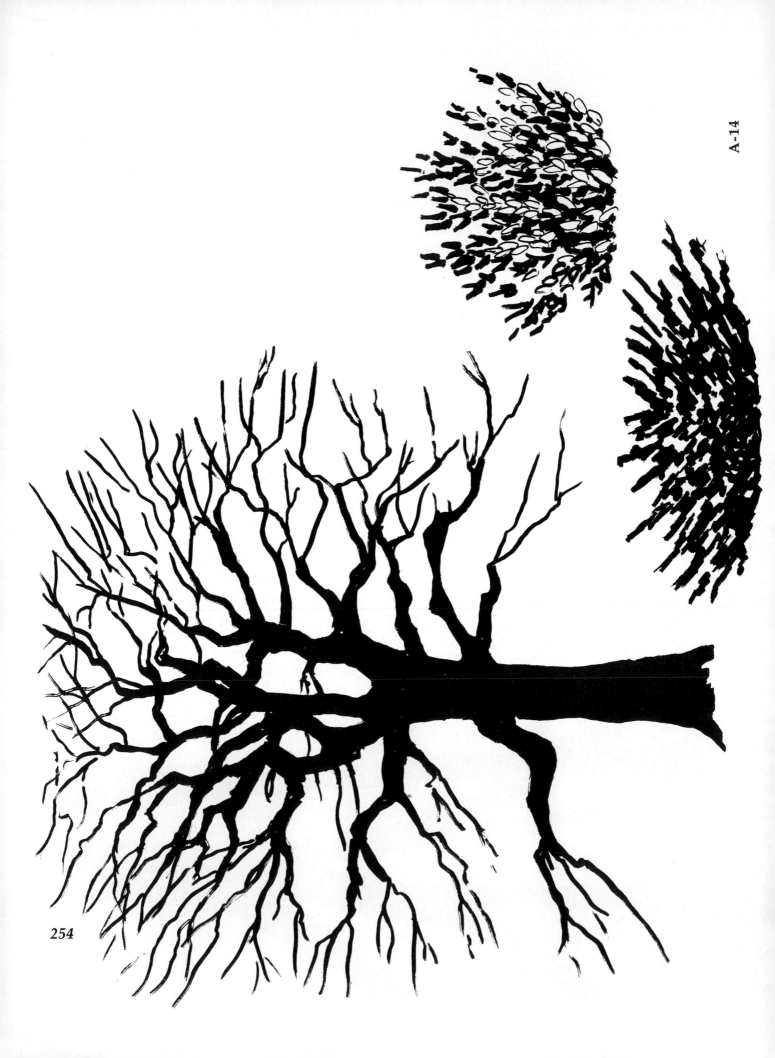

254

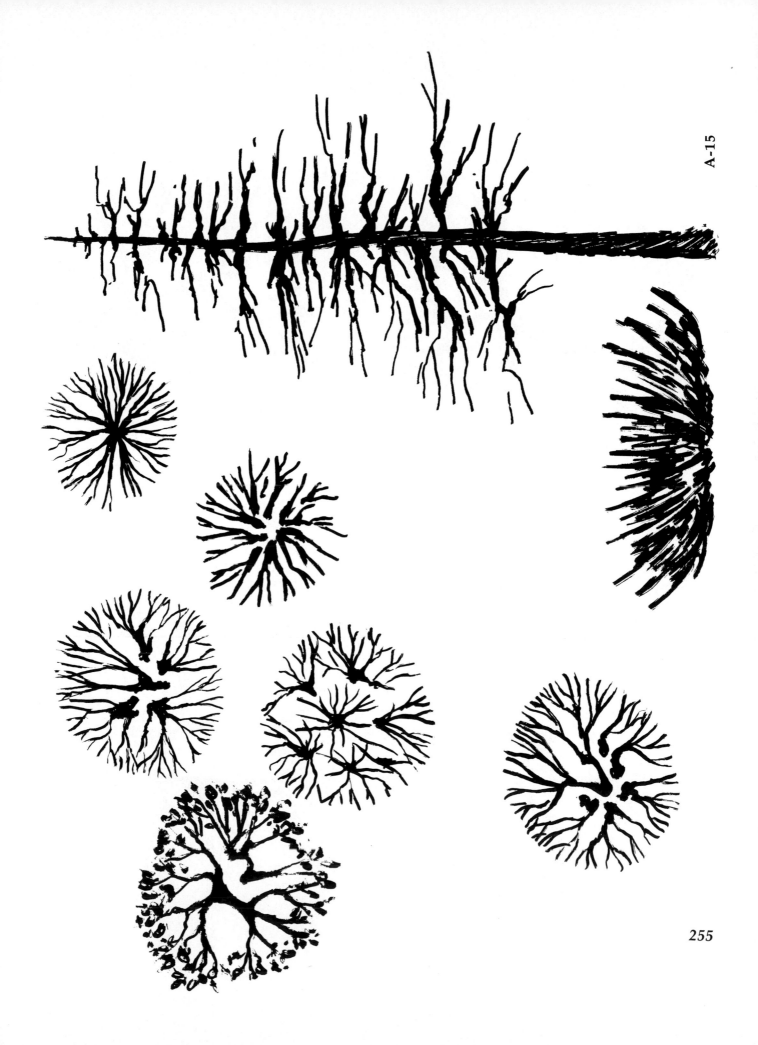

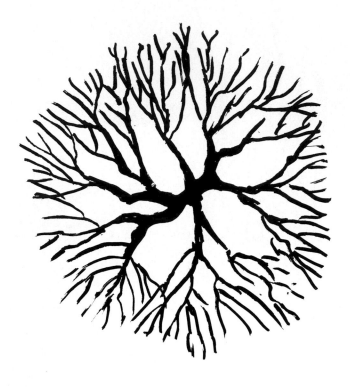

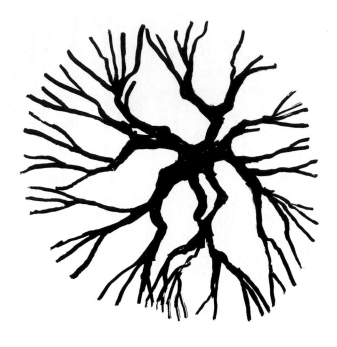

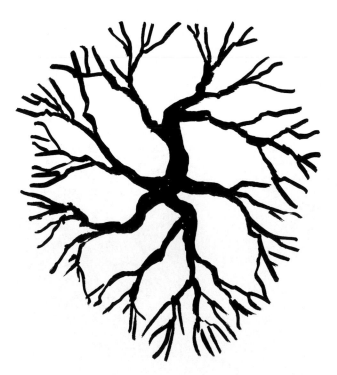

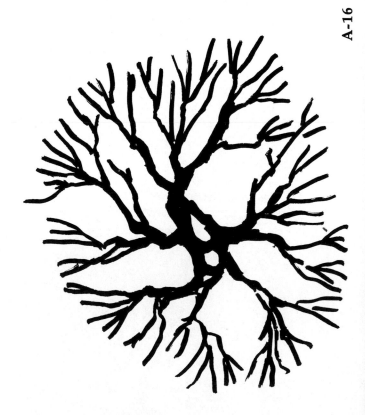

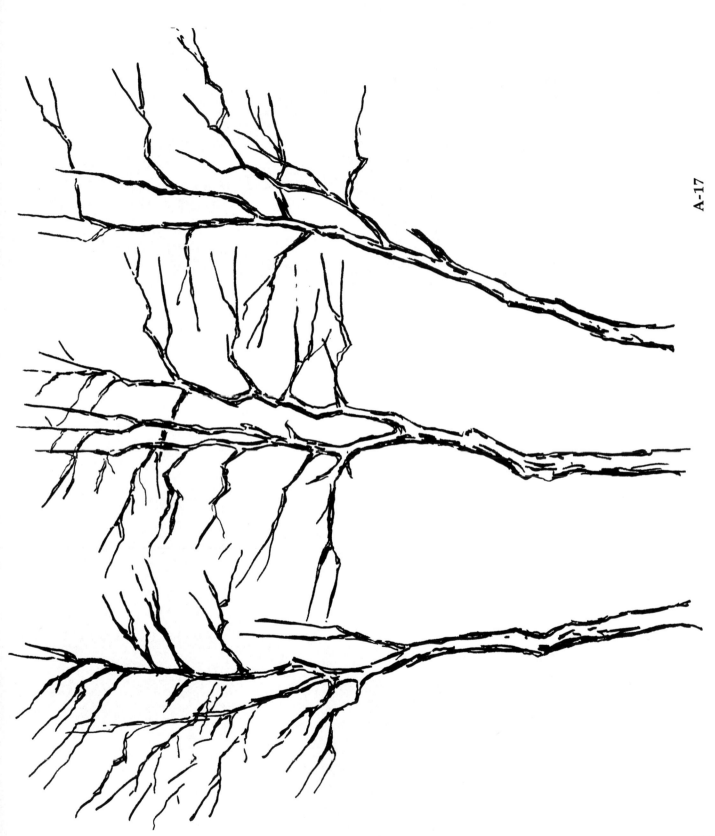

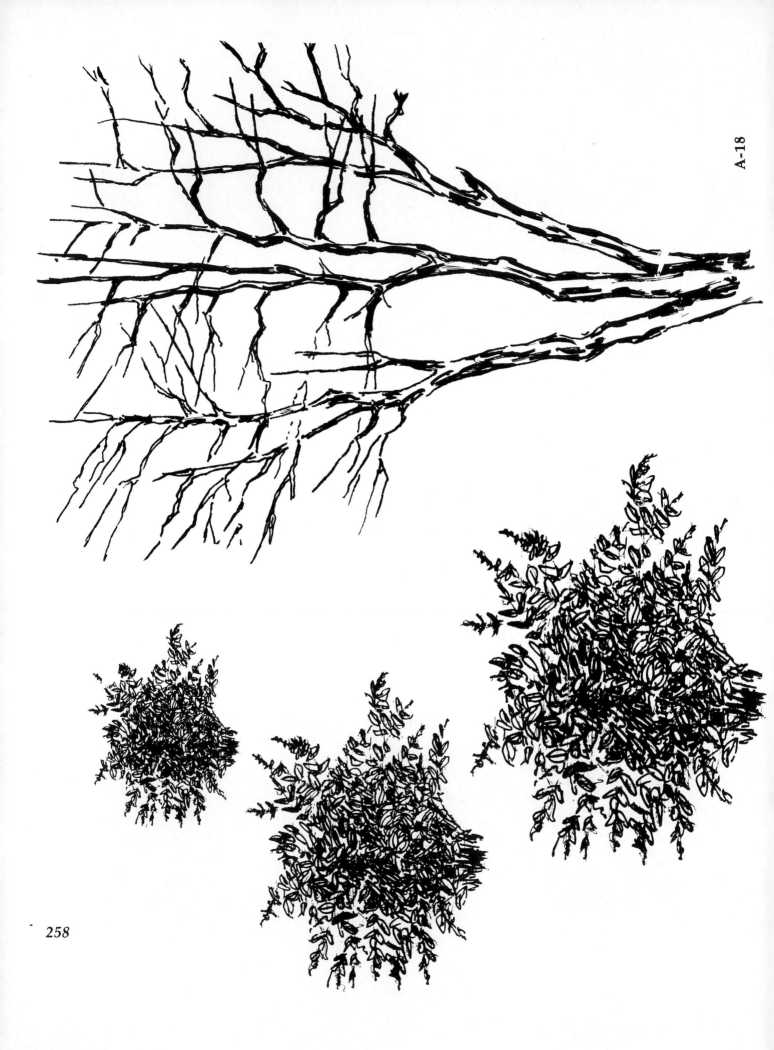

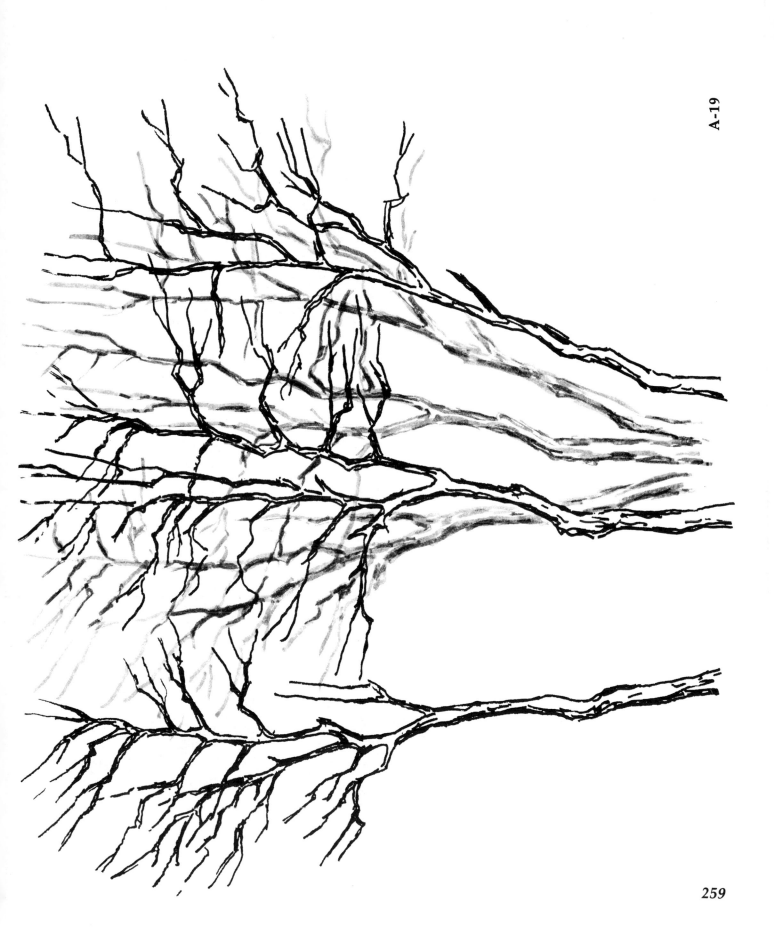

261

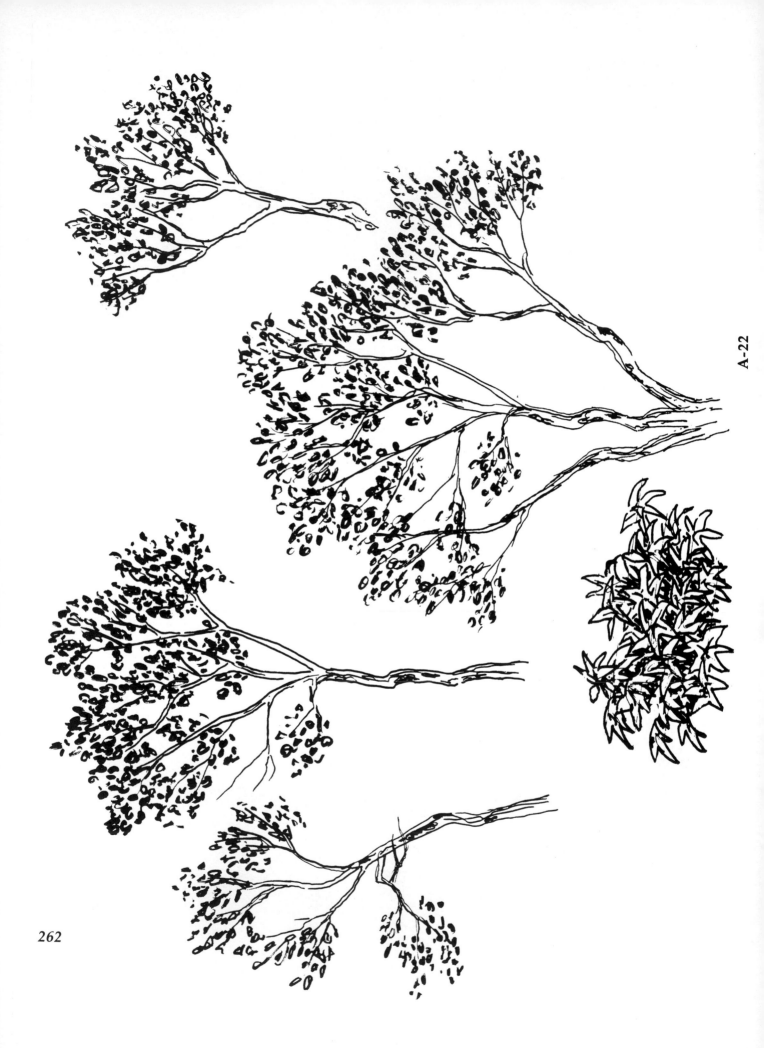

A-23

263

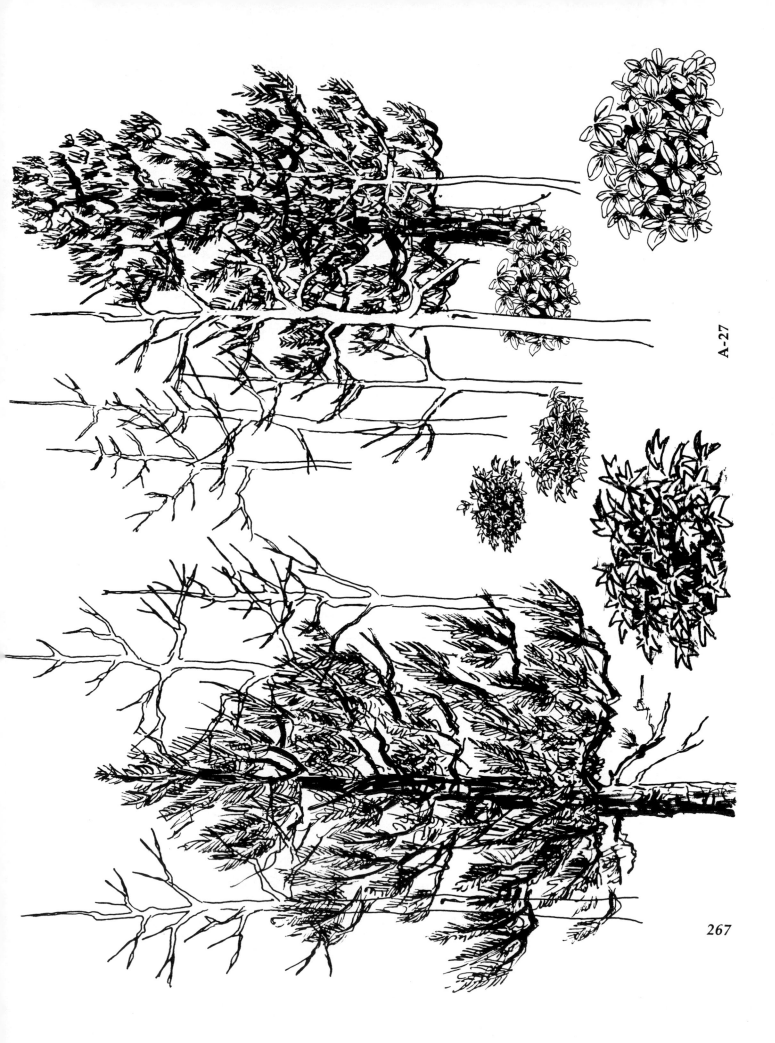

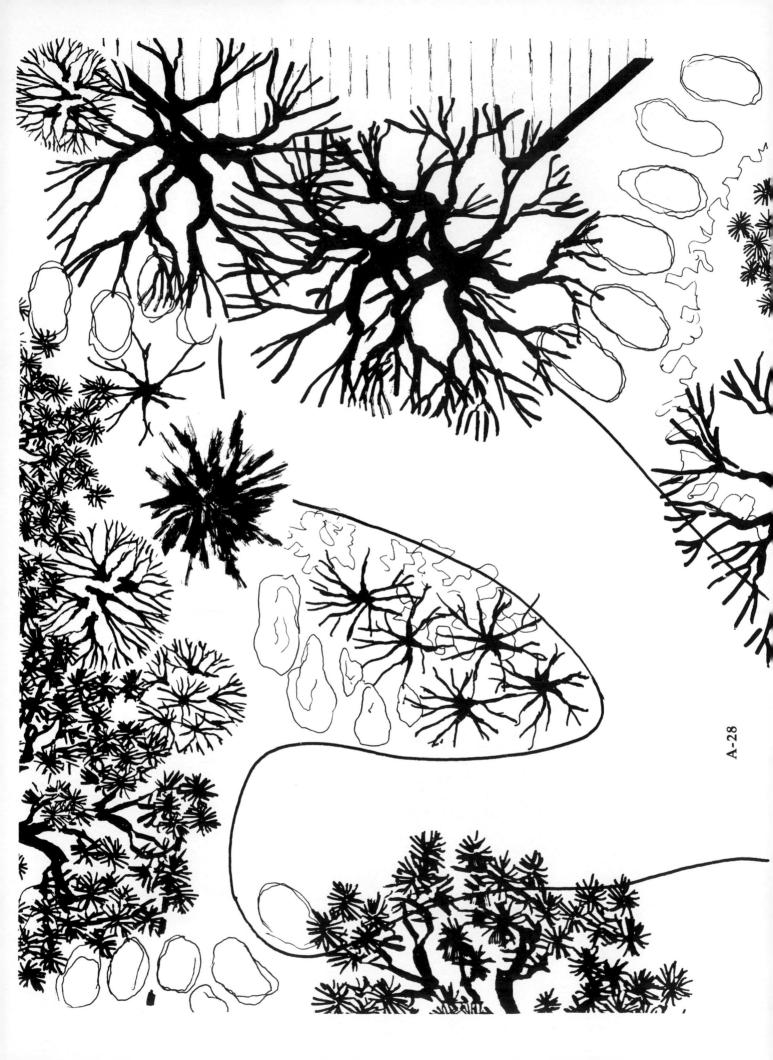

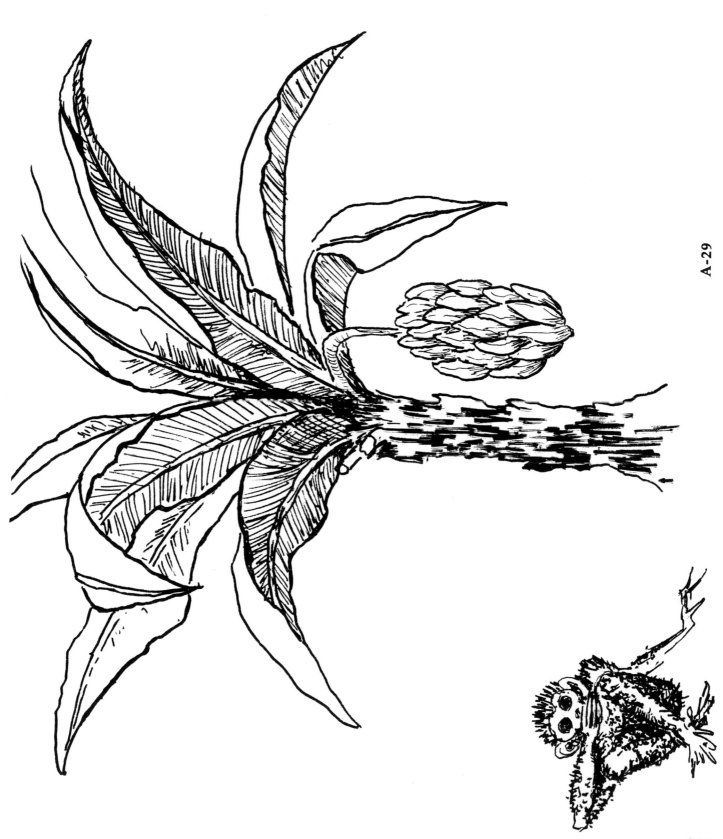

Bibliography

In this short, idiosyncratic list are a few of the books which I found useful, interesting, or simply pleasant to look through. Most are current and readily available but a few are out of print and more difficult to locate. This list is not intended to be comprehensive on any subject.

Although trees and shrubs are usually the garden's main features, plants like ground covers and perennials often play an important role. Many novel and useful ground covers and perennials can be found among alpine plants, ferns, ornamental grasses, and wildflowers; so under the heading "Specialty Plants" we have included several books on these subjects.

There is an abundance of beautiful photo essays on every scenic region in the country. This is a great blessing which I do not fully appreciate until I find myself in some other country. Deserts, mountains, and forests are described and pictured from sea to shining sea. The offering is so diverse and plentiful, and much of it is of such excellent quality that it is impossible to select a small sample that is representative—particularly since the photo essays most relevant to a garden designer's concerns are likely to be those that are about regions bearing some climatic and terrain similarities to the one in which the garden will be situated. For these reasons I have not listed any photo essays of natural scenery.

My reasons for not listing books on art are similar. There are too many good, interesting, and relevant ones, and too great a diversity of individual needs and tastes.

GENERAL

Principles of Gardening, Hugh Johnson, Simon and Schuster, 1979.

Trees and Shrubs for Northern Gardens, Leon Snyder, University of Minnesota Press, 1980.

New Western Garden Book, editors of Sunset Books, Lane, 7th edition, 1983.

Plants that Merit Attention: Vol. 1—Trees, The Garden Club of America, Janet M. Poor ed., Timber Press, 1984.

International Book of Trees, Hugh Johnson, Beazly, 1973.

Trees and Shrubs for Temperate Climates, Gordon Courtright, Timber Press, 1979.

Gardens of North America and Hawaii, Irene and Walter Jacob, Timber Press, 1986.

Taylor's Guide to Shrubs, various, Houghton Miffon, 1987.

Shrubs for Your Garden, Peter Seabrook, Scribner, 1970.

Trees for Your Garden, Roy Lancaster, Scribner, 1974.
Art Into Landscape; Landscape Into Art, Arthur Bye, P.D.A. Publishers, 1983.
Gardens; Architectural Digest, ed. Paige Rense, Knapp Press, 1983.
Tropical Gardens of Burle Marx, P. M. Bardi, Architectural Press, 1964.

ORIENTAL GARDENS

Gardens of Japan, Teiji Itoh, Kondasha, 1984.
Japanese Gardens, Wendy Murphy, Time-Life, 1979.
Classical Chinese Gardens, Qian Yun ed., Joint Publishing Company, 1982.
Chinese Gardens; History, Art and Architecture, Maggie Keswick, Rizzoli, 1978.
Garden Art of Japan, Masao Hayakawa, Weatherhill/Hibonsha, first English ed.
  1973.
Space and Illusion in the Japanese Garden, Teiji Itoh, Weatherhill/Tankosha,
  1973.
The Japanese Courtyard Garden, Kanto Shigemori, Weatherhill, 1980.
Creating a Chinese Garden, David Engel, Timber Press, 1987.
The Art of Chinese Gardens, Chung Wah Nan, Hong Kong University Press,
  1982.
The Classical Gardens of China, Yang Honghun, Van Nostrand Reinhold, 1982.

BONSAI AND SEIKEI

Bonsai—Miniature Potted Trees, Norio Kobayashi, Japan Travel Burean/Tuttle,
  10th edition, 1960.
Saikei: Living Landscapes in Miniature, Toshio Kawamoto, Kodansha, 1967.
Master's Book of Bonsai, directors of the Japan Bonsai Assoc., Kodansha, 1967.
Miniature Trees and Landscapes, Yuji Yoshimura and Giovanna Halford, Tuttle,
  1957.
Penjing: The Chinese Art of Miniature Gardens, Hu Yunhua and Shanghai
  Botanic Gardens, Timber Press, 1982.
Bonsai: Its Art, Science, History and Philosophy, Deborah Koreshoff, Timber
  Press, 1984.
Timeless Trees, Roy Bloomer, Horizons West, 1986.
Essentials of Bonsai, editors of Shufunotomo, Timber Press, 1982.

SPECIALTY PLANTS

Ornamental Conifers, Charles Harrison, Haffner, 1975, and Timber Press 1983.
Rock Gardens, Willhelm Schacht, Universe Books, 1981.
Ground Covers, Daniel Foley, Dover, 1972.
Perennials for Your Garden, Alan Bloom, Scribner, 1971.
Alpines For Your Garden, Alan Bloom, Floraprint, 1981.
Rocky Mountain Alpines, Alpines 86 Publications Committee; Jean Williams
  ed., Timber Press, 1987.
Rock Gardening, Lincoln and Laura Foster, Timber Press, 1982.
Perennials: How to Select, Grow and Enjoy, Pamela Harper and Frederick

McGourty, HP Books, 1985.

Taylor's Guide to Perennials, various, Houghton Miffon, 1987.

Taylor's Guide to Ground Covers, Vines, and Grasses, various, Houghton Miffon, 1987.

Japanese Maples, J. D. Vertrees, Timber Press, 2nd edition, 1978.

Pioneering with Wildflowers, George Aiken, Countryman, 4th edition, 1978.

Ornamental Grasses, Roger Grounds, Van Nostrand Reinhold, 1981.

Ornamental Grasses, Mary Meyer, Scribner, 1975.

Fern Growers Manual, Barbara Hoshizaki, Knopf/Random House, 1979.

Ground Covers in the Landscape, Emile Labadie, Sierra City Press, 1983.

Encyclopedia of Ferns, David Jones, Timber Press, 1987.